The International Environment and China's Twin Models of Development

The International Environment and China's Twin Models of Development

Lai Sing Lam

PETER LANG
Oxford · Bern · Berlin · Bruxelles · Frankfurt am Main · New York · Wien

Bibliographic information published by Die Deutsche Bibliothek
Die Deutsche Bibliothek lists this publication in the Deutsche Nationalbibliografie; detailed bibliographic data is available on the Internet at ‹http://dnb.ddb.de›.

British Library and Library of Congress Cataloguing-in-Publication Data:
A catalogue record for this book is available from *The British Library*, Great Britain, and from *The Library of Congress*, USA

ISBN 978-3-03911-030-8

Hochfeldstrasse 32, Postfach 746, CH-3000 Bern 9, Switzerland
info@peterlang.com, www.peterlang.com, www.peterlang.net

To the memory of my parents
Lam Wan Poh and Wong Keng Hei

Contents

Preface

This work aims to answer the basic question of what motivated Mao Zedong to formulate his strategies for the political economy of the People's Republic of China (PRC). It proposes that there was an intimate relationship between his "uprooting of the mountain" of capitalism and "that of the mountain" of imperialism and argues that it was the international environment which motivated Mao to formulate his defense-oriented development policy during the period 1953–1970. It also documents the post-Mao modernization revolution, a continuation of his four modernizations plan which started in 1971 when the international environment became more favorable to the PRC, and argues that the strategies of both the Maoist and post-Mao development were closely related to the conditions of the international environment.

The work is divided into two major parts; the first part deals with the PRC's political economy during Mao's time, which was greatly influenced by global power politics, while the second part focuses on post-Mao economic development, which has been made possible by the continued favorable international environment since 1979.

The process of the PRC's revolution during the period 1953–1969 followed his mass line strategy of "uniting with all possible" to "wipe out capitalism" in order to communize the whole nation. With the resulting astronomical power, Mao aimed to fight imperialism. Therefore, his strategy for the political economy was primarily to create a united population to counter US imperialism and the "US–USSR collusion against China". Mao launched his Great Leap Forward and commune movements in the period 1957–1958. Using the anti-Japanese Yenan experience as the model, his communization scheme to "unite with all possible", which was intimately related to the power politics of the time, accelerated in response to American and Soviet pressures. His economic-cum-defense policy was a political solution formulated for China's survival in the hostile international environment.

Guided by the capitalist or Soviet approach, Liu Shaoqi's onslaughts on Mao's collectivization drive on a number of occasions could have dangerously undermined his mass line strategy. This was a crucial period of global power politics in which the Soviet Union had turned out to be another "devil" in Mao's worldview, in addition to the United States as the primary enemy. This work argues that the origins of Mao's Cultural Revolution can be traced back to Liu's various "rightist" onslaughts.

With the favorable international environment conducive to his plan of opening the PRC to the outside world, Mao began to adopt a relaxed economic policy to "improve the livelihood of the people", starting in the crucial year of 1971. As a consequence, Mao gradually had to discard the element of moral incentives and introduce that of material incentives for China's real economic development which was the nation's primary task. A Western-style economic approach was adopted during the period 1971–1976. As a result, Mao's consistent strains of class struggle and aspiration for a more egalitarian society were no longer relevant. Likewise, his tenet of "serving the people" as well as his aim of making a communist man, which contradicted his new economic policy, eventually had to be abolished.

In view of this, this study sets out to put Mao Zedong in a proper historical perspective. Although written for the present generation, future generations will be expected to make the final judgments on Mao's psychological insight concerning his policy formulation, particularly of the Great Leap Forward, his communization goal as well as the related Cultural Revolution. It will probably take twenty to fifty years for future scholars to reach a general consensus on these very issues as presented in the first part of this study.

Holistically, this work suggests some reasons why, influenced by the different conditions of the international environment, Mao's economic strategy was not successful while post-Mao economic achievements were quite impressive.

I would like to extend my sincere thanks to Professor Ting Wai, Head of the Department of Government and International Studies, Hong Kong Baptist University for writing the Foreword. I am also grateful to Dr Russell Ong of Hull University for his comments on part of the original manuscript.

Thanks are also due to the Research Institute for International Affairs, Seoul, Korea, for permission to reproduce copyrighted materials from my article, "From Mikhail Gorbachev's Policy to China's Regional Role", *Journal of East Asian Affairs*, vol.vii, no.2 (August 1993). The materials form part of chapter six of this work.

I am also indebted to the following: Richard Booker edited part of the early version of the manuscript. Roselie Ang and Mary Beltran each put the finishing touches on part of the final version of the work.

I am grateful to Alexis Kirschbaum, Commissioning Editor of Peter Lang AG for her help in bringing the work to publication.

Regarding the romanization of Chinese characters, the pinyin system has been adopted. However, occasionally the Wade-Giles system is also used, for instance, Chiang Kai-shek, Lee Teng-hui, Tung Chee-hwa.

LAM Lai Sing
Visiting Scholar
Department of Government and International Studies
Hong Kong Baptist University
September 2006

Foreword

This concluding volume of Dr Lam Lai Sing is the culmination of his series of research on Mao Zedong Thought. It focuses on the theme that the strategies of the Maoist and post-Mao political economy were crucially influenced by the international environment. Lam's thesis espouses that, dictated by the hostile international climate, Mao's defense-oriented economic development policy during the period 1950–1970 was not very successful compared with the impressive post-Mao national development which was made possible by the stable and peaceful international environment.

The author's theory of "uprooting the mountain of imperialism" argues that, with the anti-Japanese Yenan experience as a model, Mao organized the Chinese population to communize the whole country to counter US imperialism during the period 1950–1958 and the "US–USSR superpowers in collusion against China" during the period 1959–1969. He contends that power politics was a primary determinant of Mao's economic strategy.

According to Lai Sing, the success of Mao's communization scheme crucially depended upon "wiping out capitalism". This was because the vital factor of the moral incentive of "serving the people", defined by his mass line strategy for this task, was meant to "unite with all who can be united". His aim of creating a selfless communist man was based on the same argument. Further, according to Lai Sing, Mao's rectification campaigns and movements as well as his emphasis on class struggle created for "the purpose of maintaining the ideological integrity of the population" were meant to combat a revival of capitalism and bureaucracy. However, this could not "unite with all possible" and therefore could not summon consolidated power for Mao's anti-imperialist task. Tracing the origins of Mao's Cultural Revolution of 1966–1969 to Liu Shaoqi's various "rightist" onslaughts, Lai Sing argues that Liu's "revisionist" economic approach did not take power politics into consideration.

With the changed international environment in the early 1970s when the United States was replaced by the Soviet Union as the primary enemy in his worldview, Mao, according to Lai Sing, began to inject Western economic elements into his four modernizations plan. This was to attract US-led Western capital and modern technology for improving the livelihood of the people. Apart from introducing the element of material incentives to replace that of moral incentives for China's real economic development, which was the primary national task, Lai Sing proposes that Mao realized that his consistent strains of class struggle and aspirations for a more egalitarian society and his tenet of "serving the people" as well as his aim of making a communist man were now no longer relevant to his new economic strategy, and had to be dispensed with.

In the second part of this volume, Lai Sing argues that Mao inspired the post-Mao leadership to continue organizing a quarter of mankind to carry out his modernization revolution. By introducing his "good-neighborliness" policy after abolishing Mao's outdated defense-oriented commune system, Deng Xiaoping, Lai Sing contends, aimed to "induce the whole world to help modernize China". The new century witnessed the PRC's emergence as a key player in the global economy. In early 2006, it overtook Japan as the world's largest holder of foreign currencies, with reserves of US$850 billion. It is presently the workshop of the world for computers and cars and a magnet for foreign direct investment associated with Western technology. The strengthening of the PRC's economy, Lai Sing concludes, has brought about significant improvements in the people's livelihood – the prime mover for furthering its modernization revolution.

By combining the fields of international relations, economics and contemporary Chinese studies, Lai Sing has argued his case convincingly. He has predicted that it would take twenty to fifty years for future scholars to reach a general consensus on Mao's economic policy during the period 1950–1970 as well as on the related issues of his communization scheme and Cultural Revolution. Lam Lai Sing's study will certainly spark off a debate.

Ting Wai
Professor and Head
Department of Government and International Studies
Hong Kong Baptist University
September 2006

Chapter One
Introduction

Mao Zedong is well known to students of modern China for his communization scheme, among others. In examining of the real nature of his development models and the conditions under which they materialized, we may understand another aspect of his character as a master power politician.

This work argues that the international environment at that juncture was a vital determinant of Mao Zedong's approach to his development policy. Mao's post-World War international perception led to his formulation of a strategy for the PRC's development in response to the hostile international environment. It further contends that China's defense-oriented communization model during the period 1953–70 was a vital determinant of power politics. Furthermore, contrary to the conventional school of thought that Premier Zhou Enlai initiated the post-Mao four modernizations scheme, it was Mao who introduced this scheme that is being used presently in China. The present modernization revolution, which Mao initiated in 1971, was made possible by a relatively favorable international environment. Thus Mao devised his twin national development models based on two different sets of conditions in the international environment. Using a holistic approach, this book argues why, dictated by the critically different international environments of the two periods, Mao's development scheme was not very successful in comparison with the impressive post-Mao economic achievements.

In what context should Mao Zedong's development models be considered?

This study considers China's national development within Mao's collectivization aim in the economic-cum-defense context of the period 1950–1970. This was Mao's first development model. Based on his new model formulated for the continued peaceful and stable international environment, post-Mao development has revolved mainly around the four modernizations of agriculture, industry, science and technology, and defense. Mao Zedong's second development model was adopted in 1979 by the post-Mao leadership. This study considers economic development crucial to the post-Mao modernization revolution.

The origins of Mao's four modernizations scheme can be traced to his treatise "On Coalition Government" written in April 1945 that "The task of the Chinese working class is to struggle [...] for China's industrialization and the modernization of her agriculture".[1] A month later, he argued: "one of the main reasons of China's backwardness was the lack of modern industry" and Japanese imperialism "dared to bully China because China did not have a powerful industry".[2] In the summer of 1957 Mao talked about setting this very foundation for the four modernizations plan he envisaged: "Counting from now, ten to fifteen years will be required to build a modern industrial and modern agricultural base in China [...] to obtain a fairly adequate material base".[3]

However, his scheme was shelved owing to the external imperialist threats not only from the United States, its primary enemy, but also from the "collusion of the US-USSR enemies against China" as Mao saw it. Even from the end of the World War II, Mao took the United States as China's primary enemy, with Stalin's Soviet Union as its *de facto* enemy. The collectivization scheme, which he initiated in 1953 and was central to China's defense-oriented development plan, was to pave the way to his communization goal. It was aimed at "uniting with all possible" to fight the US superpower during the period 1953–1957 and "the US–USSR enemies in collusion against the PRC" during the period 1958–1970.[4] Understandably therefore, the United States and the Soviet Union, both separately and collectively, exerted pressures on China, which intensified Mao's determination to initiate his Great Leap Forward scheme in 1958.

From December 1959 to February 1960, in Mao's conversations regarding the Russian *Text Book of Political Economics,* his thoughts on the plan of the four modernizations were revealed as follows:

> To build socialism, the basic conditions should be the modernization of industry, agriculture, science, culture and, in addition, defense.[5]

> After the second five-year plan and two more five-year plans, [...] apart from realizing the modernization of industry, agriculture, and scientific culture, (we) must achieve defense modernization.[6]

This was the first time Mao had talked about the concept of his four modernizations scheme.

During its third session held in April 1962, the Third Chinese People's Political Consultative Conference (CPPCC) adopted Premier Zhou's proposal in his "Report on the Work of the Government" to "accomplish a socialist China with modernization of industry, agriculture, and scientific culture under Chairman Mao's leadership".[7] Bolstered by improved agricultural conditions, Mao's modernization plan was now formalized. In January 1963, for the first time, Zhou referred to Mao's modernization scheme in terms of "the four modernizations of agriculture, industry, national defense, and science and technology" with the term "scientific culture" changed to "science and technology".[8] According to Premier Zhou, Mao envisaged the goals of his four modernizations scheme to be achieved in the second stage of China's long-term development plan which was to begin with the Third Five-Year Plan (FYP) in 1966.[9]

Toward the end of December 1964, Zhou referred to Mao's very plan in his report to the Third National People's Congress (NPC) on the work of the government as follows:

> To catch up with and surpassing the countries that are advanced in these respects, we may envisage the development of our economy in two stages beginning with the Third Five-Year Plan (in 1966). The first stage is to build an independent and relatively comprehensive industrial and economic structure; the second stage is to accomplish the overall modernization of agriculture, industry, national defence and science and technology (before the end of the century).[10]

However, Mao's scheme did not materialize owing to the urgency to launch the Cultural Revolution which, this author will argue in Chapter Three, was critically related to "revisionism" upheld by "China's Khrushchev", the "No.1 power holder in the Party taking the capitalist road". Ignoring the crucial importance of Mao's basic concern with the two superpowers "in (their) collusion against China",

Liu Shaoqi resorted to applying his "revisionist" economic principles to China's development, particularly during the difficult three-year period. Understandably, to Mao this was totally unacceptable. This was the reason that Liu was branded a "traitor" during the Cultural Revolution.

The rapprochement with the United States in 1972 brought twenty years of confrontation to an end. It promoted the normalization of bilateral relations and opened the way to improved relations with other Western countries and Japan, thus facilitating China's quest for modernization.

Premier Zhou, on behalf of the State Council made the report to the Fourth NPC on the work of the government on January 13, 1975, for the first time advancing China's "four modernizations" program.[11] Zhou reminded the State Councillors that it was "on Chairman Mao's instructions" that the development of the economy, as reported in the Third NPC, was envisaged in two stages beginning with the Third FYP.[12]

> On Chairman Mao's instructions, it was suggested in the Report on the Work of the government to the Third National People's Congress that we might envisage the development of our economy in two stages beginning with the Third FYP: the first stage is to build an independent and relatively comprehensive industrial and economic structure within 15 years, that is, before 1980; and the second stage is to accomplish the overall modernization of agriculture, industry, national defence and science and technology before the end of the century, so that our economy will be among the front ranks of world economies.[13]

In January 1975, in his "Report on the Revision of the Constitution" at the First Session of the Fourth NPC, Chang Chunchiao reminded the delegates of Mao's instructions to Premier Zhou.[14]

Emphasizing the four modernizations program as an integral part of Mao Zedong Thought in mid-1980, Deng Xiaoping made clear that the four modernizations scheme could find its origins in Mao's theses on the "Ten Major Relationships", "Correct Handling of Contradictions Among the People", "The Situation in the Summer of 1957" and so on. To elaborate this important point, it is worthwhile quoting Deng at length:

> We have to give a clear amount of Comrade Mao's contributions to China's socialist revolution and construction. Mao Zedong Thought is still in the process of development. We should restore and adhere to Mao Zedong Thought and go on developing it. Comrade Mao laid a foundation for us in all these respects, and the resolution should finally reflect his ideas. It should cite some of his important articles and speeches in the period of socialist revolution and construction such as "On the Ten Major Relationships", "On the Correct Handling of Contradictions Among the People" and "The Situation in the Summer of 1957". They contain the ideas, which we must continue to adhere to and develop today. We must give the people a clear understanding of what specific ideas we have in mind we say we will hold high the banner of, and adhere to, Mao Zedong Thought.[15]

Basically, Mao's theses stressed "proper relationships" among agriculture, light industry, and heavy industry. Deng adopted this idea to carry out Mao's four modernizations plan:

> In discussing our path to industrialization, we are here concerned principally with the relationship between the growth of heavy industry, light industry and agriculture. It must be affirmed that heavy industry is the core of China's economic construction. At the same time, full attention must be paid to the development of agriculture and light industry.[16]

In April 1980, speaking with some leading members of the Central Committee regarding the importance of Mao's idea of building the modern industrial and agricultural base for the four modernizations scheme, Deng elaborated:

> "On the Ten Relationships" is a fine speech. So is "On the Correct Handling of Contradictions among the People". In his article "The Situation in the Summer of 1957", Comrade Mao said that we must build a modern industrial and agricultural base in China and that only with its achievement could our socialist economic and political system be said to have obtained a fairly adequate material base.[17]

Furthermore, Mao's four modernizations plan included ideas he had adopted from his theses, not only regarding the relationship between industry in the coastal regions and industry in the interior, but also that between economic construction and defense construction.[18]

In December 1959, with the purpose of "improving the livelihood of the people", Mao initiated his plan of socialist transformation which comprised "the four modernizations of agriculture, industry, science and technology, and defense".[19] However, prior to 1971, Mao's plan could not be put into practice owing to the hostile international environment. Understandably, during the period 1953–1970, Mao gave priority to a defense-oriented national development plan by establishing the commune system.

Like many other scholars, Bernstein writes that Mao tried to achieve a breakthrough on all fronts based on the mass mobilization of the whole population and "the generation of utopian expectations (so) that a breakthrough could be reached virtually instantly and the country could leap forward into communism even ahead of the Soviet Union".[20] However, this author argues that in 1958 it was the pressures, both separate and collective, that the US–USSR superpowers exerted on China that intensified Mao's determination to initiate his Great Leap Forward scheme. More importantly, in an attempt to make the country a great steel producer, he tried to unify the masses to face the superpowers with one spirit. Furthermore, Chiou writes that the Soviet model applied to China in the First Five-Year Plan of 1953–1957, had created a "new class" of technocrats whose elitist tendency Mao distrusted.[21] Mao, he continues, therefore introduced the communization policy and the GLF in the following three years to stamp out this tendency.[22] Mao held that the Soviet approach could not "unite with all possible". With this dictum, his communization scheme, which was aimed at developing a viable political economy by combining the "agricultural and military" elements, was ideal for his aim of "annihilating imperialism". The way he perceived his communization scheme was expressed in the following lines which dramatized the unbending will of his well organized "people" in the GLF movement:

> The Five mountain ranges stretching to the heavens are dug by the gleaming mattocks;
> The three rivers tremble as the steel-like arms move.[23]

Thus, based on mass mobilization of the whole population, Mao aimed at counteracting the ambitions of the imperialists.

Mao's perception of the international arena had been gradually formulated over a period of years in response to the politics and actions of the superpowers he perceived. This had resulted in the transformation of his worldview from "friend" into "enemy", from "secondary enemy" to "primary enemy", and vice versa, and in the formulation of his scheme of collusion with the "secondary enemies" against the "primary enemy". Therefore, Mao's concept of the "three worlds" was fundamentally formulated to aim at the "primary enemy" of the imperialist First World.[24] Thus, his struggle with the primary enemy, a superpower, or the superpowers combined, was carried out in the following ways:

(a) colluding with (the imperialist) secondary enemy or enemies against the primary enemy. Enemies were divided into primary and secondary ones because "in war battles can only be fought one by one and the enemy can only be annihilated bit by it".[25]
(b) inciting the Third World nations or the Second World nations to unite against the superpower enemy or enemies,
(c) fanning revolutionary movements in the Third World.

In his scheme of fighting the imperialist primary enemy, or "annihilating imperialism", Mao argued that he needed the "people's power" or "astronomical power" (大力).[26] This was, as he himself said, "the strongest power in the world, which can be generated when all people unite".[27] Internally Mao realized this power through his policies of organizing the whole population. It is in this context that Mao's anti-imperialist mass line strategy was formulated to "unite with all possible" and "mobilize all possible factors". According to Mao, "the strongest force in the world is the force resulting from consolidation of all people" and "victory or defeat depends on whether all forces can be consolidated".[28] Therefore "uniting all those who can be united" and "mobilizing all possible useful forces" would not make sense if "concentrating the people's power" was not achieved. In order to do this, Mao must first "unite all those who can be united" and "mobilize all possible useful forces". Therefore Mao's dictum of "uniting all those who can be united" had this primary aim. Mao's policies and strategies can also be traced to the dicta of "wiping capitalism from the face of the earth" and "annihilating imperialism", his concern with "the affairs of the future generations", and so forth. These dicta entailed strategies such as "uniting all those who can be united" and "mobilizing all useful forces possible".

How do we understand Mao's concept of this mass line strategy? The Marxist epistemology of "the masses as a whole to change the world" inspired Mao to designate "the people" to play this role.[29] His "concrete analysis of the concrete conditions" convinced him that the Chinese peasantry must be won over if the revolution was to succeed, because it made up the majority of the Chinese population. According to him, "the majority is 90%–98% of the people".[30] This study argues that Mao's mass line was the means by which his dictum of "uniting with all possible" to tap astronomical power would be used to achieve the anti-imperialist tasks.[31] Thus, "persisting the Marxist-Leninist principle of intimate dependence on the masses" played an important part in shaping Mao's concept of the mass line of anti- imperialism.[32]

Mao's mass line concept and techniques of revolutionary struggle evolved in the Jiangsi period, and greatly influenced the means subsequently used to mobilize the Chinese masses in the Anti-Japa- nese Yenan period as well as the post-War anti-Kuomintang (KMT) period. Mao's practice of his mass line strategy as an approach to "unite with all possible" became clearer in the Anti-Japanese Yenan period when the Communists developed organizational and leadership techniques "for linking the military effort and rural social and economic problems in a single programme of wartime mobilization, penetrating to every village and every family and involving every individual".[33] This concept greatly influenced Mao to mobilize the Chinese masses to gain nation-wide power after 1949 for his fight against the imperialist primary enemy to which he referred in the Beidaihe Enlarged Political Bureau Meeting in August 1958.[34]

In addition, Mao applied the Marxian concept of class struggle to enhance his strategy of "uniting with all possible".

Marx's analysis of the history of all human societies gave rise to functionality. That is, by analyzing the capitalist exploitation of the working class, he created the theoretical antagonism between the bourgeoisie and the proletariat, with the aim of consolidating the energies of the exploited, who were the "majority", in order to destroy the exploiters, who were the "minority".[35] This inspired Mao's dictum of "uniting with all possible". Marx's concept of "class struggle" inspired Mao to formulate his strategy of dividing all people into two hostile opposing groups so that he could pinpoint, isolate and destroy the enemies, who were the "minority". This was to be achieved through the power generated by "the people", who were the "majority". Thus, Mao adopted this Marxian concept with his aim of "uniting with all possible" to "annihilate imperialism".

By adopting the Marxian notion of class struggle to complement his diction of "uniting with all possible", Mao sought to weed out the reactionary class enemies, both internal and external. According to Mao, the Chinese Communist Party (CCP) was to grasp the essential principle of class struggle, by relying on the working class, the poor and lower middle peasants, the revolutionary cadres, the revolutionary intellectuals, and other revolutionary elements to unite over 95 per cent of the masses and over 95 per cent of the cadres. Mao claimed that the CCP "is composed of advanced elements of the proletariat; it is a vigorous and vital vanguard organization, which leads the proletariat and the revolutionary masses in the struggle against the class enemy".[36] Thus, to Mao, class struggle was essential between the two roads of socialism and capitalism, and also in warding off the danger of a capitalist restoration and, more importantly, the threat of subversion and aggression from imperialism and modern revisionism. These class contradictions could only be resolved by relying on the theory and practice of Marxist permanent revolution.

Mao's notion of Marxian permanent revolution follows from his ideas about the struggle of man against his selfish nature, the campaigns for the rectification of thought, and the necessity of struggling against bureaucracy and corruption. In analysing Mao's rectification campaigns over a period of forty years, we found that these movements were virtually launched one after another in the context of attitude change designed to get rid of cadres, Party and non-Party members with bourgeois attitudes and specific "deviations".[37] For instance, Mao's anti-bureaucratic attitude toward cadre work showed his disgust of the bourgeois work approach, which, he felt, not only could not win over and consolidate the masses, but would also divorce the Party from the masses. These attitudes and "deviations" were considered to be obstacles to the realization of his plan of "uniting with all who could be united", from Party officials to agricultural and industrial workers. This was why Mao was so determined to create a selfless communist man. His hyperbolical plan was to generate astronomical power not merely for working toward the success of his communist revolution but, more importantly, for eliminating US and social imperialist threats.

According to Mao, the Paris Peace Treaty was an imperialist scheme, which he referred to as "the Alps".[38] He also interpreted imperialism as "a big mountain", which "lies like a dead weight on the Chinese people", and which he wanted his revolution to "topple". In "toppling the big mountain of Japanese imperialism", he could organize the "whole population". In his attempt to "topple the big mountain" of worldwide imperialism, he not merely schemed externally to unite with "all the exploited and bullied" nations around the world, but, more importantly, organized "the whole population" internally, based on the anti-Japanese Yenan experience. Therefore, Marx's magniloquence provided Mao with the method of harnessing the people's power for his Herculean task of "toppling the mountain of capitalism", the prerequisite for "toppling the mountain of imperialism". Mao's anti-imperialist strategy was to single-mindedly communize the whole population.

Mao Zedong's worldview of the period following the end of World War II to the year 1953 was characterized by the perception that the United States was the primary enemy of the PRC, while the Soviet Union was the *de facto* enemy. Following that year, the initiative for the development of his collectivization scheme, in which the country was to be united by political, economic, cultural and military bonds, was crucial. Mao's scheme would involve the whole population in developing the national economy, first, by feeding and then clothing the people so that the country's defense against the twin imperialist superpowers with one mind was possible. This approach can be traced back to the Yenan experience against Japanese imperialism. Mao's communization of the whole country was the ultimate phase of his collectivization scheme for the same defense purpose. To reiterate, Mao's commune system was based on the Yenan model as its prototype. The development of the agricultural producers' cooperatives was the prerequisite. In the context of Mao's mass line strategy, we will examine his approach of tapping the power of the Chinese masses, based on the Yenan model of communism.

During the Yenan period 1937–1945, with Japanese imperialism as the primary enemy, Mao had devised the national united front strategy of "arming all the population" to tap the people's power with the complementary strategy of "mobilizing all useful factors possible".[39] The Yenan experience was characterized by the use of guerrilla warfare as a supplement to primary and regular warfare. The effectiveness of the Communist regular forces was restricted as "the Japanese were holding on to the areas they had occupied" in the "strategic stalemate stage" of the entire process of the anti-Japanese war.[40]

With guerrilla forces spreading out all over the country, their familiarity with the geographical strategic features, and their mobility, the broad masses of the peasantry formed militia and guerrilla teams, and carried out both guerrilla and regular warfare.[41] In this way the policy of self-reliance in economic production was implemented, and both the people's livelihood and army supplies were guaranteed.[42] Thus, Mao's principle of protracted warfare was that, under the leadership of the CCP, the armed masses – that is, the militia – would play the dual role of producing essential goods and fighting the Japanese.[43] These armed masses elected their own junior team leaders, branch team leaders, and middle team leaders.[44] This was to achieve the political mobilization of the masses. To strengthen both the fighting and productive forces, Mao adopted the ancient strategy of combining agriculture and the military in which soldiers carried out agricultural activities when not engaged in fighting.[45] This strategy is well recorded in Ban Gu's (班固) *History of the Han Dynasty* (汉书) (206 BC–220 AD).

Mao's strategy of "arming the whole population" for his anti-Japanese national united front included the arming of women and youth, and mobilizing the children and all Chinese minority nationalities.[46] They were organized into the people's anti-Japanese self-defense corps without their having to give up their work in production.

The Communist anti-Japanese war first carried out the strategy of "better troops and simpler administration" in order to mobilize the masses at the lower levels effectively and thoroughly. Secondly, it implemented the policy of a "unified central leadership" with the aim of unifying all organizations under the direct control of the central government.[47] The principle underlying the three campaigns for "better troops and simpler administration" campaigns was to improve the fighting capacity of the regular troops and to effectively mobilize and organize the local forces and the militia at the grass-roots levels to carry out guerrilla warfare and develop regular warfare.[48] The third campaign was initiated in conjunction with the rectification campaign of 1942–1944.[49] Its aim was to instill the principles of the rectification campaign into the "better troops and simpler administration" movement with special emphasis on "anti-bureaucratization", which was to achieve "harmony between the army and the people" and "harmony between officers and the men".[50]

Likewise, in 1947 the united front in the people's war of liberation was adopted by the CCP, which implemented the program of "uniting the workers, peasants, soldiers, intellectuals and businessmen, all oppressed classes, all people's organizations, democratic parties, minority nationalities, overseas Chinese and other patriots to form a national united front".[51]

"Mobilizing all useful factors possible" was the basis of Mao's policies on the economy, culture, education, literature and art, foreign relations, prisoners and prisoners of war, and so forth.[52]

In sum, using the Yenan model as its prototype, Mao's communization of the whole country was aimed at achieving the ultimate phase of his collectivization scheme for defense against the twin imperialist superpowers.

To reiterate, this study argues that Mao's development policy was defense-oriented in that it was formulated to fight China's external primary enemy, the United States, during the period 1953–1957, and "the US–USSR enemies in collusion against China" during the period 1958–1970.[53] Contending with the imperialist superpowers, which, either singly or in unison, threatened China's very survival, Mao gave priority to defense-oriented national development through the commune system. Thus, characteristic of the period 1953–1970 was Mao's aim of inspiring a quarter of mankind to generate the willpower to "wipe out the mountain of capitalism". This was to communize the whole of China "to remove the mountain of imperialism" with the people's power. The mass line strategy he devised for these gigantic tasks, which required the moral requisite of "serving the people", was basically to "unite all who can be united". Mao did not attempt to create a selfless man *per se*. He wanted to create this selfless communist man for his purpose of confronting the imperialist enemy or "the superpower enemies in collusion". The emphasis on class struggle and the mass movements of the rectification campaigns was to prevent the revival of capitalism and bureaucracy, neither of which could unite the masses, and thus could not summon the people's power against China's external enemies. Thus, Mao's collectivization scheme was aimed at materializing his defense-oriented communization system.

However, the year 1971 saw the beginning of the transformation of Mao's worldview when the United States began to be replaced by the Soviet Union as the primary enemy. As a secondary enemy, the United States was now considered non-antagonistic. Mao therefore began to replace the element of moral incentive with that of material incentive in China's economic development, which became Mao's primary national task. Thus, a Western-styled economic approach was adopted during the period 1971–1976. As a result, Mao's consistent calls for class struggle and aspirations for a more egalitarian society, which were meant to weed out non-proletarian thought for "uniting with all possible" against China's primary enemy and the "Number One accomplice of the US", were no longer relevant. Likewise, his tenet of "serving the people" as well as his aim of making a communist man, which contradicted his new policy, had to be eventually abolished, as the international environment became conducive to effective national development.

Mao's approach inspired the post-Mao leadership to organize a quarter of mankind in carrying out modernization in relays. During Deng Xiaoping's time, the international environment was quite different from the Maoist period, 1950–1970. With a peaceful and stable international environment, the post-Mao national priority to develop its economy in the real sense has been made possible. As a result, Deng's four modernizations scheme inherited from Mao called for the dismantling of the outdated commune system and the abolition of the Maoist element of class struggle. Mao Zedong's "continuous revolution", which was aimed at preventing the comeback of Liuist "revisionism", was now redundant and therefore had to be abandoned.

Deng felt that China's productive forces could only be effectively developed with advanced science and technology. By formally opening up the country to the outside world, Deng planned to tap science and technology as well as vital foreign capital and administrative management, particularly from the US-led West, for its economic reform and modernization schemes. Further, in 1979, Deng formulated the "good neighborliness" policy to promote regional peace and stability to help create a new Asian economic "miracle". This policy was subsequently extended to include the South American and African continents and elsewhere around the world. The post-Mao leadership's grand strategy, with its open-door policy of "inducing the whole world to help modernize China", led to a marked "improvement of the people's livelihood". The post-Mao leadership has rationalized Mao Zedong's strategy for long-term economic development through the organization of the whole population to uplift "the mountains of economic and technological backwardness" with Western economic principles and advanced science and technology.[54] With "Mao's mass line strategy", according to Deng, "raising the living standard of the whole population was to get their support."[55]

However, Deng's "non-capitalist" state sector was preserved to play "a predominant role in the economy" in ensuring social cohesion, "by developing the collective economy" as put forward in the 1975 Constitution.[56] This element of "socialist orientation" inherited from Mao's "state capitalism" eventually proved inefficient in Deng's economic reform, resulting in great losses in this sector.[57]

As a result, Jiang Zemin, in his time, boldly implemented his "Three Represents" to allow private entrepreneurs and capitalists to bring about reform of the state-owned enterprises. This was aimed at "keeping pace with the times" in line with the popular international trend of the private economy and, more importantly, of economic globalization. Jiang's market-oriented economy was based on the rule of law and less on government intervention thus allowing foreign and private investors to take controlling stakes of state-owned enterprises. His "people" were now dominated by the capitalists and professionals. However, by adopting Deng's strategy of "one country, two systems" in an attempt to resolve the Taiwan problem, Jiang created two fronts which Mao would have avoided. Jiang's primary task was the modernization of the country.

Chapters Two and Three of this work will deal with Mao Zedong's first development model, the defense-oriented collectivization venture, which derived from the global power politics at that time. Chapter Four focuses on the watershed in the post-Mao four modernizations endeavors which had been continuously stimulated by relatively peaceful and stable international relations after 1971. Chapters Five and Six discuss the four modernizations tasks of Deng, while Chapters Seven and Eight highlight Chairman Jiang's approaches. These tasks were a continuation of the Maoist development revolution.

In sum, Mao's defense-oriented development work during the period 1953–1970 was that he organized the whole population to generate the will power to "wipe out capitalism" through the communization of the whole country for his fundamental aim of "annihilating US imperialism", China' primary enemy, which, starting in 1958, "colluded with" another superpower against the PRC. The continued Maoist modernization efforts of the post-Mao leadership was primarily related to the favorable international environment. Based on Deng Xiaoping's globally oriented strategy of inducing the whole world to help modernize China, the Jiangist modernization efforts continued to aim at "improving the livelihood of the people" for "ten thousand future generations". The Dengist four modernizations scheme, Mao's legacy, has been carried out since December 1978.

This work is divided into three main periods: the 1950–1970, 1971–1976, and the post-Mao periods, dealt with in the following period chapters:

The 1950–1970 Period: Mao's First Development Model

1. Mao's 1945–1953 worldview and the collectivization scheme,
2. The United States as the primary enemy during the period 1950–1969, with the Soviet Union as the "No. 1 accomplice" of the United States during the period 1958–1969. Mao's conception of the Great Leap Forward, the communization scheme, and the Cultural Revolution.

The 1971–1976 Watershed Period

3. The Soviet Union as the primary enemy, with the United States as a secondary enemy during the period 1969–1976: Mao's relaxed development policies.

    During the period 1958–1969, the United States was treated as the primary enemy but in the period 1969–1972, the USSR gradually replaced the US to become the primary enemy in Mao's worldview, dictated by the changing international kaleidoscope.

The Post-Mao Period: Mao's Second Development Model

4. Mao's legacy: Deng Xiaoping's economic reform and open-door policy,
5. The transformation of bipolarity and Deng's globally-oriented strategy,
6. The international environment and Jiang Zemin's Dengist globally-oriented strategy,
7. Jiang's approach to privatization,
8. China in the new century.

Chapter Two
Mao's Post-War Worldview and the Defense-Oriented Collectivization Scheme

Mao's post-World War II perception of the international environment led to the conception of his strategy concerning the new PRC's political economy. This work argues that Mao considered the post-war United States as China's primary enemy, and the Soviet Union as its *de facto* enemy. His collectivization scheme was central to the PRC's defense-oriented economic development. It was aimed at paving the way to his communization goal, with "wiping out capitalism" as a pre-requisite for ultimately "annihilating imperialism", by "uniting with all possible". Mao's political-economic policy was conceived in view of the hostile international environment. In the following, we will first consider Mao's post-war worldview.

Mao's Post-War Worldview of 1945–1953: The United States as the Primary Enemy

The end of World War II witnessed two new ideologically opposing camps in the realm of international relations, that is, the East and the West, with the former headed by the socialist USSR and the latter by the imperialist US. As Mao saw it, this was the start of an era of a bipolar world order, in the light of a general preoccupation with a likely confrontation between the two camps. In his worldview, the First and Secondary Intermediary Zones had not yet materialized during the period 1945–1949, and the Chinese Communists were still in the wilderness.

In its anti-communist stance, the United States, as Mao saw it in August 1946, was making worldwide large-scale military arrangements and setting up its military bases worldwide to contain the Soviet Union. Mao also argued that "attacking the USSR would be out of the question until the US had subjugated the rest of the world".[1] He stressed that after World War II, "it was not the Soviet Union that was the first to suffer US aggression, but those countries where these military bases were located".[2] Although Mao had yet to carry out his "new democratic revolution" against the Kuomintang (KMT), his worldview gradually took shape in this light.[3] His post-war worldview was that the US anti-communist stance was a "smoke-screen" for its attempt to "subjugate the intermediary world".[4] This meant that the US policy had several targets, the three main ones being Europe, Asia, and the Americas. China, according to Mao, was the center of gravity in Asia. Therefore, by seizing China, the United States would possess all of Asia.[5]

Therefore, just a month before the establishment of the PRC, Mao wrote that "the US aid to China during and since the close of the World War II, totalling over 5,914 million US dollars, given to help Chiang Kai-shek slaughter several million Chinese [...] had one purpose, namely, that it consistently maintained those fundamental principles of the US foreign policy toward China which included the doctrine of the Open Door and opposition to any foreign domination of China".[6] Thus, as Mao saw it, the US grand design for the containment of China and the domino theory primarily directed to encircle it had long been planned.

With the success of his socialist revolution, Mao initiated a collusion with the Russians and, in his plan, with the "oppressed peoples" of the world against US imperialism. Mao argued that the Sino-Soviet Treaty and Agreements were aimed at "opposing the possible imperialist invasion".[7] Therefore Mao's worldview was shaped by the world situation as he perceived it, which contributed to his later attempt to form a united front with "all who can be united" against the United States primary enemy.[8]

John W. Garver argues: "the leaders of the People's Republic of China had the option in late 1949 and early 1950 of developing a working relationship with the United States and Mao's choice not to pursue that option lost Taiwan for the PRC".[9] However, back in January 1945, according to Harrison E. Salisbury, Mao "had sent a personal message to President Franklin Roosevelt saying that he and Zhou Enlai were ready to come to Washington and negotiate an arrangement" for Sino-US cooperation.[10] Salisbury's research shows that Mao had "never gotten a reply".[11] Therefore, Garver's claim that the US policy in late 1949 and early 1950 "to wash its hands of the Kuomintang to condone an anticipated PLA takeover of Taiwan" was far from convincing.[12] Moreover, Mao had concluded in his report "The Present Situation and Our Tasks" to a meeting of the Central Committee of the CCP towards the end of December 1947 that the United States had inevitably become the PRC's primary enemy: "Irreconcilable domestic and international contradictions menace US imperialism everyday. This situation has driven the US imperialists to draw up a plan for enslaving the world".[13] Further, in his articles "Cast Away Illusions, Prepare For Struggle", "Farewell, Leighton Stuart", "Why It Is Necessary to Discuss the White Paper", "Friendship Or Aggressors?" and "The Bankruptcy of Idealist Conception of History", all written in August 1949, around the time when "the US washed its hands of the KMT" as Garver claims, Mao concluded from the US State Department's White Paper and Dean Acheson's Letter of Transmittal that "the imperialist nature (of supporting Chiang Kai-shek and anti-communism) of the US policy towards China had been sealed".[14] According to Mao, "The White Paper is a counter-revolutionary document, which openly demonstrates US imperialist aggression and intervention in China":[15]

> As stated in Acheson's Letter, the United States in this last war has given the Kuomintang government material aid to the value of "more than 50 percent" of the latter's "monetary expenditures" and "furnished the Chinese armies" (that is, the Kuomintang armies) with "military supplies". It is a war in which the United States supplies the money and guns and Chiang Kai-shek supplies the men to fight for the United States and slaughter the Chinese people. [...] The war to turn China into a US colony has been an important component of the US imperialist policy of world-wide aggression since World War II.[16]

It was therefore very difficult for Mao to think otherwise.

The Soviet Union as the *De Facto* Enemy in Mao's Worldview

This work proposes that from 1945, after World World II to the beginning of the Korean War, the Soviet Union gradually became the *de facto* enemy in Mao's worldview, while the United States was the primary enemy. This meant that, strictly speaking, there was no real "angel" in his worldview. However, Mao believed that in enhancing China's efforts to counter US imperialism, it was necessary to side with the Soviet Union at this crucial stage. Thus, in 1946, he artificially made the USSR the "angel" in his worldview or the "defender of world peace" as he put it. However, by scheming and manipulation, the Soviet Union under Stalin had virtually annexed Outer Mongolia from China only a year earlier, and the US–USSR predominance at the Yalta Conference permitted Russian entry into Xinjiang province. All this had occurred against the Chinese will. Furthermore, Mao revealed in 1969 that Stalin had tried to make Xinjiang and Manchuria Moscow's "colonies".[17] However, circumstances dictated the necessity of siding with the Russians against the United States, its primary enemy, at this crucial stage. Although this was to tap Sino-Russian combined forces against the United States, Mao undoubtedly considered the Soviet Union China's *de facto* enemy. He would have to complete his socialist revolution before he could defend his country from any imperialist intrusion. At this stage US imperialism was too strong all around the globe in its confrontation with the socialist camp.

Mao's interest in Outer Mongolia can be traced back to the time of the Edgar Snow interview in 1936[18] and other occasions as well. In July 1936, Mao told Snow that following the victory of the Chinese revolution, Outer Mongolia was to "automatically become a part of a socialist federation of China".[19] The Soviet Union recognized Chinese suzerainty over Outer Mongolia as a result of the Mutual Defense Pact signed in 1936.[20] Snow writes that during the Bolshevik revolution the Russians helped create the Mongolian People's Republic (MPR) after overthrowing the Lama priesthood.[21] According to Snow, though the Soviet government continued to "recognize the PRC's nominal sovereignty over *all* (emphasis existing) Mongolia, the Soviets made an armed alliance with Outer Mongolia and stationed troops there".[22] In 1945, Snow continues, by signing the Sino-Soviet military alliance against Japan with the KMT government, Stalin obtained Chiang Kai-shek's full recognition of Outer Mongolian independence.[23] That alliance, according to Snow, died a natural death once Mao achieved victory, but Outer Mongolia retained its independence and was still a military ally of Moscow.[24] In February 1949, Mao asked the Soviet leaders for their opinion about the amalgamation of the MPR with China.[25] Stalin replied that he did not believe the MPR would give up its independence in exchange for autonomy as part of China even if all Mongolian areas including Inner Mongolia were to be united.[26] Under the terms of the Chinese alliance with the Soviet Union in 1950, Mao had accepted the independence of Outer Mongolia "unwillingly" with the crucial consideration of "socialist unity".[27] In 1954, during Khrushchev's visit to Beijing, the Chinese had offered a new amalgamation "deal", but the Soviet delegation refused to discuss it.[28] In 1956, the Chinese declared that Outer Mongolia should be returned to China, and in the publication of Beijing's World Atlas, the MPR was made part of China.[29]

Salisbury traced the origins of the dispute between Mao and Stalin back to 1927 when the latter supported Chiang Kai-shek even after "he turned on the Communists in the massacre that year at Shanghai".[30] According to Mao, China's revolution was "successfully carried out against Stalin's objection".[31] From the beginning of 1937 to August 1938, through Wang Ming, Stalin tried to stop Mao's attempt to carry out the revolution.[32] During the anti-Japanese Communist-KMT united front period of the 1930s, Salisbury argues, Stalin sent Chiang planes, arms and military advisers but only a planeload of propaganda leaflets to the Communists.[33] Salisbury further writes that in 1946 "when Chiang began preparing an all-out drive against the Communists, Stalin urged Mao to enter into a coalition with Chiang and take a secondary role".[34] Thus, Mao realized that "to get Stalin's financial assistance is just like trying to get a piece of meat from a tiger's mouth".[35] Moreover, as is well known, Stalin tried hard to prevent Mao's victorious armies from completely destroying Chiang in the late 1940s. Thus, at the end of 1948, seeing Lin Biao's army sweeping down south from Manchuria, Stalin quickly sent an envoy to Xibaipo to dissuade Mao from crossing the Yangtze River. Stalin's attempt to create two Chinas was obvious. The paranoid Stalin could have considered that a liberated China would be a grave threat to the Soviet Union.

It has been alleged that Stalin conspired with Gao Gang (高岗) to set up an "independent kingdom" in Manchuria. This was plausible. In the days of the Comintern, Stalin appointed and sometimes even executed leaders of other parties. He also used the Cominform to expel Marshal Tito of Yugoslavia from the movement as a result of the conflict between them in 1948. Gao committed suicide in 1954 rather than face charges of treason, with the discovery of his secret alliance with Stalin. According to Mao, "Stalin bribed Gao Gang with a car and Gao sent Stalin a birthday telegram on August 15 every year".[36] Mao described the Gao-Rao (Shushi 饶漱石) anti-Party betrayal as a "shocking earthquake of grade eight".[37] In his paper "To Recall the Gao-Rao Event" published in 2005, Yang Shangkun confirms that "Gao-Rao anti-Party betrayal was backed by Soviet great power chauvinism".[38] In his memoirs, Khrushchev claims that "Because of Stalin's betrayal of Gao Gang, we lost a true friend who supplied us with valuable information about the true attitude of the Chinese leadership toward the Soviet Union".[39] It seemed that the Chinese bitterly tolerated the Russian animosity and betrayal for the sake of "socialist unity" in the face of the threat of US imperialism.[40]

Perhaps nothing was more revealing than the Korean War of 1950–1953, which, Harrison Salisbury convincingly argues, was Stalin's plot to embroil China in a war with the United States in order to destroy the new PRC.[41] Snow contends that the "well-planned, well-supplied offensive (by North Korea) could have been undertaken" with prior consultation with and approval by Stalin.[42] All this was obvious, in addition to the arguments above. To reiterate, the Russians firmly believed that China's victory in its liberation war was a real menace to them.

Having secured the Sino-Soviet military treaty in mid-February 1950, Stalin's deadly plot was able to "dispel" his apprehensions that "China might follow the Yugoslav road".[43] Salisbury's well-documented account shows that in the second half of February 1950, having secretly instigated his protégé, Kim Il-sung of North Korea, to attack South Korea, Stalin promised Mao that the Soviet Union would send its air force to aid the Chinese land action in the war. Kim returned to North Korea in early March 1950 and the fighting erupted along Korea's 38th parallel on June 25 that year. However, Stalin "triple-crossed the Chinese", as Salisbury put it, by breaking his promise while the Chinese forces were already pouring toward the Yalu border.[44] Salisbury's research shows that with this very scheme, "Stalin lured the Chinese down a path of no return".[45] Stalin's plot certainly gained the upper hand in the tripartite US-USSR-PRC relationships. However, even without Stalin's "promise", Mao would still defend North Korea. Any military strategist would accept the necessity of "stopping" the eventual war spillover into Manchuria. This the Chinese described as "damage to the lip would make the teeth vulnerable to the cold" (唇亡齿寒). Mao believed that he had no choice but to go to war, contrary to Garver's argument.[46] This was because, according to Mao, "if the whole of Korea was taken away by the Americans, the whole Far East would be exposed to considerable danger".[47]

The Korean War of 1950–1953 and the US Containment of China

In mid-October 1950, direct Sino-US military confrontation began as the US-led United Nations forces crossed the thirty-eighth parallel. Rolling back the Americans with "tactical counter-attacks on all fronts" indeed gave the new PRC a sense of strength, generating more confidence for its subsequent contention with the "invincible" US superpower. As Mao said, "the Chinese people are now organized, they are not to be trifled with".[48] On the basis of the US grand strategy of anti-communism, the day after the Korean War broke out, the United States dispatched the Seventh Fleet to "neutralize the Formosa (Taiwan) Straits". At the same time, President Truman announced increased aid to the French in Indochina and strengthened US forces in the Philippines. By dragging in the issues of Taiwan, Vietnam, and the Philippines, the United States was determined to contain China. With the crystallization of the United States' China policy of containment and the domino theory, there were, as John Welfield put it, "the unprecedented and sustained build-up of US nuclear, naval, and air power in Asia and the Pacific from the Aleutians, through Japan, Korea, Taiwan, and Southeast Asia to Australia; the formation of an extensive network of interlocking military alliances such as the Southeast Asia Treaty Organization; the efforts to isolate the PRC militarily, diplomatically, economically; persistent large-scale military intervention in North and Southeast Asia".[49] Therefore, to Mao, the United States' China policy of containment was central to its worldwide containment of communism. Thus, according to Mao, in an attempt to neutralize Communist Chinese influence in Asia's intermediary zone, the United States sought economic, and therefore military, domination.[50] This was contrary to Akira Iriye's simplistic argument as follows:

> Not only ideologically but militarily American interests were seen to be deeply involved. The US must now resist any further alteration of the status quo by force (after the Korean War). "The loss of Taiwan", as MacArthur reminded the Congress, "might well force our western frontiers back to the coasts of California, Oregon and Washington". Similar considerations motivated a departure in policy toward Indochina. America's involvement in Vietnam began in 1950, with the initial aid to the French of $150,000,000.[51]

Long before the monumental US aid to South Vietnam was proposed, President Eisenhower's speech concerning US policy at a Governors' Conference on August 4, 1953, had lent credence to Mao's argument:

> Now let us assume that we lost Indo-china. If Indo-china goes, several things happen right away. The peninsula, the last bit of land hanging on down there, would be scarcely defensible. The tin and tungsten that we so greatly value from that area would cease coming. All of India would be out flanked. Burma would be in no position for defense. All of that position around there is very ominous to the US, because, finally, if we lost all that, how would the free world hold the rich empire of Indonesia. So, when the US votes $400,000,000 to help the war, we are not voting a give-away program. We are voting for the cheapest way that we can to prevent the occurrence of something that would be

of a most terrible significance to the US, our security, our power and ability to get certain things we need from the riches of Indo-China territory, and from Southeast Asia.[52]

Therefore, Mao's position was a reaction against the US imperialist global scheme as he saw it. Understandably, he initiated collusion with the Soviets, and in principle, with the "oppressed peoples" of the world to form a united front with "all who can be united" against US imperialism, China's primary enemy.[53]

However, on January 12, 1954, giving the Council of Foreign Relations "an overall view" of the foreign policies of the new Eisenhower Administration, Secretary of State John Dulles announced the United States' "great strategic change", which was initiated in 1953 during the Korean War to further isolate the PRC.[54] This was Eisenhower's so-called "peaceful transformations" about which Mao cautioned his colleagues, pointing to the US aim of "colluding with the Soviet Union against China".[55] Less than a fortnight later, Pospelov, Secretary of the Soviet Communist Party's Central Committee, responded that "Russia would do everything to ease international tension and solve all disputed problems by peaceful means".[56] Quoting Lenin's theory of the Soviet struggle for easing international tensions, he emphasized that "the Soviet Union could exist together peacefully with capitalist countries".[57] On January 27, Dulles made it clear to Soviet Foreign Minister Molotov that he should prevent "the Chinese Communist aggressors" from joining the Berlin Conference, which was to be convened a few days later, "for the purpose of dealing with the peace of the world".[58] As Mao perceived it, this development not only was a watershed in the Sino-Soviet relations, but threw light on the gradual "US–USSR collusion to the disadvantage of the Peoples' Republic of China".[59]

The de-Stalinization movement at the 20th CPSU Congress in February 1956 put further pressure on Mao. To him, the movement could dangerously exert a destabilizing influence on Mao Zedong Thought and his leadership. Thus, in his speech "On the Correct Handling of Contradictions Among the People" at the Enlarged Eleventh Session of the Supreme State Conference on February 27, 1957, Mao stated that "revisionism or right opportunism is a bourgeois trend of thought which is even more dangerous than dogmatism". The PRC denounced Soviet "revisionism" as a cowardly acquiescence to Western, especially US domination. Following the Soviet launching of the first intercontinental ballistic missile and space satellite, Mao stated in the Conference of Communist Parties on November 18, 1957: "The international situation has now reached a new turning point" that "the forces of socialism are overwhelmingly superior to those of imperialism".[60] On this basis, Mao suggested to consolidate "the Sino-Soviet alliance and the Socialist camp in the face of the US hostility".[61] Understandably, the Russians and their European comrades refused to accept his assessment of the international situation.

Even Mao's link with the Third World was weak *vis-a-vis* the primary enemy. At the 1955 Bandung Conference, China attempted to marshal the animosity already nursed by the Third World against US imperialism into an Afro-Asian alliance under the slogan of anti- old or new colonialism.[62] Moreover, at the 1957 Cairo Conference, the Chinese, in the name of the liberation movements of the "Moscow Declaration", encouraged the Afro-Asian alliance to expand its united front on anti-colonialism and anti-imperialism.[63] After the Conference, the Chinese strongly fanned anti-imperialist revolutionary flames in many Afro-Asian nations in an attempt to wean aligned nations from the West, for instance, by supporting the Indonesian communist movement, the Iraqi rebel government, and the demand by the Laotian Communists for the formation of a coalition government.[64] Support for all these movements was geared to the Chinese policy of anti-US imperialism. The outcome of the Bandung Conference enabled China to establish diplomatic relationships with thirty Afro-Asian nations.[65] Although the PRC's diplomatic achievement in making these nations neutral prevented them from joining any anti-communist alliance, its anti-US activities were not effective in facing the superpower. With the emergence of the Soviet "revisionists", Mao's aim of colluding with the USSR superpower against the stronger US superpower in the bipolar world did not work out. Therefore, he resorted to organizing the whole Chinese population, because "the richest source of power to wage war lies in the masses of the people".[66]

It is important to note that in mid-June 1953 Mao estimated that the transition period of the Party from the founding of the PRC to the basic completion of socialist transformation would take "ten to fifteen years, or a little longer".[67] However, in the opening speech at the National Conference of the CCP in March 1955, Mao cautioned his colleagues that "China was still surrounded by imperialist forces" and urged that they "must be prepared against all possible emergencies".[68] "If the imperialists should unleash a war in the future", he continued, "very likely they would launch a surprise attack, as in World War II".[69] Therefore, he concluded, "we must be prepared, mentally and materially, to avoid being caught unawares by such a sudden turn".[70] As a result, from the summer of 1955, Mao changed the above-mentioned time-table and accelerated the process of transformation. Thus, the second half of 1955 saw an upsurge of the cooperatization effort of the agricultural producers. At the end of that year, the number of cooperatives reached 1.9 million from 650 thousand previously. In his speech "On the Ten Major Relationships" at an enlarged meeting of the Political Bureau of the Central Committee of the CCP in April 1956, Mao emphasized the following: "For enemies are still around, and we are being bullied and encircled by them. We must strengthen our national defense and for that purpose we must first of all strengthen our work in economic construction".[71] It is in this context of Mao's international perception of the United States as China's primary enemy and the Soviet Union as its *de facto* enemy that his defense-oriented strategy for China's political economy need to be considered.

Devising the national united front strategy was vital as great masses of peasants were available as defence against the aggressors. In the Beidaihe Enlarged Political Bureau Meeting concerning "the Resolution of the Question of the People's Communes in the Peasantry", August 17–30, 1958, Mao introduced the principle of a defense-oriented commune system, which was characterized by the unified mobilization of the whole population. This was based on the PRC's various wartime experiences.[72] Characteristic of Mao's military-based communism was the concept of an "equalized livelihood" for the population in which soldiers and the people were to be treated equally and the military officials and the soldiers were also to be treated the same. Using this system, the Communists were able to defeat Japanese imperialism and the KMT. On many occasions, Mao also emphasized that the "leftist communist wind" of "robbing the peasants" or illegally ordering them about was absolutely prohibited. Thus, Mao's mass line strategy was formulated to develop the collectivization scheme. His defense-oriented economic development strategy, based on the Yenan model, was to ultimately lead to his communization goal. In the following, the development of the agricultural producers' cooperatives (APC) will be discussed.

The 1953–1957 Period: Mao's Development of the Agricultural Producers' Cooperatives

When the Communists took over the mainland in October 1949, the economy was badly disrupted. Both industrial and agricultural production had plummeted while the transport and distribution systems had been badly damaged. Furthermore, inflation had skyrocketed beyond control. As Eckstein writes, "under the impact of deficit financing, military requirements, a narrowing tax base, the economy (had been) caught up in an accelerating process of hyper-inflation".[73] To promote financial stability, the new PRC government issued the so-called people's currency (*renminbi*) and banned the circulation of foreign currencies as a medium of exchange.[74] Gradually, prices and wages were stabilized through drastic reduction of the paper money in circulation. A new taxation system was devised. During the recovery period, Mao's policy helped to rehabilitate the economic life of the people and restored agricultural and industrial production. The government launched an agrarian revolution in June 1950 to target landlordism, confiscating landowners' holdings and farm implements for redistribution to landless peasants.[75] The nationalization of industrial and other non-farm enterprises, together with land reform, collectivization and compulsory purchases of farm products, were initiated during the rehabilitation period. Certainly, this was the first step to winning the majority of the population in carrying out the huge task of national economic reconstruction and in countering US aggression and the hostility toward China already nurtured by the Soviet Union. By 1951, hyperinflation had been arrested, fiscal and monetary stability had been restored, and agricultural and industrial production had recovered speedily.[76]

In mid-October and mid-December 1951, Mao gave instructions for the gradual development of the agricultural cooperatives.[77] The PRC was then in the midst of the Korean War. By December 1952, the land revolution had been completed. This paved the way for Mao's collectivization scheme to improve the people's livelihood and, more importantly, to unite the masses against US imperialism, Mao's primary enemy, and guarding against the *de facto* enemy.

Understandably therefore Mao's collectivization scheme, which had begun in 1953, was the basis for building a defense-oriented economy. Characteristic of the Chinese peasantry were small-scale individual economies. These would not only fail to unify and cement all the individual scattered units, but also breed capitalism. This, in turn, would lead to exploitation, thus rendering his mass line strategy difficult to improve the people's livelihood, repel US imperialism, and guard against the looming Soviet enemy. Thus, according to Mao, "by-passing" capitalism was needed. In promoting "by-passing" of capitalism in his collectivization scheme, Mao argued that agricultural cooperatives were aimed at "consolidating the CCP's alliance with the peasants on the basis of proletarian socialism and not of bourgeois democracy".[78] This was meant to "isolate the bourgeoisie once and for all and facilitate the final elimination of capitalism".[79] To Mao, proletarian socialism could unite and consolidate the masses, but bourgeois democracy could not, "like a pot of loose sand", as he put it. In "wiping out capitalism", which breeds individualism, and uniting the masses against the United States, cooperativization, the basic principle of collectivization, was his answer. This was especially the case in view of the then Chinese conditions where frequent national disasters rendered the land incapable of producing sufficient food for the vast population and where land management was primitive. Although land reform had improved their livelihood, Mao continued, the Chinese people remained beset with difficulties. The wealthy were in the minority, and the majority – more than 70% of the whole population – were poor.[80] Thus, Mao's rationale was to cement all people together by “cooperativizing”. In mid-December 1951, according to Mao, there were three hundred or more agricultural producers’ cooperatives, and two years later, the number grew to more than 14,000, a 46-fold increase.[81] In June 1955, the number reached 650,000.[82]

Mao's policy of “uprooting the mountain of feudal landlordism”, a continuous process inspired by the agrarian revolution in Hunan in 1927, ended in October 1952. However, the 1950–1952 land reform was also aimed at promoting the rich peasant economy essential for post- war national economic construction. The land reform movement de- monstrated that Mao’s tapping of the people’s power achieved by his strategy of “uniting with all possible” temporarily included the rich peasants. Mao’s land reform program during the periods 1946–1949 and 1950–1952 was the precondition for his gigantic task of “wiping out capitalism”. However, this program, initiated to temporarily protect the rich peasants, indicated the essence of China’s post-war national economic reconstruction. On the surface, socialist cooperativization seemed to be an economic solution. However, more importantly, in terms of national defense, this strategy was basic, because the whole population “must be prepared against all possible emergencies”.

In sum, with the primary aim of restricting capitalist development and minimizing individual land ownership in the short term and eventually abolishing it, Mao’s uprooting of feudal landlordism in terms of land reform – an integral part of transforming agriculture to pave the way to collectivization – was a precondition for his task of "wiping out capitalism” and a basic strategy for “uniting all who can unite” against US imperialism as well as the looming socialist enemy.

The Defense-Oriented Collectivization Scheme

Mao’s collectivization scheme was divided into three phases, namely, the phasing out of the rich peasant economy, the implementation of mutual aid teams (MATs) which were the foundation for his cooperatives, and the commune system. The first two phases paved the way for Mao’s defense-related commune system which will be discussed in the next chapter. In the following, Mao's policy of the rich peasant economy will be examined.[83]

Following the defeat of feudal landlordism, the phasing out of the rich peasant economy was seen as crucial for Mao's collectivization drive since he was primarily concerned with preventing capitalist development. Phasing out the rich peasant economy was essential to realizing Mao's egalitarian goal for national defense through his cooperativization scheme, which called for the support of the whole population and the formation of one class. Winning over the well-to-do middle peasants to isolate the rich peasants and landlords and thereby abolish their economy was imperative as the former groups constituted 20 – 30 per cent of the whole populace, while the poor and lower middle peasants made up 70 per cent.[84] These well-to-do middle peasants were supported by the rich peasants and landlords. How did Mao phase out the rich peasant economy?

As noted above, before the full cooperativization drive could be implemented following the success of the revolution, the rich peasant economy was indispensable for the rehabilitation of the economic production of the peasantry; and thus the existence of the rich peasants had to be tolerated temporarily. Thus, the 1950 Agrarian Reform Law was characterized by the policy of protecting the rich peasant economy – a policy which was even more lenient than the pre-1949 land policy toward the rich peasants. Mao's policy witnessed the change from requisitioning their surplus land and property to one of maintaining the rich peasant economy.[85] This was designed to boost rural production which was essential to the development of a viable national economy as well as to isolate the landlords. This was because "as the war has basically ended on the mainland and the situation is entirely different from that in the period 1946–1948 (when the People's Liberation Army was locked in a life-and-death struggle with the KMT [...] and the issue had not yet been decided)".[86]

Basically, the objective of Mao's collectivization scheme was "to organize public and private labour, mobilize the mass production enthusiasm and increase labour efficiency [...]", because, he argued, "if labour forces of *all* peasants are organized for collective labouring in terms of mutual aid (and cooperativization)", capitalism would crumble due to the astronomical cementing effect of the masses.[87] As a result, the mass line strategy would eliminate capitalist exploitation. In ensuring the realization of people's power, Mao injected into the peasantry a catalyst – the spirit of "serving the people selflessly". Further, in ensuring the success of the collectivization scheme, Mao introduced a state of egalitarianism where (theoretically) everyone was equal politically and economically. Mao's egalitarianism was a means but not an end in his battle against capitalism by involving all and making them united. He considered it "imperative to attain unity between the middle and the poor peasants, consolidate the co-operatives, expand production and achieve socialist transformation in the entire country".[88] This was "to establish the dominant position of the poor peasants and the new lower-middle peasants in the leading body of a cooperative, with the old lower-middle peasants and the new and old upper-middle peasants as the auxiliary force".[89] This was because they were the majority. Thus, in his attempt to "wipe out" capitalism, Mao was to realize astronomical power by winning over the majority of the people in carrying out economic production. With this policy, *all* Chinese could then become well off *together* and united against the powerful enemy or enemies outside China. The realization of an egalitarian peasantry following the completion of land reform was therefore a precondition for ensuring the achievement of Mao Zedong's scheme of collectivization.

In the urban areas, immediately after the takeover, the Communists nationalized the KMT-owned heavy industries – iron and steel, cement, electric power, petroleum, railroads and highways, and air transport. They also took over foreign-owned firms.[90] The protection of industry and the commercial enterprises of landlords and rich peasants [Article 4 of the 1950 Agrarian Reform Law (ARL)], except where they were run by "bureaucrat-capitalists and counter-revolutionary local tyrants", was spelled out in the land reform program in the early 1950s. The provision governing this was spelled out in Article 12 of the 1947 Outline Land Law. According to the 1950 ARL, land reform was to pave the way for China's industrialization. The industrial and commercial enterprises of the landlords and rich peasants were complementary to the peasant economy for the early rehabilitation of China's economic production. Thus, on many occasions, Mao stressed the necessity for private industry and commerce run by landlords and rich peasants.[91]

However, although Chinese private capitalists and businessmen were permitted to operate their own business, these were restricted in order to prevent capitalist development. Restricting the private capitalist economy was to improve "the livelihood of the workers and other working people on the basis of increased production".[92]

The Five Antis Movement in 1952 was directed explicitly at lawbreaking by capitalists, but its larger target was the national bourgeoisie as a class. This movement showed that the road that revolutionary China pursued was to socialism, not capitalism.[93] It was considered as "the first preparatory step toward the socialist transformation of Chinese capitalists".[94] The result of the movement strengthened the state-controlled economy.[95] By the end of 1952, only a third of wholesale trade, a little more than half of retail trade, and barely a third of factory production remained in the hands of private enterprises.[96] In 1955–1956 "three million capitalist industrial and commercial enterprises were converted into joint state-private enterprises".[97] This meant that the state invested in the enterprises and assigned personnel to share in the management together with the capitalists.[98] By 1956, most industries in China had been socialized. New cooperatives were formed by the amalgamation of wholesale, retail trade and handicrafts.[99] By September 1956, Zhou Enlai could claim that 99 per cent of formerly privately owned enterprises had entered into partnership with the state.[100] The socialist transformation of capitalist industry and commerce was basically completed by 1957. China now had only two types of ownership of the means of production, namely, socialist ownership by the whole people and socialist collective ownership.

From the MAT to the Realization of People's Power

When the collectivization campaign was completed in 1957, a hundred million peasant households had been organized into 750,000 higher-level APCs. How did Mao adopt the mutual-aid teams from the traditional Chinese peasantry as the basis of his cooperativization plan to tap all available labor forces so as to realize people's power?

Through cooperative arrangements among peasants in the form of small production teams, the MAT was adopted to achieve maximum production efficiency. This cooperative teamwork had been a simple informal work exchange system practised by Chinese peasants throughout the centuries. The principle involved was that peasants helped each other for mutual benefit. During peak seasons, a peasant family was handicapped by a shortage of workers, and if laborers were hired they would be idle in the off-peak seasons. Mao argued that "teams for the exchange and hire of labour were usually formed by peasants with insufficient land. Besides exchanging work among themselves for mutual aid, their members also hired themselves out collectively to families which were short of labour power".[101] Hiring was normally carried out by offering their own labor in return when the latter needed hands during peak seasons. Wong's research shows that ox-cooperatives were also "promoted in order to overcome the scarcity of draft animals".[102]

Thus, the people's power conceived by Mao for "wiping out" capitalism was to be realized by making everyone better off through cooperation for mutual benefit. In addition, supply cooperatives, credit cooperatives, and consumers' cooperatives were established to increasingly restrict the private economic opportunities of rich peasants and channel economic resources to the cooperative sector. To strengthen the ties between the urban and rural economies to guarantee the flow of commodities and capital between them, the "relation contract" was initiated.[103] Further, the local clans undertook construction and maintenance of communal projects such as water-works through cooperative peasant teamwork efforts. As early as 1934, Mao had already decided that, to abolish capitalism, cooperativization was the answer.[104] This was because "coordinated with the state enterprises", cooperative activities "will become a tremendous force in our economy and will gradually prevail and assume leadership over the private sector".[105]

Socialized agriculture was active even in the CCP-held border areas in north China during the anti-Japanese war period; and MATs were used to tap available labor and other scarce resources in stepping up production for the increased war effort. With a tradition of rural cooperatives, these areas achieved impressive records of economic production. Mutual aid was developed after 1949 in both old and newly liberated areas. Mao organized MATs in 1950 and completed co-operativization within a short span of eight years. To ensure the success of Mao's cooperativization scheme, the various rectification campaigns and movements carried out to develop the "proletarian consciousness" were critical. This "proletarian consciousness" was meant to "unite all who can be united" against US imperialism. Since "wiping out capitalism from the face of the earth" entailed "uniting all that can be united", Mao's project of changing human nature from selfishness to selflessness became more crucial. Mao thought that self-less people could be more easily united than selfish ones.

The principal objective of his rectification campaigns and movements, which was to develop "proletarian consciousness" and to correct deviant thoughts and attitudes, was to strengthen close ties with the masses. It is important to note that rectification of cadre work *style* was a major aspect in this scheme. Failings in cadre work style can be traced to "vestiges of evil ideology of the oppressing class, namely, remnants of petty bourgeois individualism".[106] Mao referred to cadre shortcomings such as "bureaucratism", "subjectivism", "sectarianism", and formalism in propaganda work.[107] Other shortcomings were patriarchal despotism, authoritarianism, the sentiment of mountain stronghold and so forth. Mao argued that the origin of all these failings in cadre work style could be traced to the attitude of arrogance and self-centeredness. All these would lead to divorce from the masses.[108] It was in this context that the following section will consider Mao's rectification campaigns, which ensured the success of his mass line strategy.

Ensuring the Success of the Mass Line Strategy

Mao's schemes for attitude change were basically designed to rid cadres, Party and non-Party members of bourgeois attitudes and specific "deviations". These were considered to be obstacles to the realization of his Herculean scheme of "uniting with all who can be united", from Party officials down to agricultural and industrial workers. This was to generate people power for not only his communist revolution but also his anti-imperialist fight. In this section, based substantially on Frederick Teiwes' work concerning the 1950 Rectification Campaign, Party Rectification and Party Building of 1951–1954, the "Anti-Bureaucratism-Commandism Movement of 1953 and the 1957–1958 Anti-Rightist Struggle and Rectification Campaign, it is argued here that Mao's rectification campaigns and movements originated in the Yenan period to ensure the success of his mass line strategy.

The nationwide victory marshaled a new era of Chinese social transformation. More struggles against non-proletarian thoughts such as "arrogance, the airs of a self-styled hero, inertia and unwillingness to make progress, love of pleasure and distaste for continued hard living" were envisaged for the goal of a socialist revolution.[109] These were the human weaknesses that Mao abhorred. Thus, the leadership "must be taught to preserve the style of plain living and hard struggle" so that it would not be divorced from the masses.[110] Commandism practised by basic level leadership had resulted in widespread popular dissatisfaction.[111] The Rectification Campaign of 1950, the first such campaign of the PRC, focused on the weaknesses of basic level leadership. Thus, commandism was singled out for attack in this Party rectification work in order to strengthen "relations between the Party and the masses in both rural and urban areas".[112]

The 1950 rectification campaign, according to Teiwes, was carried out over three years under the Party Rectification and Party Building Program to deal with basic level Party organizations in the rural areas.[113] The Three Antis Campaign of 1951–1952 was initiated to co- ordinate with this movement but focused on the urban areas.[114] The Five Antis Movement, on the other hand, aimed at law-breaking capitalists particularly the national bourgeoisie who had defrauded the state and the public.[115]

The National Organization Work Conference of March–April 1951 expressed concern that the Party had rapidly expanded by 2.7 million members in the previous two years without careful examination of new recruits, and thus included some "bad elements".[116] This led to the training of selected cadres to conduct rectification among basic level leadership in the autumn of 1951, since a leading core of grass-roots communist cadres skilled not only in administration and leadership but also in displaying ideological commitment was needed. Thus, the 1951–1954 movement stressed thought reform. "Bureaucratism" and "liberatism" were also attacked. Rich peasant thinking and capitalist tendencies were growing out of control in many places as a result of the temporary tolerance of capitalistic practices, such as the "four major freedoms" of buying and selling land, hiring labor, lending money, and leasing land.[117] Together with the traditional corrupt behavior of rural cadres, these were immediate problems to be tackled in the movement.[118]

Mao saw that bourgeois values, attitudes, and lifestyle had a direct link with the corruption of Party and government cadres. Thus, the key targets of the Three Antis Campaign were urban cadres, particularly those in the financial and economic departments who had been involved in corruption, waste, and bureaucratism.[119] The Three Antis Campaign was merged with the Five Antis Movements in January 1952 to tackle bribery, tax evasion, theft of state property, cheating on government contracts, and stealing state economic secrets for private speculation.[120] Teiwes argues that the two campaigns were closely related as the corrupt urban cadres, especially those in the financial and economic departments, dealt directly with the bourgeoisie.[121] The important role given to private industry and commerce in reviving the national economy had inevitably led to close relations between the cadres and the bourgeoisie. The Three Antis Movement also stressed the link between corruption and bourgeois exploitation of the working class. In educational institutions, the Three Antis Campaign was coordinated with the ideological reform of intellectuals, which began in October 1951. The movements resulted in increased central government control over both state and private economic enterprises, the breaking up of alliances between officials and businessmen, and the undermining of the prestige and security of private businessmen.[122]

All these were important factors in the further curbing of bourgeois influence in the subsequent movements.

In 1953, the Movement of "Anti-Bureaucratism-Commandism" against "bureaucratism", "commandism" and the violation of law and discipline was targeted against the rural areas.[123] It was an extension of the Three Antis campaign. Since the Three Antis Movement was focused on the urban areas, the campaign of "Anti-Bureaucratism-

Commandism" was aimed at the intermediate and lower levels in the rural areas. According to official statistics, about 3.83 million people in the Party apparatus (excluding the military organs) took part in the Three Antis campaigns.[124]

Crude basic level leadership methods such as "commandism" were widely used in the rural areas around 1952 and 1953. Instead of relying on persuasion, cadres used brutal methods to force their will on the people.[125] Another example was that cadres forced peasants to join mutual aid teams and subsequently APCs. A kind of bureaucracy existed, for example, "subjectivism", in which many leading cadres believed that merely issuing orders would achieve cooperativization speedily, alienated them from those working under them.[126] Great efforts were thus made to combat these shortcomings during the movement.[127]

Impediments to Mao's Collectivization Scheme

In Mao's worldview, China's primary enemy was the United States, with the Soviet Union as its *de facto* enemy after World War II. He considered it imperative to consolidate the great masses of the Chinese population by accelerating the process of his collectivization scheme. This scheme, however, motivated the Liuist "rightist" onslaughts on a number of occasions. Mao considered the 1957 rightist movement to be detrimental to the scheme and the Party leadership. Externally, according to Mao, the Soviet-dictated First Five-Year Plan of 1953–1957 was not compatible with the scheme and could not tap the people's power in countering the superpower enemies. The following section will examine the internal and external acts of hindrance to Mao's collectivization endeavors. They were:

(a) the "rightist" Liu Shaoqi's onslaughts,
(b) the 1957 rightist movement, and
(c) the Soviet "great power chauvinism".

Mao's determination to speed up the process of collectivization led to onslaughts by the "rightists" on a number of occasions.

First, the completion of land reform witnessed a new trend in the peasantry. By the end of 1952, three-fifths of all peasant farms were still privately owned and the remainder "had joined seasonal MATs with only a very small share belonging either to permanent MATs or to APCs".[128] According to Mao, in the "oppose rash advance" (反冒进) campaign led by Liu Shaoqi in the spring of 1953, the rightists attempted to "sustain private ownership" and practice the "four big freedoms", which were to "facilitate the growth of a small number of rich peasants and follow the capitalist road".[129] As a result, many peasants had sold their land to the rich peasants and the renting and leasing of portions of land and farm capital to the poor by the rich peasants had become common, since all this was allowed by the 1950 Agrarian Reform Law (Article 6). The development of the rich peasant economy was thus uncurbed and rural capitalism was resurgent.

According to Mao, mutual aid teams by themselves were not enough to stop peasants from selling their land, but only cooperatives and big ones of one or two hundred households could do so and could eliminate the need of peasants to rent out land.[130] Mao argued that cooperativization could make his anti-imperialist mass line strategy workable. Therefore, by October 1953, he had curtailed the rights of the rich peasants with the intensification of his cooperativization drive, and agricultural cooperation had been developed in 60 to 70 per cent of the old region and 20 to 25 per cent of the new region.[131]

Secondly, in June 1953, Mao criticized the Liuist emphasis on a "new democratic program" as inhibiting socialist transformation.[132] This was because Liu Shaoqi, who "firmly established the new democratic social order, hindered the progress of the socialist cause" of "burying the capitalist system and all other systems of exploitation once and for all".[133] Therefore, Article 4 of the PRC Constitution published in September 1954, was to ensure that "through socialist industrialization and socialist transformation, gradual annihilation of the exploitation system to establish socialist society in China (would be) guaranteed".[134]

Thirdly, criticizing the rightists' campaign of "oppose rash advance" in opposition to the cooperatization scheme in the spring of 1955, Mao as editor of the book *Socialist Upsurge in China's Countryside* wrote: "(The rightists wanted) the resolute contraction of co-operatives".[135] As noted above, Mao's objection to the rightists' campaign was that "the well-to-do and fairly well-to-do middle peasants, who constituted 20 to 30 per cent of the rural population, are quite strong" in that "behind the well-to-do middle peasants were landlords and rich peasants who gave them support".[136] Mao considered that the rightist attitude encouraged the growth of capitalism. This was because the "oppose rash advance" movement in 1956 "dampened the enthusiasm of the masses" which could jeopardize the mass line strategy and his anti-imperialist task.[137]

Furthermore, with China's abundant labor, scarcity of capital, and technologically undeveloped condition, Mao could forgo mechanization before agricultural collectivization was realized *for the sake of uniting the masses*.[138] He argued that if China's agriculture "could not make a leap from small-scale farming with animal-drawn farm implements to large-scale mechanized farming, then the contradiction between the ever increasing need for commodity grain and industrial raw materials and the generally low output of stable crops" could not be resolved.[139] Liu Shaoqi condemned Mao's policy as a "rash advance" toward full collectivization before the realization of the stage of agricultural mechanization.[140] However, Mao argued that Liu's policy of mechanization based on the Soviet experience as a guide could not make full use of the available population by mobilizing all human forces (and even animal forces) in the crucial drive for cooperativization.[141] According to Mao, the production and use of agricultural tractors and other farm machinery should only be considered on the basis of an agriculture where large-scale cooperative farming prevailed.[142] He criticized the Liuists for failing to see that China was now carrying out a revolution not only in the social system, a change from private to public ownership, but also in technology, a change from handicraft to large-scale modern machine production, and that the two revolutions were interconnected.[143] Further, according to Mao, they failed to realize the link between the large funds, which were needed to accomplish both national industrialization and the technical transformation of agriculture, and the fact that a considerable part of these funds had to be accumulated through agriculture.[144] Mao also argued that the large-scale expansion of light industry required the development of agriculture as well as of heavy industry and that only socialist cooperative agriculture could give peasants far greater purchasing power than they now possessed.[145]

The important point Mao emphasized was that by "taking the stand of the bourgeoisie, the rich peasants or the well-to-do middle peasants with their spontaneous tendencies towards capitalism", the Liuists thought "in terms of the few" and "failed to think in terms of the interests of the whole country and people".[146] Thus, in his February 1957 thesis "On the Correct Handling of Contradictions Among the People", Mao criticized the Liuists "who vainly hope to restore the capitalist system" and whose "right-hand men are the (Soviet) revisionists".[147] It is important to note that from then on Mao identified the Liuists with the "capitalists" as well as the Soviet "revisionists".

The 1957 Rightist Movement

Nineteen fifty-seven was the crucial year when the advanced APC was set to be transformed into a commune. Mao was anxious about the rightist opposition to the Party leadership led by the Liuists through their various "anti-rash advance" movements. Thus, the 1957 Anti-Rightist Struggle and Rectification Campaign was launched to safeguard Mao's "three red banners" – the Party's general line for socialist construction, the Great Leap Forward, and the people's commune – from rightist attack. His "three red banners" were crucial to defense against the external aggressors.

James P. Harrison argues that Mao appeared to have wanted the intellectuals to "educate" the Party cadres in strengthening their ties with the masses, while Goldman contends that launching a new attempt in industrialization required the support of the intellectuals and professionals.[148] Thus, starting from 1956, the intellectuals were given a degree of academic freedom. In addition, they were allowed to criticize officials in order to improve the bureaucracy. Zhou Enlai proposed certain reforms in order to arouse their enthusiasm. It was in this context that the Hundred Flowers Campaign was initiated in May 1956 to invite the people to criticize the ruling elite freely. According to Mao, "as scientific truth, Marxism fears no criticism" and Marxists should suppress bourgeois tendencies not by force but by argument, using the slogan "long-term co-existence and mutual supervision". In consolidating the unity of the whole population, Mao made his "Contradictions" speech at the end of February 1957, stressing the continuation of contradictions under socialism and "certain contradictions existing between the government and the masses", although these, he argued, were primarily "non-antagonistic" and "among the people".

However, the intellectuals and professionals began to call for more access to Western publications and ask for the London "Hyde Park" type of free speech forums. Some pro-Western economists even questioned the relevance of Marxist economic theories in the PRC. In early June, Party leaders found that criticism was being directed against the guiding policies and leadership of the Party – a direct response to the growing student unrest. Moreover, the "democratic" parties demanded that they be allowed independence from the CCP. In May 1957, Mao warned that the inner Party "revisionists" and the "right-wing intellectuals outside the Party acted in concert" and that the anti-Party "revisionists" inspired by the Soviet "revisionists" were "more dangerous than dogmatism".[149] The "rightists" were accused of "paying lip-service to socialism, but actually admiring capitalism and Euro-American type of government".[150] The PRC was being encircled by the United States. As Mao saw it, by sheer accident, the "blooming and contending" campaign had led the anti-Party elements to expose themselves. Top CCP leaders decided that the "blooming and contending" campaign was unacceptable if left unchecked. The period of free criticism was suspended and Mao launched the Anti-Rightist Movement against "bourgeois liberalism" in the public media.[151] This certainly shattered the assumption of united national support for the Party. Mao criticized the bourgeois rightists, such as Zhang Bojun (章伯钧), Luo Longji (罗隆基) and the leaders of the Democratic Alliance and the Peasants-Workers Democratic Party as "bourgeois reactionaries". In his September 1957 "Report of Rectification" to the Third Plenum, Deng Xiaoping attacked the "bourgeois rightists" for arguing that "laymen cannot lead experts, that Marxism is dogmatism, and that socialist countries are inferior to capitalist countries".[152] Reflecting bourgeois ideology and opposing centralism and Party leadership, the "revisionists" were considered inspired by external "revisionist" ene mies.

In the realm of international relations, China's primary enemy was the United States, and Mao could not afford to let the "rightists" undermine the Party leadership. This movement was primarily aimed at the bourgeoisie and intellectuals in the urban areas and members of the democratic parties. The Anti-Rightist Campaign showed Mao's increasing concern that educated youth, China's future generation of leaders, had insufficient revolutionary consciousness. The campaign purged about half a million intellectuals, who were sent to the countryside and factories for reform.[153]

Zhou Enlai admitted that shortcomings had been pointed out earlier and declared that they were recognized by the highest leadership, who called for continued efforts to handle correctly "contradictions among the people" and to overcome "subjectivism, bureaucratism and sectarianism" which could not "unite with all possible".[154] Therefore, the "rectification and improvement" movement was launched in September 1957 to replace the Anti-Rightist Campaign.[155]

Teiwes argues that official statements had interpreted that the aim of the "rightists" was to overthrow the existing system and restore capitalism, and that the rightists were proposing institutional change including rotating democratic parties in power, establishing a genuine coalition government of all parties.[156] However, this study argues that it was not merely this which caused Mao's anxiety. For the "rightists" were hardly in a position to achieve their aims. It would be more likely that Mao was more concerned about the impact the "rightists" would make, particularly through the press, on the society at large. The primary enemy's containment activities were in full swing. The year 1957 was a crucial year when the advanced APC was to be transformed into the defense-oriented commune. By mid-summer of 1957, it was reported that the events of the Hundred Flowers Campaign had adversely affected the rural situation, and criticism of the Party by "bourgeois rightists" had encouraged landlords, rich peasants, and counter-revolutionaries to engage in anti-Party activities.[157] Equally important, the inner-Party "revisionists were more dangerous than dogmatists". All this threatened Mao's dictum of "uniting with all possible" against the external primary enemy.

Thus, as articulated in his revised version of his "Contradictions" speech, Mao's "Anti-Rightist Struggle" focused on the theme of "uniting with the people but not dividing them", in other words, to "unite with all possible".[158] In addition, in July at the Qing Dao Conference Mao called on Party members to carry out a rural socialist education movement to combat "individualism, departmentalism and absolute egalitarianism" among cadres and to correct "right opportunist" ideas within the Party.[159]

Understandably, Mao's rectification and improvement movement launched in September 1957 on the eve of the transformation of the advanced APC into a commune was aimed at uniting the great masses to counter the external pressure from US imperialism and Soviet "revisionism".

The Soviet "Great Power Chauvinism"

Toward the end of the First Five-Year Plan (FFYP) in 1957, agricultural stagnation and poor harvests led to food shortages and became the critical bottleneck in furthering industrial development. The result of this Soviet-dictated FFYP was that industry had grown by 18 per cent but agriculture was only at 4.5 per cent, a declining rate. However, much of industry depended on agricultural raw materials. While the urban population had grown by about 30 per cent during the period 1952–1957, the rural population had increased by only 9 per cent; and government collections of grain were jeopardized. Moreover, natural disasters aggravated the situation. The pressures on agriculture were further intensified, Soviet credits were largely exhausted and the accumulated debt had to be repaid.[160] It was difficult for the country to maintain an export surplus of agricultural products and amortize the debt.[161]

In the early 1960s, Mao claimed that "in the aspect of economic construction, we had to resort to copying everything Russian particularly the Russian heavy industrialization".[162] Mao revealed that "(t)his was completely necessary and that we lacked the capability to be independent".[163] This revelation was contrary to Eckstein's argument that "the Chinese Communists had very few indications of a conscious search for an organizational model and a development strategy suited to Chinese conditions" and that "it was apparently taken for granted that the Soviet model could be adopted more or less ready-made".[164]

In the Sino-Soviet dispute in 1963, the Chinese accused the Soviet Union of practising "great power chauvinism in requiring the Chinese to use the Stalinist model of economic development" in the early 1950s which stressed heavy industry to the neglect of agriculture.[165] In the name of the "international division of labor", the Chinese went on, the Russians "imposed their will on others, infringing on the independence and sovereignty of fraternal countries".[166] In the international situation of the time, China had virtually no choice.

First, the Chinese needed the Russians to extend economic aid for their industrialization efforts. In May 1953, the Soviets offered the Chinese 156 aid projects, which became the core of their First Five-Year Plan of 1952–1957.[167] The Russians also extended loans to the Chinese to buy, on deferred payment, about two thousand completed industrial plants, military equipment and other commodities.[168] During the 1950s, the Soviets sent more than ten thousand technical experts to the PRC to train the Chinese. In addition, China sent more than thirteen thousand students to the Soviet Union for advanced training. The loans greatly helped China to establish a solid industrial base.[169] The Chinese allocated a significantly larger share of investment resources into heavy industry. According to K.C. Yeh, 46 per cent of the gross fixed investment was put in industry and only 20 per cent in agriculture.[170] K. Chao writes that during the whole FFYP period, about 89 per cent of the investment funds were allocated for industrial construction.[171] Chinese industrial growth strategy was critically dictated by Soviet ideology.

More importantly, as discussed above, in reacting to the start of an era of the United States' anti-communism and containment of the PRC, Mao resorted to initiating collusion with the Soviets against US imperialism. Mao revealed in September 1962 that the signing of the Sino-Soviet Friendship and Cooperation Treaty in Moscow in 1950 was concluded only after a tough two-month period of negotiation.[172] This was because, according to Mao, Stalin was not willing to sign the

Treaty.[173] Under the hostile international conditions, Mao thought it necessity to consolidate China's alliance with the Soviet Union against the United States. With the hostile containment policy of the United States on China, military considerations such as armament production were another vital factor underlying the Chinese "heavy industry first" policy. This explained why the Chinese were reluctant to give up the priority assigned to heavy industry. In his celebrated thesis "On the Ten Major Relationships" written in April 1956, Mao argued: "In the period of the FFYP, military (and administrative) expenditures accounted for 30 per cent of the total expenditures in the state budget".[174] This proportion, he claimed, was much too high. However, he argued that "still bullied and encircled by our enemies, we must strengthen our national defence".[175]

In December 1955, Mao became unhappy about China's total reliance on the Soviet development model, which stressed tight centralization and heavy industry to the neglect of the initiative of the people (the mass line) and agriculture. By 1956–1957 the relative neglect of agriculture had resulted in the slowdown of its growth rate and basic food supplies.[176] Certainly this strategy could not harness the people's power.[177] Mao evidently realized this because "only when we speed up the development of agriculture, light industry and heavy industry at the same time can we suitably improve the livelihood of the people".[178] However, although the Chinese government reallocated investment funds to industries which supported agriculture, its priority was still on heavy industries, particularly the defense industry. This was because although Mao proposed in 1956 in his thesis on the "Ten Major Relationships" that attention should be paid to industry and agriculture at the same time, he could only carry out this plan in 1960.[179]

In short, with the hostile international environment, Mao had no choice. The unbalanced economic strategy not only jeopardized the development of agriculture and light industry for the livelihood of the whole population, but also could not tap the mass power to face the PRC's external enemies.

To sum up the three impediments to Mao's plans, first, Mao's collectivization scheme led to the Liuist "rightist" onslaughts on a number of occasions. Second, he felt that the 1957 rightist attack would dangerously undermine his scheme and the Party leadership. Thus, the anti-"rightist" purge was aimed at consolidating the whole population to face the external pressures of US imperialism and Soviet "revisionism". Third, the Soviet-dictated First FYP, which emphasized tight centralization and heavy industry to the neglect of the initiative of the mass line and agriculture, led to a slowdown of the growth rate and shortage of basic food supplies. It not only jeopardized the PRC's economic development, but also could not harness the people's power to face the superpower enemies.

Conclusion

Treating the United States as the primary enemy and the USSR as the *de facto* enemy in Mao's worldview after World War II, Mao's foreign policy was to collude with the latter against the stronger former. With Mao's January 1954 perception of the gradual "US–USSR collusion to the disadvantage of the PRC", his domestic policy was to devise a national united front strategy for China's defense against US imperialism and guard it against the *de facto* enemy. Mao's mass line strategy was to serve his collectivization drive aimed at "uniting with all possible". The drive was meant to ultimately lead to his defense-oriented communization goal, which will be discussed in the next chapter. All in all, Mao designed his political-cum-economic strategy to create a united population to fight US imperialism and "US–USSR collusion". However, the Soviet-dictated First Five-Year Plan of 1952–1957 jeopardized the development of agriculture and light industry and thus could not tap the people's power to face China's enemies. Internally, according to Mao, the Liuist onslaughts on his collectivization drive on a number of occasions were attempts to restore the capitalist system. Starting from February 1957, Mao identified the "rightist" Liuists with the Soviet "revisionists". He considered the various Liuist onslaughts to be detrimental to his collectivization scheme and therefore to his mass line strategy. China was in a hostile international environment in which the Soviet Union turned out to be another "devil" in January 1954, in addition to the ferocious United States as the primary enemy. The origins of Mao's Cultural Revolution can thus be traced to the Liuist onslaughts on his collectivization scheme.

Chapter Three
1958–1969: The US as Primary Enemy with the USSR as "No. 1 Accomplice of the US" – Mao Launches the Great Leap Forward, the Commune and the Cultural Revolution

The previous chapter surveyed Mao's collectivization drive in order to "wipe out capitalism" which preceded his defense-oriented communization initiative. With the realizationn of his cooperativization efforts in about eight years, Mao launched his Great Leap Forward (GLF) and commune movements in the years of 1957 and 1958. His communization project, which used the anti-Japanese Yenan experience as a model, was accelerated in response to US and Soviet pressures in this period. While the United States had always been considered China's primary enemy, the twin superpowers were found to be colluding against China in 1958. In this chapter, we will consider how Mao increased his communization endeavors amid Soviet-influenced "revisionist" objections and Liu Shaoqi's "revisionist" maneuvers, which eventually and inevitably resulted in Mao's launching of the Cultural Revolution. First, let us consider the Sino-Soviet relationship.

1958–1969: The US as Primary Enemy with the USSR as "No. 1 Accomplice of the US"

In Chapter 2, I discussed US Secretary of State Dulles' 1954 announcement of "peaceful transformations" and the subsequent Soviet positivist response. This was taken as a sign of superpower collusion against the PRC which alarmed Mao. Following the Korean War, the new US foreign policy was aimed at further isolating the PRC, in addition to its encirclement activities in East Asia. Furthermore, as Mao was aware, the de-Stalinization movement in the 20th CPSU Congress in February 1956 was detrimental to Mao Zedong Thought and his leadership. In April 1965, the Chinese accused this CPSU Congress of "postulating US–USSR friendly cooperation to dictate to the whole world", apart from "combating Stalin's personality cult".[1] The Chinese further claimed that "the 20th Congress was the origin of the evils of Khrushchev's alignments with imperialism and oppositions against China".[2] Therefore, in July 1957, in his speech "On the Correct Handling of Contradictions Among the People", Mao began to denounce Soviet "revisionism", which he described as a bourgeois trend of thought that is even more dangerous than dogmatism".[3] Thus, needless to say, in mid-November 1957, following the Soviet launching of the first ICBM and space satellite, Mao's attempt to consolidate the Sino-Soviet alliance and the socialist camp with his estimate of the international situation that "the forces of socialism were overwhelmingly superior to those of imperialism" was unsuccessful. On May 13, 1958, the *People's Daily* referred to Mao's statement in the "Contradictions" speech. Mao's targets were Liu Shaoqi and Khrushchev, in the view of the *PD* editor that "it was not only directed to the situation in our country, but also fits the international situation well".[4]

Latent hostility between China and the Soviet Union, according to Mao, was aggravated by "Khrushchev's intention to control the Chinese coast from the autumn of 1958 onward through a common navy".[5] Mao later added that "Khrushchev's arrival at the end of July was because of this".[6] In my published work *Mao Tse-tung's Purposive Contention with the Superpowers: The Theory of Ch'i*, I argue that Khrushchev was not prepared to stand firmly by Mao's August 1958 Taiwan Straits offensive.[7] With great restraint to avoid direct confrontation with the US navy, Mao initiated the Taiwan Straits Crisis to discern how far Khrushchev would commit his new power in support of China's interests.[8] In his thesis "Mao Zedong and the Bombardment of Quemoy" published in 2005, Commander Ye Fei (叶飞) recalls: "Mao ordered that the target of bombardment be Chiang Kai-shek's warships but not the US navy".[9] However, Khrushchev's fruitless Beijing visit on July 31 before the Crisis of August 23 had already confirmed his decision regarding Soviet non-commitment to China's interests. As Snow revealed in his celebrated *The Other Side of the River*: "Khrushchev's quite gratuitous and maladroit tip-off to the US that the bomb would be withdrawn from Mao's hand if he followed through with an offensive to close down the Quemoy-Matsu bases".[10] In his book published in 2000, Khrushchev's son, Sergei Nikitich, confirms that Khrushchev "flatly refused to participate in military actions in the Taiwan Straits".[11] The Taiwan Straits Crisis not only demonstrated US determination to dominate Asia through its containment-of-China policy and the domino theory, it was the turning point in the Sino-Soviet relationship. The crisis confirmed that "the US and USSR (had) colluded to the disadvantage of the Chinese" in the face of the Sino-Soviet Friendship Treaty and Agreements.[12] A new enemy, "the No. 1 accomplice of the US", was now confirmed witnessing Mao's new worldview as a result of the changing international kaleidoscope. As Mao saw it, the "US–USSR collusion" was a blow to China both politically and strategically. In Mao's worldview, it represented a united front against China.

Khrushchev's "ambition to blockade the Chinese coast", to borrow Mao's term, was plausible. For the Soviets needed to dominate the PRC, not only because of the US–Soviet detente, but to eliminate this potential threat to Soviet supremacy. In a meeting between Mao and Khrushchev in Beijing in August 1958, Khrushchev did not get what he "intended".[13] The Sino-Soviet relationship turned sour and the Soviets aborted the Sino-Soviet agreements and withdrew all their technicians a few months later. This culminated in the Khrushchev–Eisenhower Camp David Meeting in 1959. These events reinforced Mao's anxiety although officially Sino-Soviet friendship was still intact.

After 1958, a new angle of tripartate Sino–US–USSR relations emerged that took into account the potential Soviet threat to China. In other words, the PRC had to contend not only with the US, but also with the USSR, now a confirmed "devil". In 1959 the Soviet sided with the Indians against the Chinese in the Sino–Indian border conflict. In addition, in November 1963, the Chinese claimed that after the Indians had initiated armed provocations against China in 1960, the Soviets began to supply India with military aid.[14] Because of

"US–USSR collusion", it proved difficult for Mao to benefit from Sino–USSR collaboration for his anti-imperialist agenda. The pressures, exerted on the PRC by the superpowers both separately and collectively, intensified Mao's determination to rely on his mass line strategy *to consolidate the people* at home to fulfill his GLF plan, the first step of his communization goal. Understandably, therefore, in the 15th Supreme State Council Meeting on the international situation in early September 1958, Mao emphasized the importance of military training in the communes.[15]

The Defense-Oriented Great Leap Forward

During the spring and summer of 1958, the first year of the Second FYP, disappointed with and in defiance of the Soviet-imposed development strategy, Mao launched the GLF in his own view on China's economic development. Goodman claims that Mao's GLF initiative was "a significant ideological challenge to the Soviet Union's claims to be furthest along the road to communism".[16] This study argues that with the Soviet economic model abandoned, Mao's GLF program was aimed at achieving phenomenal progress on all fronts through the mobilization of peasants and workers, men and women, civilians and soldiers, to "enter communism", which was meant to be defense-oriented in the face of the external imperialist enemies. Military considerations thus underly China's "heavy industry first" policy. In the 15th Supreme State Council Meeting on the international situation in September 1958, Mao clarified his communization objective "to arm the whole population".[17] This study contrasts with Lardy's pure economic approach on Maoist policy particularly concerning "Mao's firm belief in his mobilization of existing resources primarily labor within the rural economy to provide a breakthrough for more rapid growth".[18]

The problem the PRC faced in the formulation of the Second FYP was how to maintain the rate of industrial growth and also improve agricultural performance. Mao was not prepared to divert investment resources from industry to agriculture, with a consequent decline in industrial growth. Mao subsequently claimed that "national defence is too indispensable; and we are being bullied and encircled by our enemies".[19] Chen Jian argues that "Mao's constant use of international tensions" was "for the purpose of domestic mobilization in the Great Leap Forward", while Lieberthal contends that the GLF was "based on almost utopian optimism about what the CCP, with its methods of mass mobilization, could accomplish".[20] However, my study is that Mao's domestic mobilization in the GLF was to unify the great masses of the people against possible attacks by China's external superpower enemy or enemies "in collusion". It was along these lines that his new development strategy was speeded up in the second half of 1958.

Under great pressure from the US and USSR superpowers, Mao argued for the need of a more productive steel industry. In the 15th Supreme State Council Meeting concerning the international situation in early September 1958, Mao called for the GLF and industrialization to move quickly, an urgent issue at the height of the US pressure on China. He noted that "(o)ur private industry is estimated to be only 1.7 billion yuan, that is, less than US$7 billion. With this little bit (of capital) how couldn't we be bullied? That the imperialists bully us is not without reason".[21] He argued that, with the availability of steel as a base, defense industries would be possible. According to Mao, "we must firmly grasp the three-line construction. After we have established steel, defense, machinery, chemical industry, oil (fossil fuel), we will not fear even if war breaks out".[22] In early 1958, the NPC announced the GLF agenda for the next three years, with the aim of increasing steel production by 19 per cent, electricity output by 18 per cent and coal output by 17 per cent in 1958.[23] It is not surprising that he had an obsession with steel as an indicator of collective strength, as evidenced on many occasions particularly during the GLF period, as can be seen in his speeches collected in the book *Mao Zedong Si Xiang Wan Sui*. The following are examples:

> If we can produce 11 million tons of steel next year, and 17 million the year after next, we will shake the world. If in five years, we can reach 40 million tons, then in 15 years, we will surpass the US (May 1958).
>
> We must achieve the production of 11 million tons of steel this year. [...].We must increase ++ tons next year in order to reach ++ million tons. A year of hard work will give us ++ million tons of steel, that is, we will rank third after the USSR and the USA (September 1958) [24]

Even as early as in September 1950, Mao argued that US imperialism which "had an abundance of steel demonstrated its military advantages".[25]

In this industrialization drive, Mao took a further step toward socialist transformation by creating the people's communes. The Second FYP was abandoned in mid-1958 when the nationwide GLF and commune movements were launched. By November 1958, he had organized 26,000 people's communes convening 98 per cent of the peasants from the merger of 750,000 higher-stage cooperatives that combined industry, agriculture, trade, education, and military affairs with government administration and commune management. On average, each rural commune consisted of some 30 cooperatives of about 5,000 households or 25,000 people. With the slogan "politics in command", the GLF was a landmark mass mobilization of labor for irrigation, reclamation, and flood control tasks designed to raise agricultural yields and output with minimum input of capital.[26] Mao relied on mass mobilization of China's astronomical manpower in his quest for an instant breakthrough on all fronts. In an attempt to consolidate the masses, Mao mobilized ninety million peasants to build backyard steel furnaces, with the neglect of expertise. The shoots of communism appeared in 1958 in the form of the multi-functional communes, which were meant to provide a transition from socialist collective ownership to ownership by all. Mao's strategy was to transform the narrow collective ownership of the land of the communes and capital goods into ownership by all the people in the full socialist form. In this way, social coherence was to be guaranteed and the mobilization of a united population to repel possible attacks by external enemies could be possible.

With the purpose of consolidating the entire population, the Rectification Campaign of 1957–1958, launched following the Third Plenum, was related to the Great Leap Forward movement and people's commune movements.[27] The realization of GLF aims, the amalgamation of APCs and the development of the commune necessitated indoctrinating the masses once again with selfless communist spirit. To ensure the success of these movements, the dictum "uniting with all possible" was applied as the theme of mass mobilization.

Mass mobilization, together with the GLF emphasis of maximum use of local resources, led to administrative decentralization. Characteristic of the rectification and improvement was the partial phasing out of the centralized bureaucratic economic apparatus in favor of decision-making autonomy for localities. Thus the *xia fang* or downward transfer of cadres was needed. First appearing in the early 1940s, the downward transfer of cadres to lower levels had been popularized since 1957. This was originally designed to change cadre attitudes through physical labor to break down the distinction between mental and manual work. Apart from serving as both administrative decentralization and strengthening local units, the downward transfer movement was aimed at bringing cadres into direct contact with the masses to overcome bureaucratism, and at avoiding their divorce from the masses through participation in labor. Moreover, efforts were made in the movement to bring intellectuals and workers and peasants together. This was "to unite with all possible".

Mao's economic strategy now was not that of the heavily industrial, capital-intensive, Soviet economic model, which allowed for agricultural stagnation. This model was not suited to the Chinese conditions of abundant labor, little capital, and little agricultural surplus for industrial capital. He instead initiated a policy of "walking on two legs", which stressed agriculture and industry. Meanwhile the traditional and modern sectors were preserved in that medium and small-scale labor-intensive industries based on indigenous technologies were developed with the modern industrial sector.[28]

In the following section, based in part on my published work *Mao Tse-tung's Ch'i and the Chinese Political Economy With Special Reference to the Post-Mao Modernization Revolution*, I will discuss Mao's commune system as an organizational technique of tapping the power of the people to face China's imperialist enemies.[29]

In order to "wipe capitalism from the face of the earth", Mao considered organizing the people to "unite all that can be united". This technique can be traced to the anti-Japanese war period, when Mao organized the anti-Japanese government in the Shen-Kan-Ning Border Areas. The political-economic-military principles that guided this process became crucial to the commune system Mao set up in 1958. In other words, the Border Areas *as a whole* became a prototype for this commune system. Mao's idea that the nation be organized as a "combination of production and militia" therefore materialized in relation to communes as individual units.

During the period of revolutionary struggle against Japanese imperialism, militancy was the key to political organizations in the Border Areas. This principle applied to the 1958 commune drive to combat the "US and Soviet collusion at the disadvantage of the PRC". In the communes, all young men were expected to become a soldier. Men eligible by age and demobilized servicemen were organized into the militia underwent continuous military training.[30] In a speech delivered in Beijing on September 30, 1958, Mao also stressed that the militia was both a military organization and a labor organization".[31] Reflecting the Yenan experience, workers, peasants, traders, students and soldiers of the nation were systematically integrated into Mao's communes so that "the broad masses of the people become workers when entering factories, peasants when going to the fields, and soldiers when taking up arms".[32]

The consumption-related activities such as cooking, washing and child-rearing were shifted from a household to the communes, releasing female labor for work in farming activities.[33] These shifts toward increasing collective activities were aimed at enhancing Mao's dictum "uniting all who can unite". To further enhance the dictum, principles of income distribution were fundamentally changed, with a large share of net earnings distributed on a per capita basis to minimize the income differentials within the communes.

Further, in November 1958, Mao asserted the importance of the production of commercial goods appropriate for exchange in the communes, in addition to those of self-sufficient production.[34] According to Mao, commercial production served the cause of socialism in that it provided the state not only with goods, but with accumulated capital.[35] Previously, in September 1953, Mao had emphasized that state capitalism would transform capitalist industry and commerce.[36] This would serve the nation's economy and raise the standard of living of the people.[37] More importantly, Mao argued, this was "to unite a few hundred million peasants".[38]

Evolved from the traditional cooperative system for organizing peasant labor forces, the commune model was developed in the early 1940s by Communists who organized production teams and combined the production systems with the local militia in each community unit (village) under a unified command. The organizational structure and management of the 1958 communes corresponded to that of the Shen-Kan-Ning Border Government model. Defined as "both economic unit and basic unit of state power", the commune was organized to strengthen the control functions of the Party at the lower levels and to give new functions to the local governments such as the *xiang* (township) and the *xian* (county). Thus government decentralization at the higher levels was balanced by centralization at lower levels. Linkage between the political and economic administrations also made possible to tap the people's power from the whole populace. Judging from the MATs of the Yenan period developed in the post-liberation period into the basic agricultural producers' cooperatives, which in turn were developed into the advanced APCs, it is clear that the people's commune was, for Mao, the most logical way of tapping the people's power of the whole population to fight powerful external enemies.

The commune was a higher form of socialist organization with the structure roughly approximating a sub-unit or district within the county. It was essentially a township comprised of a market town (sometimes even several small towns) and its satellite villages. Within each large village or brigade were production teams made up of between 20 and 60 households, depending on the district. The mix of private and collective activities was shifted toward the latter. Private farming plots were eliminated under the commune system; households within certain sections of the village now worked the land as a team.[39] During the non-farming period, household members might serve on other brigade teams, work in commune industries or services. While the commune in 1958 typically was a township (*xiang*) comprised of a number of villages (*cun*), Mao's ideal commune also included gradual development into "the federation of people's communes at a county level to become one with the people's council of that county".[40] Mao's original 1958 commune was based on the idea of "one *xian* one commune" system. The original form of the actual commune was a huge organization (5,500 households each), about 25 times the size of the higher-stage APCs formed in 1955–1956 which took over the functions of the local government and claimed to have achieved "communism" by providing "to each according to his needs". Thus the commune project revealed Mao's strategy that the task of China's socialization aimed at reaching ownership-by-all of the means of production and eventually a consolidated communist society.

Therefore, to eradicate capitalism and guard against possible imperialist intrusion through consolidated power generated by the masses of the whole nation, Mao organized the communes. With the notion of "serving the people" as catalyst, Mao's communization plan served as a means to realize consolidated power by first "wiping out capitalism" for his ultimate aim of fighting imperialism.[41] Thus we can see that Mao's method of acquiring this power had been at work since the Yenan period. This phenomenon persisted throughout the decades in his anti-feudal, anti-capitalist and ultimately anti-imperialist tasks.

The Concept of Moral Incentive to Unite the Entire Population

In the following section, I will elaborate how Mao furthered his commune system for the purpose of consolidating the entire population by introducing the moral incentive of "serving the people selflessly".

The principal objective of Mao's commune system was to promote "proletarian consciousness" so that close ties with the masses could be strengthened. First, all bourgeois thought and culture were to be suppressed. In addition, individual interests were to be subdued to the common interest, private property renounced, the ethical education of all carried out by the state. This is reminiscent of the Yenan anti-Japanese imperialist "unified leadership" through which public enterprises, peasant cooperatives, a collective self-reliance economy, education, the choice of rank and possession, and the arts and literature were all placed under the exclusive and absolute control of the state. Based on Mao's idea that social life must be the collective life; this consummation of his ideal of justice, is to be attained by a system of communism and the common education by the state. Furthermore, the system incorporated into a nation's whole structure would enable astronomical power to become generative vis-a-vis powerful external enemies.

The realization of Mao's communist ideal necessitated indoctrinating the masses with selfless communist spirit. Division of labor had a drawback from Mao's viewpoint with respect to his mass line philosophy. By creating an egalitarian society, he applied the moral incentive of "serving the people" in order to win over the majority. Social cohesion, as Mao saw it, could only result from collective contribution, not competition for individual gain.

To Mao, egalitarianism meant social coherence, mass participation, and serving the people – a vision that could be fulfilled only when individuals first served others. Its complete antithesis, the pursuit of private profit, would produce social individualism and thus divisiveness rather than social coherence. On this view of the nature of man, one owes a responsibility not merely to oneself, but to one's neighbor. This was Mao's approach to realizing consolidation of the great majority of the people. This social coherence was to be guaranteed by establishing a commune system in China. This rationalized Mao's hyperbolical ideal of "the will of each thinking in terms of all" – an effective method of consolidating "all possible" to produce an astronomical result. In response to Marx's call for the selfless brotherhood of communism, Mao put the notion of egalitarianism into practice. Heir to Marx, Mao envisioned a cohesive society where each would live to "serve the others" and no rights to private property would be asserted. In order to implement this concept effectively, Mao saw that as vanguard of the proletariat, the party system was vital with effective leadership. Thus China was to become a conglomeration of communes where people elected their own leadership.

An important factor hindering this desired social coherence, Mao explained in "Dialectical Materialism", was "idealist philosophy", or the "reactionary ideology of the ruling classes". This ideology, according to Mao, was rooted in the material process of production with the technical and social division of labor. "With the development of the productive forces of society", Mao argued, "the division of labour saw the emergence of persons elevating themselves entirely and exclusively to intellectual labour" who "became the exclusive privilege of the ruling class, while manual labour became the oppressed classes".[42] As a result, it was difficult to "unite with all possible" to eradicate capitalism in order to fight imperialism effectively. Thus, to eliminate the distinction between manual labor and intellectual labor was one of the preconditions for eliminating capitalism.

To make his commune system effective in the long-term in generating astronomical power to eradicate capitalism, "minimizing or abolishing the difference between town and city, between rural worker and factory worker, between manual and mental labour" was needed. This was to make the feudal peasant educated, literate and scientifically-minded – the counterpart of an educated, literate, technical factory worker.[43] Therefore the social organization of the future communist society was to be centered in the commune and designed to be at once city and countryside, trade market and production center.[44] This meant that the commune would take over all local government functions, and would be the instrument for elimination of private ownership of the means of production. Each commune would thus become a small individual state whilst in addition to being united to all the others by cultural, economic, political and military bonds.[45]

Thus Mao's grand strategy was the formation of the basic unit on which to build the structure of a nation and through which Herculean power could then be generated for the purpose of fighting imperialist intrusion, similar to the Yenan model designed for dealing with Japanese imperialism.

Mao's Communization Model Challenged: The Soviet-Backed Right Opportunism and Liuist Revisionism

Mao's determination to wipe out capitalist thought and prevent the "restoration of capitalism" associated with the primary enemy and the "No. 1 accomplice of the US" was challenged. "Right opportunists" and Liuist "revisionists" were opposed to his defense-oriented communization agenda. While the former's widespread opposition was Soviet-encouraged, the development policy of the latter was identified as capitalist motivated and Soviet "revisionist" oriented. Mao was thus under great pressures both externally and internally. In the following, I will deal with the dismissal of the "right opportunists" and then with that of Liu Shaoqi, "China's Khrushchev", the primary targe of Mao's Cultural Revolution.

The 1959 Dismissal of Soviet-Encouraged "Right Opportunists"

The 1959 dismissal of the "right opportunists" on the surface revolved around policy differences over the "three red banners". However, this campaign – a "rectification of the whole Party" – was a major effort to combat widespread opposition led by Peng Dehuai over the CCP's economic policies. More importantly, this widespread opposition was backed by "revisionist" Khrushchev as Mao implied in his letter to the editors of *Shikan,* Zang Kejia and Yuan Shuipai on September 1, 1959.

Mao's astonishing economic plans, together with unfavorable weather conditions, first caused disaster to agriculture and then severely curtailed the supply of agricultural raw materials to industry. The economy took a serious leap backward starting in 1959. The "right opportunists" then launched their anti-Mao attack.

With Soviet backing, the "right opportunists" attacked Mao's policies of the GLF and people's communes as "left adventurist" errors. However, as early as February 1959, Mao had already noted the "leftist wind of communism" after the establishment of the commune system in the autumn of 1958.[46] Mao warned that this "leftist wind" or "communist style" of "robbing the peasants" in terms of "equal distribution, moving the ownership of certain properties of the production teams upwards without compensation, and reclaiming banking loans from the peasantry", which was detrimental to his mass line strategy, had to be stopped.[47] The "right opportunists" ignored Mao's warning prior to the Lushan Conference.[48] In late June of 1959, on his way to the Lushan Conference, Mao called for the ignoring of unrealistic targets set by higher levels leadership and identified comprehensiveness and balance as critical issues.[49] The "right opportunists" disregarded Mao's statement and charged that the GLF was a scheme of "petty-bourgeois fanaticism", as Peng Dehuai put it, based on a "pitch black" general perspective.[50] Mao was aware that this opposition was detrimental to his strategy of uniting all of the people – crucial to his "three red flags" – he needed the spirit of single-mindedness of the masses if his schemes were to succeed. He argued that through pouring cold water on the "revolutionary zeal" of the Party and hundreds of millions of people, Peng Dehuai's challenge would have had a negative effect on Mao's defense-oriented plans.[51] Mao's real concern regarded de-emphasis of the mass line through promotion of capitalist elements to the masses. Viewing collective production as excessively rigid and detrimental to the productive enthusiasm of peasants, the "right opportunists" advocated measures promoting "small freedoms" and individual production. The result, the Maoists argued, would be a "retreat to scattered individual labor" and the danger that capitalism would be restored in the peasantry.[52] The emergence of the Russian "revisionism" had inspired the "right opportunists" to challenge Mao's "three red flags". Understandably therefore, in a Hangzhou meeting in November 1959, Mao, referring to Dulles' three talks of 1954 on US-proposed "peaceful transformations", warned that Dulles' agenda had seeped through the very foundation of socialism.[53]

It became quite obvious that what Mao actually objected to were: firstly, "right opportunists" colluding with the Russians to oppose his "three red flags". The harmful effect of the bourgeois "expertise" of the "right opportunists" regarding Mao's "redness" and "mass line" strategy was considered great. Further, the revolutionary fervor of the masses, without which Mao's "three red flags" and hence his socialist revolution would collapse, would be extinguished. The effect would be extremely detrimental as it would involve hundreds of millions of people, thus weakening his anti-imperialist stance. Thus Mao's struggle against the "right opportunists" began with a call for opposing bourgeois ideas and for increased efforts to achieve the "three red flags" goals. Since the plenum, the press had been filled with denunciations of "right opportunist" views such as "bourgeois anti-socialism" and "criminal activities against the building of socialism". The rectification campaign was an effort to stop the danger of "right opportunist ideology" spreading throughout the nation. The 1959 rectification campaign showed that Mao was determined to wipe out capitalist thought at any price and, more importantly, the detrimental external influences of the Khrushchev-backed "right opportunist" Peng.

Mao's View on High Treason

According to Teiwes, during his 1959 spring tour to the Soviet Union, Peng Dehuai "expressed misgivings" regarding Mao's GLF and commune schemes to Khrushchev. Khrushchev in turn "allegedly encouraged Peng to return to China to oppose Mao" and subsequently "attacked the Chinese communes in a speech in Poland".[54] Mao's outrage at Peng's unprincipled behavior described as "treason" was understandable.[55] Undoubtedly the Chinese regarded what Peng did as "most despicable", likening it to "a family member who eats at home but crawls outwards" (吃里爬外). The international situation in 1959 was crucial as was evident when the Soviet Union was confirmed as the "No.1 accomplice of the US primary enemy" in Mao's worldview. Mao considered Peng's "collusion" with the Russians an attempt to "push over Mt. Kunlun" as an act of high treason.[56] Therefore Peng's fate was sealed as a result of the 1959 rectification campaign against "right opportunism". The case against Peng and his supporters resembled that of Gao Gang and Rao Sou-shi of 1954. In his "speech at the second plenary session of the Eighth Central Committee of the CCP", on November 15, 1956, Mao denounced Gao's high treason as "having illicit relations with foreign countries"(里通外国).[57]

During the months of August and September 1967, three articles were published on subsequent dates in the *Beijing Review* that accused Peng of carrying out "his heinous crimes" of anti-Party activities particularly with respect to the GLF and communization movements.[58] Attempting to appeal some of the charges against him particularly those of having secret ties with the Soviet Union and organizing an anti-Party clique, Peng wrote a letter to the Central Committee and Mao during the period of "the wind of reversal of verdicts". This period involved re-examination of wrongful verdicts and the rehabilitation of individuals found falsely charged in the 1959 anti-rightist struggle.[59] Mao responded that rehabilitating Peng was out of the question.[60]

Mao referred to many acts of treason committed in ancient China. For instance, the overthrow of Zhou Wang (纣王) of the Shang dynasty (16th century B.C.–1066 B.C.), according to Mao, was due to the treacherous Shang minister Wei Zi's (微子) "illicit relations with the foreign Zhou (周) dynasty".[61] With his critical appreciation of the ancient text *The Various Kingdoms of the Eastern Zhou Dynasty* (东周列国) written by Feng Meng Long (冯梦龙), Mao talked about the "overturning of a country with treason".[62] Mao's comments on this issue occurred around December 1959 after the Lushan Meeting. This meeting focused on the anti-"right opportunism" struggle against Peng, described as "ganging up with Khrushchev" against Mao's commune system.[63]

Mao's psychological insight can be seen in his great reverence for the patriotic Yue Fei (岳飞) (1103–1141), the celebrated general of the Song dynasty (960–1279), who is considered as China's preeminent national hero. I discovered that Mao's calligraphy of Yue's lyric *Man Jiang Hong* (满江红) is displayed in the gallery beside Yue's tomb in the Hangzhou city of Zhejiang province (浙江省).

The Dismissal of Liu Shaoqi, "China's Khrushchev"

To account for the purge of Liu Shaoqi, the "No. 1 power holder in the Party taking the capitalist road" during the Cultural Revolution, we must first deal with the difficult period of 1958–1961 and the aftermath.

The Difficult Period of 1958–1961
and the Emergence of the "Capitalist-cum-Revisionist" Economy

During the "difficult period of 1959–1961", the Liuist economic policy was officially carried out.

In the initial stage of the GLF, differentiated and incentive rewards were increasingly replaced by an egalitarian wage system, causing a negative effect on labor productivity.[64] At the same time, the Maoist leadership turned from the approach of modern industrial technology and large-sized plants emphasized in the First Five-Year Plan to indigenous production methods and small plants, which turned out to be detrimental to the economy.[65] Harmed by a succession of agricultural setbacks starting in 1959 due primarily to unfavorable weather conditions that lasted for three years ("the worst in the century") and by the sudden withdrawal of Soviet advisers and technicians, agricultural output significantly declined and the economy was badly disrupted. As farm output worsened in 1960, Mao's mass labor mobilization plans were abandoned and the GLF discontinued.[66] This resulted in a sharp decline in commercial crop output for light industry and subsequently a fateful blow to heavy industry. As a result, sources of investment funds dissipated.[67] The winter of 1960–1961 witnessed the worst food, agricultural and economic crises in the PRC since it came to power. Economic development was virtually brought to a standstill.

During the "difficult period of 1959–1961", a series of natural disasters exacerbated by the disastrous GLF led to a liberalization of agricultural policies and Liuist "revisionist" policies were officially carried out. Measures were taken to increase material incentives through the "*san zi yi bao*" system, which allowed private plots and free markets, increased the number of small enterprises responsible for their own profits, and in some cases allowed peasants to leave communes to engage in private farming. The average size of the communes was also reduced through the transfer of much decision-making authority from the communes to production brigades and teams. Research works of Skinner and Richman confirm that by 1964 there was a reappearance of former economic patterns based on material incentives for China's peasantry, while Hoffmann's study reveals the reappearance of free markets in 1959 and the small private plots in 1960,[68] which created links between individual effort and compensation.[69] At the height of international hostility, this "revisionist" economic policy, which threatened the mass line, was certainly not acceptable to Mao. Further, at both conferences Liu Shaoqi criticized the economic problems that resulted from Mao's GLF.[70] Liu had partially "reversed the verdicts" of the anti-rightist struggle and GLF, restoring Party positions to those dismissed. Thus, the "struggle between two lines" flared up at two enlarged Party and Central Committee work conferences in January–February 1962. At the first conference Mao emphasized the need for continued "protracted, complex and at times [...] violent class struggle" because of the persistence of bourgeois ideology, and for guarding against a "capitalist restoration" such as had been occurring in the USSR.[71] Mao would have launched his Cultural Revolution at this stage. However, his Socialist Education Movement proceeded for an unusually protracted period, from the winter of 1962 to March 1966. My findings show that a series of events that occurred in the international arena largely prevented the launching of Mao's initiative. The following will survey these events.

As discussed above, in Mao's perspective in the late 1950s, the Soviet Union had become a confirmed "devil" while the US was still seen as the primary enemy. Sino-Soviet relations then worsened, exacerbated by a series of events that occurred between the two communist giants. This included the 1960 Khrushchev attack on Mao at Bucharest, the Sino-Soviet border arms build-up in 1962,[72] and finally the 1963 Sino-Soviet dispute after it became public knowledge. Published in the *Beijing Review* in mid-July 1961, the united front strategy reappeared to counteract confirmed "colluding US–USSR imperialism" with the emphasis of Mao's commune project.[73] It is in this context that in the following section we will consider the international environment before Mao found the opportunity to launch his Cultural Revolution.

According to Li Jie's research, in the later half of 1962, China faced the possibility of simultaneous large-scale invasions by the US and the USSR.[74] Mao also raised the possibility that the twin superpowers would jointly attack China, one from the north and the other one from the south.[75] The US–USSR threat was real. Moreover, the Moscow Test Ban Treaty was signed by the US, USSR and UK in 1963. The Chinese considered the Soviet role in the signing of the June 1963 Test Ban Treaty with the US (and the UK) as a betrayal of the Sino-Soviet alliance, for not only did the Chinese need to develop their own nuclear capacity,[76] but, more importantly, they believed the growing US–USSR detente and cooperation was aimed at them. Allowing Chiang Kai-shek to be a signatory to the treaty, the Chinese argued, meant that the Soviets conspired with the US against them.

On June 10, 1963, President Kennedy delivered a speech in which he said that the US and the USSR "had a mutually deep interest" and expressed the hope that "the leaders of the Soviet Union (would) adopt a more enlightened attitude".[77] Immediately the *Evening Star* had this to say: "The time might come when the US would be allied with Khrushchev and company in a common front against the Peking peril".[78] Khrushchev replied: "Kennedy's speech makes a favorable impression. We have noted with satisfaction the call for better relations between the US and the USSR".[79]

In July 1964, the Chinese claimed: "At the 22nd Congress of the CPSU, the revisionist Khrushchev clique developed their revisionism into a complete system not only by rounding off their anti-revolutionary theories of 'peaceful co-existence', 'peaceful competition' and 'peaceful transition', but also by declaring that the dictatorship of the proletariat is no longer necessary in the Soviet Union and advancing the absurd theories of the state of the whole people and the party of the entire people".[80] The Chinese criticized the Russians arguing that, with the abolition of the dictatorship of the proletariat behind this camouflage, Soviet leadership under Khrushchev paved the way for the restoration of capitalism.[81] The Chinese were obviously concerned about "US–Soviet collusion" against them.

In April 1965, the Chinese accused the new leadership of the CPSU of following Khrushchev's "general line of foreign policy to uphold peaceful co-existence" and "US-Soviet collaboration for the solution of the problems of the world".[82] The Chinese further stated that the 20th Congress of the CPSU "was the first and the most significant sign of the emergence of Khrushchev revisionism.[83] In the same year, a new Soviet book entitled *The USSR and the USA – Their Political and Economic Relations* "lavishly praised the Soviet government's perfidious activities of colluding with the US", according to the Chinese, which the author claimed were not only "in accord with the interests of the Soviet and American peoples", but were "vitally necessary for the destiny of all mankind".[84]

In these circumstances, in which the PRC stood in opposition to the world's strongest powers combined, the government had no alternative but to initiate resistance to the "colluded" superpowers by relying on Mao's people's war. In the influential "Problems of Strategy in Guerrilla War Against Japan" (first published in May 1938 by Mao), the *Beijing Review* of August 27, 1965 republished Mao's theory of the people's war. This issue emphasized the vital practical importance of Mao's strategy for the Chinese people in their struggle against US imperialism.[85] The ideas expounded in the article, the editor hinted, "played a great guiding role" in China's possible war against the United States, which had "colluded" with social imperialism. It particularly pointed out "the important strategic role of guerrilla warfare". The article elaborated that "(t)oday it is very clear that the theory of a people's war found in Comrade Mao Tse-tung's article is of vital practical importance for the Chinese people [...] against US imperialism and its lackeys". We can see why Mao had clung to his communization drive the entire time. Ross writes that during the Vietnam War, "Mao was so alarmed by the American threat that he placed the Chinese economy on a war footing".[86]

Externally Mao initiated resistance to the "colluding" superpowers by working on the extremely weak basis of uniting with the intermediary world to form the so-called "united front".[87] The grouping included the nations of Asia, Africa and Latin America as the First Intermediary Zone and the capitalist nations of Western Europe, Oceania, Canada and so on as the Second Intermediary Zone. Beginning in February 1963, the Chinese organized the Afro-Asian-Latin American Consolidation Conference with Afro-Asian-Latin American peoples in an attempt to establish an anti-US-USSR united front. In 1965 Lin Biao's essay of "world countryside to encircle the world cities" expounded the Chinese policy of strengthening the world's subversive activities, especially communist insurgency and the establishment of an anti-US united front in Southeast Asia in an attempt to break up US containment. Between 1958 and 1965, China won formal diplomatic recognition by 22 non-communist governments, with 17 of them from Africa.[88] The Chinese also tried to improve relations with the Second Intermediary Zone of mainly Western European nations, regardless of whether they had previously had ties with the PRC, through diplomacy, trade, and cultural activities.[89] Launching a diplomatic offensive in an attempt to neutralize Western European anti-Communist solidarity through attractive trading conditions, the PRC was able to establish trade relationships. In January 1964, Sino-French diplomatic relations were established. The number of Western nations, that had recognized China, now increased to eight, and other West European nations also relaxed their attitudes. In a sense, therefore, China was quite successful in breaking up Western anti-Communist solidarity. Through commodity exchange and trade with the United Kingdom, France, Italy, West Germany, Canada and Australia, China imported not only food staples, but also manufactured items such as steel, machinery and airplanes. Because these West European nations granted political and economic credits to

China, it was enabled to end its diplomatic isolation and improve its economy. More importantly, this ended the Western nations' embargo against the PRC instigated by the United States.

It is important to note that while the Johnson administration initiated US involvement in formal combat in the Vietnam War during the second half of the 1960s, Leonid Brezhnev, who had replaced Khrushchev as Party leader in the Soviet Union, was focusing on domestic problems. This brought the Chinese some relief in the international arena. In January 1964 and again in mid-September 1965, on both occasions, Mao told visitors that "globally the US–Soviet contradiction can never be resolved".[90] He reached this conclusion prior to launching the Cultural Revolution in October 1965.[91] US support of South Vietnam after 1954 was part of its strategy of containing communism throughout the world. Since 1965, the United States, China's primary enemy had been bogged down in the Vietnam quagmire, however. There was increasing domestic opposition to the War particularly by young people, who dominated anti-War demonstrations in the United States. Protests began in the spring of 1965 and grew in intensity as the numbers of young men sent to Vietnam increased. With relief, Mao was able to dismiss the Liuist "revisionists" by launching the Cultural Revolution.

Overtures of the Cultural Revolution

To return to July 1961, attacking "the Tito clique of Yugoslavia's self-management of enterprises", which were placed under "independent" management of the so-called "workers collectives" in the enterprises concerned (through the "workers' councils" and "administrative committees"), the Maoists actually aimed at their real target of Liu Shaoqi's "revisionist" approach.[92] Under the rule of the Tito government, the Yugoslav economy was subjected more and more to the economic system of the capitalist world. The "revisionist" approach, for instance, stressed "material incentives" and encouraged capitalist methods of management.

Mao began his counter attack at the Central Committee work conferences in Beidaihe in August 1962. Bolstered by improved agricultural conditions, he began to curb some particularly liberal features of the Liuist pro-Soviet, "revisionist" policy established during the difficult period. At the Tenth Plenum of the 8th Central Committee, held in September 1962, having won the adoption of resolutions halting decentralization and liberalization of the communes, Mao renewed his emphasis on "politics in command" under the slogan "never forget class struggle". Hence his Socialist Education Movement of 1962–1966 was launched in the rural areas to curb excessive emphasis on material incentives as understood in Liuist "revisionist" policies.[93] Steps were taken to restrict "small freedoms" including prohibiting the division of land among households, cutting back on excessive private plots, and tightening control over free markets and private speculative activities.

The Socialist Education Movement proceeded in several stages. Firstly, from the winter of 1962 to mid-1964, the Party attacked errors in commune operations, especially basic level cadre corruption and the neglect of the mass line. This stage emphasized a "four clean ups" campaign to rectify politics, ideology, organization and the economy.[94] Secondly, Mao's "first ten points" plan of leadership by "poor and lower-middle" peasant rural work associations adopted by the Central Committee work conference in May 1963 had been revised by Liu at the September conference to emphasize lower-level Party leadership and material incentives. In the December 1964 Central Committee work conference, Mao's "twenty-three points" were utilized to attack the Party's handling of the Socialist Education Movement for misinterpreting Mao's techniques of "investigation" and the mass line.[95] The "twenty-three points" were described as measures against Liuist "spontaneous capitalist tendencies" prevailing in rural areas. Thirdly, the movement to study of Mao Zedong Thought, initiated in August 1965 and directed at cadres and the masses alike, stressed "self-reliance" and "self-sacrifice" as well as the importance of collective interests. Fourthly, the movement of "criticism and self-criticism" was carried out from mid-October 1965 to March 1966 to rid *xian* Party secretaries of their "mandarin-like work styles" and "negative behavior of looking for stability" which had arisen from "selfishness" and "conservatism" thus disenabling them to "unite with all who can be united". It was in this period of Mao Zedong Study movement and of emphasis in politics to "take command" that the Socialist Education Movement merged into the Cultural Revolution.

The Great Proletarian Cultural Revolution of 1966–1969

In 1981, the CCP issued a resolution on its history in which the "grave 'left' error" of Mao's Cultural Revolution was "responsible for the most severe setback and heaviest losses suffered by the Party, the state and the people, since the founding of the People's Republic". The resolution elaborated that Mao had confused right and wrong and "the people with the enemy". The resolution was too simplistic to be convincing, however.

For four decades Mao had been continuously combating the basic human defect of individualism – petty bourgeois thought – and more importantly, revisionism, in order to consolidate the Chinese masses against the external enemies. This culminated in his Great Proletarian Cultural Revolution of 1966–1969. This movement demonstrated his breaking of the Liuist political-economic apparatus with great power. The Liuist approach could not "unite all who can be united" in the face of the threats of the twin superpowers.

In the following section, we will first survey various schools of thought concerning the origins of the Cultural Revolution.

Focusing on domestic, elite politics relevant to the Hundred Flower and GLF movements in his trilogy, Roderick MacFarquhar neglects the role of the superpowers in relation to the strategies of the Maoist defense-oriented political economy.[96] MacFarquhar traces the origins of the Cultural Revolution to the year 1956 and Mao's "visions of leaping economic progress" after his initial success in collectivization and in reaction to Khrushchev's de-Stalinization, which "embarrassed Mao", triggering the Sino-Soviet dispute.[97] According to MacFarquhar, "(t)he Hungarian revolt Khrushchev's (anti-Stalin secret) speech triggered prompted Mao to challenge Khrushchev's competence to set the ideological guidelines for the world communist movement".[98] As Sino-Soviet relations worsened, MacFarquhar continues, Mao "pondered how to avert a similar betrayal of the revolution in China (instigated by Liu Shao-qí)".[99] He thus argues that the collapse of Mao's "hopes for a collectivist utopia at home and a fraternity of communist nations abroad" made Mao "focus all his energies upon the nation's spiritual metamorphosis" to tear down and rebuild the nation.[100] Similarly, many sinologists have noted consistent strains in the Mao Zedong Thought, in particular his emphasis on class struggle, opposition to bureaucracy and aspirations for a more egalitarian society.

True, Mao's decision to prevent China from taking the "revisionist" Soviet road is well known.[101] The threats from the combined superpowers were real; and Mao needed to formulate an effective national defense-oriented political-cum-economic strategy for China's survival. No one has stressed that each of the above- mentioned strains was only a means but not an end. They were designed to realize his dictum of "uniting with all who can be united" in his political-cum-economic approach primarily for defense purposes vis-à-vis the powerful competitors.

Even different interpretations of the Cultural Revolution advanced by principal specialists in the early 1970s did not touch on this dictum. In his major work *Maoism in Action: The Cultural Revolution*, Chiou compiled their views as follows: [102]

The editors of *Fortune* magazine believed that Mao's campaign signaled the end of his version of Communist theory and practice, with L. LaDany and Robert S. Elegant posited that it was a sign of "Mao's loss of governing power". This school of thought, however, eventually died out. In contrast, the editors of the *Monthly Review* challenged Barry Richman's "bets" against the workability of the Maoist classless society that the Cultural Revolution espoused. Ellis Joffe, Benjamin Schwartz, Tadao Ishikawa, Kikuzo Ito and others of this school all contended that Mao was "the guiding spirit and guiding hand of the campaign", and argued that Mao's predetermined aims sought "the realization of his immortal revolution to eliminating his political opponents". Neale Hunter and later Chiou concurred with this group's pro-Mao argument that "the Cultural Revolution was Maoism in action". Chiou elaborated that the movement as an example "to show how Mao had attempted to apply his principles and create a new China, a new classless society and a new selfless people". According to Chiou, Mao had to resolve China's basic or "impossible problems" before it could become a nation that was not "another revisionist Soviet Union or another capitalist modern nation". And finally, Chalmers Johnson and Richard Pfeffer adhered to the popular "incremental decision-making theory" that Mao initiated the campaign but "unintended consequences diverted his forces from their long-term goals into emergency salvage operations".

However, although the second and third schools of thought had merits, these arguments did not consider the crucial external factors related to Mao's movement. And all these schools of thought were meaningless without taking account of the importance of national defense in the face of US imperialism and Soviet "revisionism" which first emerged in January 1954.

The official explanation of the Cultural Revolution described it as a final battle in a long-term struggle between two lines: the Maoist line and the "revisionist" line of "China's Khrushchev", the "No. 1 power holder in the Party taking the capitalist road", head of state and (Mao's) heir apparent Liu Shaoqi". Liu was accused of being a "traitor" and "lackey of imperialism and modern revisionism". The Great Proletarian Cultural Revolution of 1966–1969 thus witnessed the displacement of the "leading persons in authority (who are) taking the capitalist road" and reinstatement of the fervor of popular revolution, mass participation and self-reliance. Most scholars agree that Mao launched the Cultural Revolution to forestall a "capitalist restoration" in China, and eradicate ideological degeneration within the CCP. However, I argue that Mao's Cultural Revolution to combat "economism" or "capitalistic backsliding" which deviated from a true Marxist- Leninist-Maoist path to tap the people's power. Mao objected to Liuist "revisionism" and "capitalist restoration" because they could not "unite all who can be united" to face the ferocious superpowers singly or in unison.

This book also argues that the origins of Mao's Cultural Revolution can be traced back to Liu's consistent onslaughts on Mao's collectivization initiative starting in 1950. During the Cultural Revolution, Liu was accused of opposing labor-exchange teams, multi-aid teams and the development of collective economy.[103] Mao's acceleration of the process of his defense-oriented collectivization led to the onslaughts of the "rightists" led by Liu Shaoqi on a number of occasions as discussed above. First, in the spring of 1953, Liu led the "oppose rash advance" campaign against Mao's collectivization drive. According to the Maoists, in the "oppose rash advance" campaign, the "rightists" nurtured the development of a rich peasant economy leading to the resurgence of rural capitalism. This led to many peasants selling their land to the rich peasants. According to Mao, this situation undermined his mass line and only cooperativization could stop peasants from selling their land to the rich peasants. Second, in June 1953, Mao criticized the Liuist emphasis on "the new democratic program" as "hindering the progress of the socialist cause of burying the capitalist system and all other systems of exploitation once and for all". Third, criticizing the Liu-led "oppose rash advance" campaign to hinder the progress of his cooperatization plan in the spring of 1955, Mao claimed that the rightists wanted "the resolute contraction of cooperatives" to encourage the growth of capitalism and that Liu led the rightists to launch another similar campaign in 1956 in an attempt to dampen "the enthusiasm of the masses". Fourth, with the Soviet experience as guide, Liu was reported to have condemned Mao's "rash advance" toward full collectivization before the stage of agricultural mechanization was realized. Mao argued that Liu's policy of mechanization could not make full use of the available population by mobilizing all human forces in the crucial stage of cooperatization before the stage of mechanization was begun and that the production and use of agricultural mechanization should only be based on an agriculture where large-scale cooperative farming prevailed. These Liuist initiatives, according to the Maoists, undermined Mao's dictum of "uniting all those who can be united". Given the then hostile international situation, Mao made clear that he could not afford to "think in terms of the few and fail to think in terms of the interests of the whole country and people".

Mao therefore avowed that the GPCR was merely the first of many such cultural revolutions – one of a continuing series of ideological rejuvenations needed to keep the communist spirit free of cancerous capitalistic poisons, which prevented the ability to "unite with all possible"; these were the revolutions, which would constantly refresh China's true Marxism-Leninism-Maoism by reaffirming anti-economism, anti-intellectualism and anti-elitism.

Mao felt that even in a classless society "restoration of capitalism", revisionism and "the emergence of a new class" might hamper the dictum of "uniting all who can be united". He therefore initiated movements such as the rectification campaigns, "socialist education" and "*xia fang*", to continuously inculcate proletarian culture, ideas and attitudes among the people and to keep the revolutionary zeal alive. This is Mao's so-called "uninterrupted revolution". To Mao, it was essential that the bourgeois (and feudal) roots be dug out.

In analyzing Mao's rectification campaigns over a period of forty years, it is found that these movements were launched virtually one after another primarily to combat bourgeois attitudes and approaches. This showed Mao's determination to promote a selfless communist man and to unite the populace. These campaigns showed that Mao was obsessed with eradicating capitalist thought at any price, as bourgeois culture and approaches were detrimental to his strategy of "uniting with all possible". Mao thus did not aim just to create a communist man *per se*. My argument is that Mao endeavored to make a selfless man to defend against a potential imperialist intrusion.

Mao's main objection to the economic strategy of Liu Shaoqi and associates during the three-year difficult period was to their advocacy of material incentives such as private plots, bonus payments, specific material rewards and free marketing. In 1959, the Liuist-styled decentralization of the Maoist commune organization took place. In the summer of 1960, as a result of the failure of the GLF, the so-called "three-level management" was modified to "three-level ownership", with the production brigade as the basic unit of authority for production management. In early 1961, the production brigades were made independent of the commune and were able to plan their production, while the communes were left with control only over their own enterprises. The production teams also were given specific guarantees to stabilize their position within the framework not of the communes but of the production brigades. Communes still had at its disposal a small labor force engaged in commune-owned industries but had no right to conscript labor from the brigades or teams as it had been in 1958.[104] To Mao, these changes were characterized by divisiveness that severely undermined his dictum of "uniting with all possible". After 1962 Liuist measures were taken to stimulate agricultural recovery so that the patterns of production and distribution virtually reverted back to the advanced APC stage, with the commune providing only an overall administrative framework. In that year, another development catalyzed the downward shift from the brigade to the production team as the basic accounting unit in the countryside, a further decentralization of administrative power, thus neutralizing Mao's dictum further. This development meant that the production team virtually assumed full responsibility for organizing production, showing a slip back to the "old" MATs and the elementary cooperatives.[105]

Liu's well known material-oriented development theme appeared as early as 1949 in his "Tienjing Talks". During the Cultural Revolution, Liu was accused of advancing the idea of welcoming capitalist exploitation and developing capitalism.[106] In 1956 and 1957, his industrial policy stressed private capitalism as expressed in his speeches such as "Admitting Private Capitalists to Establish Factories for the Support of the Socialist Economy". This philosophy was further advanced in his 1959 speech "The Use of the Old-Styled Capitalism to Develop Commodity Economy" and his 1964 speech on "Learning from Capitalism in Organizing Socialist Production".

Mao's objection to Liu's pure economic policy was that it failed to take into account the crucial international situation. Although Liu's tightly structured and hierarchically centralized Party apparatus did play an important role in revitalizing the nation's fragile economy in the "three bad years", his bureaucratized elitist Party machinery based on technocratic "expertise", centralism and a "careerist" professional cadre undermined Mao's revolutionary "redness", "democratic centralism" and revolutionary cadre approach.[107] Mao argued that Liuist economic policy would create a gulf between the masses and the Party and, in the long run, a capitalist trend of exploitation of the majority by the minority, thus hindering the "uniting all who can be united". This made counteracting potential imperialist intrusion impossible. China was confronting the "US–USSR cooperation". Without considering the grave international situation China faced, Liu's pure economic strategy was aimed at "liberating and developing the productive forces" as advocated in his work "National Industrialization and Raising the Levels of the People's Livelihood". As early as February 1957, in his "Contradictions" speech, Mao criticized Liu who “vainly hoped to restore the capitalist system” with the “Soviet revisionists as his right hand men”.

Uniting with the great majority of the people necessitates the inculcation of proletarian culture and attitudes among the masses. However, characteristic of Liu’s bourgeois approach, which was at variance with the socialist economic base, was the factor of bureaucratization in his Party organization. Mao considered that this would inevitably lead to revisionism, for bureaucracy breeds “bureaucratism“ owing to its inherent hierarchical, elitist, “expertist”, “careerist”, “professional” and “centralist” (rather than “democratic centralist”) elements. These elements, which would give rise to competition, inequality and hence exploitation, could not unite with the majority of the masses. In contrasting Mao’s “redness” with Liu’s pro-Soviet revisionist “expertise”, the latter was designed for the minority and could not help amass the power of the people needed for his anti-imperialist endeavors. However, “redness” was designed for “uniting with all possible” with one mind. This called for Mao’s approach of “politics in command”.

However, Mao believed that “redness” and “expertise” can co-exist but that the former could enhance the latter in order to reap positive results. Mao evidently argued that with the approach of “redness” and “politics in command”, science and technology would only be effective on a large scale if “all” united. This was because Mao’s mass line approach was initiated to raise not only the standard of living for everyone at the same time, but also the long-term well-being of the collective, a crucial anti-imperialist tool. The element of collective selflessness needed to be promoted to encourage Mao’s mass mobilization.

The Cultural Revolution witnessed the adoption of a Maoist style of guerrilla military even further. For instance, soldiers were assigned the work of running farms and helping communes.[108] It was in this context that Robinson wrote: “The old guerrilla tradition, that the Army is fish swimming in the waters of the people, is cherished more than ever”.[109]

Finally, in the following section, I will consider Deng Xiaoping's position during the Cultural Revolution.

Our discussion above has shown that Mao launched the Cultural Revolution primarily to circumvent Liu Shaoqi who, beginning in 1950, had consistently and systematically opposed his political economic policy. In addition, Liu had planned to put the future of Mao's communization project in jeopardy. Therefore Liu's fate was sealed right from the beginning. Although Deng was "the No. 2 capitalist roader", there was hardly any evidence to show that he had systematically tried to jeopardize Mao's general political economic policy. He sincerely believed that Mao's GLF was wrong.[110] With his capitalist approach, he was trying to rescue hundreds of millions of people in the peasantry dying of starvation during the "three bad years" of crop failure. Deng's famous statement regarding "the black cat and the white cat" demonstrated his intent to rescue the famine-strickened population. Certainly he was a pure "non-capitalist" as shown in his approach to the acute problems concerning the state-owned enterprises confronted in the post-Mao modernization revolution. Thus Deng, who was held in a different category than Liu during the Cultural Revolution, was spared. Moreover Mao had always recognized Deng as "a rare talent". Therefore Deng was only banished to Nanchang, capital of Jiangxi province late in October 1969 with his wife Zhuo Lin (卓琳).

In March 1973 Deng's Vice-Premiership was restored. In addition, in January 1975, he was made Vice-Chairman of the CCP, Vice-Chairman of the Central Military Committee as well as Chief-of-Staff of the PLA.

Conclusion

Upon the completion of his anti-capitalist cooperativization plan in 1957, Mao accelerated his communization endeavors. In his commune scheme, Mao developed organizational and leadership techniques to link military efforts and rural economic and social strategies in a basic program of mobilization to penetrate to every village and every family involved every individual. Based on the Yenan model as a prototype, this was meant to "unite with all possible" in response to pressures from the United States and the Soviet Union. Thus Mao's economic-cum-defense strategy was a political solution for China's survival in the hostile international environment. Liu Shaoqi's strategy, which was purely economically oriented, in contrast, neglected then crucial, realistic power politics. In his "revisionist" approach which was dangerously detrimental to Mao's mass line, Liu ignored the simple fact that since 1953, the Soviet Union had emerged as the *de facto* "devil" and "No. 1 accomplice of the US primary enemy" in Mao's worldview during the crucial period 1958–69. Liu's "rightist-cum-revisionist" plans and his opposition to Mao's communization endeavors inevitably led to Mao's launching of his Cultural Revolution.

Chapter Four
1969–1976: The USSR as Primary Enemy and the US as Secondary Enemy – Mao's Relaxed Development Policies

The previous chapters surveyed Mao's first development model in relation to the then hostile international environment. In this chapter, we will consider aspects of Mao's modernization initiatives, which responded to the relatively favorable international environment begin ning in 1971. They were aimed at "improving the livelihood of the people". Mao's four-modernizations scheme, his second development model, was introduced in the Fourth Five-Year Plan of 1971–1975. First, let us consider the international environment of the period 1969–1976.

The USSR as Primary Enemy and the US as Secondary Enemy: 1969–76

Mao's perception of the Soviet Union as primary enemy and the US as non-antagonistic secondary enemy began to come into focus as early as 1969 as a result of the hostile new Soviet policy, which was not officially acknowledged until October 1, 1972.[1]

Sino-Soviet relations worsened throughout the 1960s as the Soviets reinforced their forces along the Sino-Soviet and Sino-Mongolian borders and signed a treaty of friendship and cooperation with Mongolia. This suggested a military alliance directed against China.[2] Sino-Soviet relations clearly took a new turn in August 1968, with the Soviet invasion of Czechoslovakia. While other elements remained roughly the same as in 1965, the Chinese worldview from 1968–1969 gradually shifted, with the Soviet Union replacing the United States as the primary enemy. It was not merely the Russian invasion of Czechoslovakia, but, more importantly, the announcement of the Brezhnev Doctrine of Limited Sovereignty in November 1968 that accelerated the Chinese perception of possible Russian military action against the PRC. This underscored the Chinese fear that the Indo-Pakistani War was taking place, as the Soviets claimed, "in direct proximity to the border of the Soviet Union",[3] and therefore "involve(d) the interests of Soviet Union". According to the Chinese, this was the sort of Japanese argument which had led to the Japanese invasion of North China before the Second World War. Similarly it was also the Russian argument that justified the Russian invasion of Czechoslovakia in 1968.[4] Obsessive Chinese fear of Soviet nuclear attack resulted in the construction of vast, fully-stocked "underground cities" in Beijing, Shanghai, Canton and other major population centers. This was followed in mid-1969 by what the Chinese perceived as a Soviet revival of John Foster Dulles' containment policy of the 1950s – the advocation of an "Asian Collective Security System". As a result of the skirmish on the Sino-Soviet border in 1969, a massive military concentration in the Soviet Far East and Outer Mongolia was established, and this seemed to confirm the intentions of the USSR as advanced in the Brezhnev Doctrine. After attempting to foster military alliances with the PRC's neighbors similar to their agreement with India in 1971, the Russians increased their military and political pressure in Asia. It thus became increasingly clear that the USSR had replaced the US as the "most ferocious" primary enemy of China. In mid-September 1969, the PRC government declared to the world that it was prepared to fight a nuclear war against the Soviet Union.

The Chinese believed that the Russians were aiming at establishing hegemony over the Eurasian landmass, though China in the East and the Atlantic alliance in the West were obstacles to this ambition. The Chinese argued that the USSR's strategic plan was to establish an entire ring of pro-Soviet nations around China's borders, with naval bases and a fleet operating from the Soviet Union stretching from East Siberia through the Soviet Western Asian region, and joining the nations fringing the Indian Ocean, from Asia Minor to Southeast Asia. Thus Mao needed to re-orient his foreign policy with respect to the two superpowers, in order to combat the Soviet threat as

China's primary concern. Facing China's two-front threat, Mao, with Zhou Enlai's assistance, sought reduced Sino-US tensions and an international united front against Soviet hegemony.

In the following section, I will first argue about the shift in Chinese perception of the US superpower from that of China's primary enemy to that of secondary enemy.

In January 1965, in answering Edgar Snow, who had asked if there was any hope for improved Sino-US relations, Mao had said "yes". He implied that the major threat to China came from the Soviet Union and that there were corresponding prospects for Sino-US co-operation.[5] Further, understanding that the US-Soviet conflict was the paramount global contradiction, on two occasions, in January 1964 and mid-September 1965, he told visitors "this contradiction can never be resolved".[6]

Washington's prolonged Vietnam War had incurred heavy financial and human losses and produced a profound social and political crisis. This compelled the United States to re-evaluate its foreign policy in relation to China. In an article in the October 1967 issue of *Foreign Affairs* entitled "Asia After Vietnam", Richard Nixon wrote: "efforts to contain China should not become a permanent policy leaving the PRC to live in angry isolation". In his *Memoirs*, he also wrote: "The most pressing foreign problem I would have to deal with as soon as I became President was the war in Vietnam".[7] To manage its Vietnam problem, the US would have to deal with China, because China provided crucial support to Hanoi.[8] Henry Kissinger wrote that US leaders now understood the importance of having "contact with [...] one quarter of humanity".[9] In his inaugural address on January 20, 1969, Nixon again signaled his interest in improving relations with the PRC: "We seek an open world, a world in which no people, great or small, will live in angry isolation".[10]

On November 26, 1968, Beijing proposed to Washington a resumption of ambassadorial-level talks in Warsaw. Three days later, Lyndon Johnson, the outgoing President, encouraged by president-elect Richard Nixon, accepted China's proposal. Although the actual resumption of the talks was delayed, this was the first sign of détente in Sino-US relations. On July 21, 1969 the United States cancelled certain sanctions against the PRC and relaxed limitations on travel to

China.[11] In August 1969 Nixon lifted the travel and trade ban, allowing his Secretary of State William Rogers to signal interest in opening a dialogue. Crucially, in November 1969, he also terminated regular Seventh Fleet patrols in the Taiwan Straits.[12]

On October 1, 1970, Mao received Edgar Snow on the Tiananmen rostrum and had his photograph taken with Snow at his side. The photo appeared on the front page of the *People's Daily* along with Mao's statement that "people from all over the world including the people from the US are our friends".[13]

Responding to the Kissinger-Nixon Doctrine of the early 1970s, which called for the gradual withdrawal of the US from Southeast and Northeast Asia, the Chinese saw a golden opportunity for the normalization of Sino-US relations in the face of the Soviet threat. The so-called "ping-pong (table tennis) diplomacy" of 1971 led to Henry Kissinger's secret mission to Beijing that year and to the decisive changes of China's relations with the superpowers, with President Nixon's China visit in 1972 a subsequent relaxation in the Chinese attitude toward the United States, for instance, inviting Americans to visit China. The rapprochement with the United States brought twenty years of confrontation and mutual suspicion to an end, and eventually reduced US military presence in the Asia Pacific region. More importantly, it promoted the normalization of bilateral relations and paved the way to improved relations with other Western countries and Japan. These developments facilitated China's quest for modernization, while helping to contain Soviet expansion. This initiative seemed to further the establishment of trade relations with the United States, Japan and Europe, and, more importantly, a gradual adoption of elements of the Western "individualistic" liberal economic model.[14] The Chinese were eager to acquire Western capital and modern technology for Mao's modernization initiatives, particularly as the economic consequences of several years of domestic turmoil were becoming all too apparent.[15]

US–Sino rapprochement was needed by both sides in the face of the threat of expansionist Soviet Union, their respective adversary. In mid-February 1973, during a meeting in Zhongnanhai, both Mao and Kissinger confirmed that their countries "face(d) the same danger" and that their "target (was) identical".[16] Clearly, in the first half of the 1970s, Soviet expansionism was Mao's principal concern, superseding the Taiwan issue. As Mao told Kissinger in 1972: "The small issue is Taiwan, the big issue is the world".[17] With the United States also now relegated to the secondary position, the USSR became China's primary enemy.

The Sino–Soviet border talks, which lasted more than a year and a half, failed, and the prospect that Sino–Soviet hostility might be relieved, faded.[18] The period 1972–1976 witnessed the Chinese attempt to break out of the "Soviet containment" ring through the following actions:

First, the Chinese elevated the Second Intermediary Zone, vitally comprising Europe and Japan, into the Second World as evidenced in Mao's conversation with Zambia's President Kaunda in February 1974 on the question of the "three worlds".[19] Europe and Japan appeared to be considered the primary areas of potential weakness, where the PRC could disrupt the Soviet containment ring *from the outside* before it could be successfully established. In this light, it was clear that the Chinese attack on "superpower hegemony" in Europe was primarily meant to incite Western Europe to stand up against Russian hegemony. Similarly, the Chinese incitement of anti-Soviet feeling in Japan was understandable. Second, Deng Xiaoping's speech in the United Nations in April 1974 under the cover of anti-superpower hegemony aimed to win over as many nations of the First and Second Intermediary Zones as possible. The Chinese scheme was aimed at setting not only West Europe and Japan against the Soviet Union, but at persuading the "friendly" Africans to exert more pressure on the Soviet southern flank, thus posing a threat to the Russian Black Sea maritime outlet.

The Chinese tried to persuade the relevant Third World nations to defuse the Soviet strategic points along its containment ring. This explained why the PRC, since entering the United Nations, had aligned itself firmly with the Third World by stressing coordination of economic and armed struggles, and "setting up, or taking over, international conferences and organizations to institutionalize this economic and geo-political warfare".[20]

In the early 1970s, the Chinese established their counter-containment ring. The Soviets now began to reconcile with the NATO nations. By the mid-1970s, they had strengthened their cooperation with the

French and validated the Soviet–West German Treaty, the West Berlin Agreements, the Polish–West German Treaty, and the East–West Germany Basic Relations Treaty, etc. With great effort, they had taken part in the preparatory talks of Helsinki's European Security and Cooperation Conference and Agreements, and of Vienna's European Arms Reduction Conference. This indicated that the Soviets had tried to relax tensions in Europe. The Chinese considered that easing tensions between East and West in Europe would enable the Russians to pay more attention to their eastern front, however. Nixon's Year of Europe, that is, his doctrine of self-sufficiency of 1973, was designed to establish a new Atlantic Charter of self-reliance within the EEC while the ongoing US–USSR detente would assure West Europeans that the Soviet threat to their security would be minimal. But the Chinese tended to see the desired new Atlantic Charter as a rationale for US withdrawal. They feared that the achievement of a true USSR–US detente in Europe would leave the Russians free to concentrate their military might along the Sino-Soviet borders. Thus, the Chinese encouraged West Europeans to resist the US-imposed Year of Europe, wanting the NATO alliance to counter-balance Russia's western front. In the East, moreover, the Soviet threat to Chinese borders was real. Therefore Chinese land troops, bomb shelters, population decentralization, and so on were prepared for this eventuality.

In East Asia, with the urgent need to counteract the Soviet "Asian Collective Security System", China needed to acquire Japan's acceptance of an anti-hegemonic clause as a basis for Sino-Japanese reconciliation. This explained why "the PRC intimated that she preferred maintenance of Japan's security arrangements with the US".[21] Certainly this was an attempt to resist the USSR's plan of containment of China through Japan. The new Sino–Japanese communique repeated the anti-hegemonic clause in the Nixon–Zhou statement in Shanghai was an indication that China, Japan and the US now came to accept the new terms of international relations in the Asia Pacific region.

Even in Eastern Europe, beginning in the early 1970s, the Chinese had begun to strengthen their already cordial relations with Albania, and to improve their relations with Yugoslavia, Romania, and others. This was aimed at disrupting the Soviet control of the East European communist nations so as to puncture the Soviet containment ring throughout that part of the world. Since the visits to Beijing by Romania's Ceausescu and the Foreign Minister of Yugoslavia in the summer of 1971, the Chinese had attempted to intrude, diplomatically, in the Warsaw Pact states. This was to encourage revival of the idea of regional Balkan cooperation, which without doubt would weaken the cohesion of the Soviet bloc. From the beginning of 1973, the Chinese started to improve their relations with Bulgaria, Hungary, East Germany, Poland, Czechoslovakia , and others.[22]

To conclude, dictated by the new international environment, China now treated the Soviet Union as its primary enemy with the United States seen as a non-antagonistic secondary enemy. Chinese maneuvers in the Second and Third worlds were aimed at disrupting Soviet containment of China and establishing a counter-containment ring. Mao was now in a position to advance his new economic strategy in line with the Western economic model. While aiming to open up China to the outside world to tap capital and science and technology from the US-led Western world for his modernization initiatives, he also adopted the Western liberal "individualistic" economic features to "improve the livelihood of the people" overall. The new international environment made all this possible. In the next section, we will delve into Mao's perception of the importance of science and technology before discussing his new development strategy.

Mao's Perception of the Importance of Science and Technology

Mao considered modernization and science and technology inseparable. In February 1940, speaking on the importance and formation of the Natural Science Research Committee in the Shen-Kan-Ning Border Areas, he said: "Natural science can solve the problems in (our) daily life concerning the four essential items of clothing, food, housing and transport".[23] According to him, China was so weak because it lacked Western inventions such as the railroad, telephone, telegraph and steamship.[24] Despite important Chinese inventions, he argued, the lamentable state of natural science in China over the centuries was that it was not developed systematically.[25] Understandably, therefore, on January 31, 1941, in a letter to his sons, An Ying and An Ching who were both in Moscow, Mao emphasized that they "should major in disciplines of natural science with those of social science as minors, while still young".[26]

In August 1959, while emphasizing that economic development should emphasize science, he encouraged the editors of the *People's Daily* to publish more papers on scientific discussions.[27] During the period of December 1959 through February 1960, commenting on the Russian text book *Political Economy*, he often urged his comrades "to learn how to apply industrial technology" to their economic tasks. On one occasion in 1959, Mao commented that under the CCP leadership, China's industrialization and the development of its socialist production forces had already begun.[28] It was in this context that in December 1959, with the basic purpose of "improving the livelihood of the people", Mao initiated his plan of socialist transformation based on "the four modernizations" of industry, agriculture, science and technology, and defense.[29] In March 1960, stressing the importance of the peaceful and stable international situation for "China's modernization of agriculture, industry, scientific culture and defence", in his own words, he urged the Chinese to "strengthen scientific reform and technological revolution".[30] In December 1963, Mao argued that "without science and technology, the production forces will not be developed".[31]

As noted above, prior to 1971, Mao's plan could not have been put into practice, owing to the hostile international environment. Thus, during the period 1953–1970, Mao made the commune system a priority in his defense-oriented national development.

In August 1977, commenting on Mao's view of science and technology, Deng Xiaoping stressed the importance of China's productive forces:

> Comrade Mao said that a battle had to be waged for science and technology, and that unless it was won, the country's productive forces could not be further developed.[32]

In addition, in his speech on the opening ceremony of China's Science Conference in mid-March 1978, Deng referred to Mao's statement saying that "China will have become a powerful industrial socialist country (in the 21st century) [...] and ought to make a greater contribution to humanity".[33] Deng clearly emphasized that Mao meant to make "a greater contribution" in the sphere of science and technology.[34]

"Improving the Livelihood of the People"

With the new international environment conducive to his scheme to open up his country to the outside world, Mao initiated relaxed policies to improve the livelihood of the people. In this section, we will first deal with Mao's original plan in the mid-1950s of transforming the lives of the people, a quarter of mankind, through the modernization of agriculture and industry.

As far back as April 1945, Mao had already argued the importance of industrialization as follows: "Without industry there can be no solid national defence, no well-being for the people, no prosperity or strength for the nation".[35] It was quite understandable that Mao should assert the importance of the modernization of China's agriculture and industry. This was the same view of Marx that the growth of natural science had enabled modernization, through industry, to transform the life of man. Following this reasoning, with the influence of science and technology, Marx envisaged the true emancipation of mankind.

In February 1957, in discussing China's path to industrialization, Mao stressed the importance of agriculture to the growth of heavy and light industry. This was because: "As China is a large agricultural country, *with over 80 percent of its population in the rural areas*, agriculture must develop along with industry, for only thus can industry secure raw materials and a market for building a powerful heavy industry".[36] (Emphasis added) However, in his celebrated paper "The Situation in the Summer of 1957", Mao urged the Chinese to "build a modern industry and modern agriculture and the way is to seek truth from facts and *follow the mass line*". (Emphasis added). This was because, according to him, "without good relations between the Party and *the masses*, the socialist system cannot be established or, once established, be consolidated" *for the very purpose of defense against the primary enemy.*[37] In the summer of 1957, the United States remained China's primary enemy but the Soviet Union began to emerge as the "No. 1 accomplice of the US imperialism". Thus Mao had to concentrate his efforts on his political mobilization to realize his communization scheme.

With the new international environment favorable to the PRC in the early 1970s, Mao was in a position to launch his modernization efforts, aimed at "improving the livelihood of the people" in the real sense. His modernization initiatives were meant to open up China to the outside world in order to tap capital inflow and science and technology particularly from the US-led Western world. A characteristic of "improving the livelihood of the people" with science and technology of the US-led Western world was a hallmark of Mao. This was the very spirit that drove Mao to "strive for the Four Modernizations with one mind to remove Mt. Tai".[38] This was the same spirit the post-Mao leadership exhibited when urging the people to "remove China's two mountains of economic and technological backwardness".[39] This spirit was important to Mao and the post-Mao leadership, because it not only stimulated their visions to realize their modernization scheme, but also provided the theoretical base to acquire the astronomical power to carry out the plan. This meant that only in a peaceful and stable international environment could the "mountains of economic and technological backwardness" be uplifted with the Western economic principles and the advanced science and technology of the world especially the US-led Western countries. Deng Xiaoping called this "ning ju li" (凝聚力), that is, "concentrated power" or "astronomical power".[40]

It has been argued unceasingly that Mao's political campaigns and movements carried out since 1950 to "wipe out capitalism from the face of the earth" led to the neglect of effective economic development. In addition, it is argued, too much national time was spent on class struggle, which aimed at changing human nature to embrace selfless communism. This school of thought has also argued that since 1957 there had been very little improvement in economic performance in both rural and urban areas and that stagnant rural living standards persisted thirty years after the CCP had seized power with peasant support. Despite the egalitarian Maoist policy, it goes on, inequalities persisted. This school of thought has often argued about the "ten lost years" and even the "twenty lost years" caused by Mao's Cultural Revolution. It has also contended that compared with the modernization of other countries in the region, particularly Japan and the Four Little Dragons, China's progress had been marginal and that certainly the Cultural Revolution helped lay the foundation of change that began in December 1978. This school of thought has often referred to riotous disturbances in Beijing in April 1976 to illustrate social disappointment with leftist Maoist policies. Bernstein writes that what disturbed the post-Mao leadership were "immense imbalances, inefficiencies and poor results", which "included disparities in growth rates among the three major sectors of heavy industry, light industry and agriculture, and the neglect of services, which sharply lowered the quality of life".[41] Yuen Chen writes that the Marxist central planning and management are naturally inefficient and production was incommensurate with the needs of society under Maoist leadership.[42]

This is a distorted picture, however, neglecting the importance of the hostile international situation which deprived Mao of his priority of improving the livelihood of the people, as argued above.

With the perceived change of the international environment, the Fourth FYP witnessed Mao's new policy of opening up the country to the Western world to tap foreign capital and science and technology. To be in tune with US-led Western economic principles, the Maoist economic model in the Fourth FYP of 1971–1975 stressed relaxed policies providing individual and material incentives, for instance, for individual labor as well as decentralized production, which encouraged local self-reliance. Thus, starting in 1971, Mao's Fourth FYP emphasized the improvement of "the people's livelihood" overall, with commune members now allowed to farm small plots for their personal needs, to engage in limited sideline production at their households, and in pastoral areas to keep a small number of livestock for their personal needs.

Mao's Modernization Initiative: The Fourth Five-Year Plan of 1971–1975

The 1971 New Year Day Editorial of the *People's Daily* focused on Mao's long-term plan of his four modernizations for changing "our country's economic, scientific, and cultural backwardness within several decades enabling it rapidly to reach advanced world levels".[43] Mao's long-term plan was in tune with his call for "striving to build a great socialist country" in mid-September 1954. The New Year Day call marked the beginning of his four modernizations scheme to stimulate "the mass upsurge" in development of the national economy.[44] To reiterate, his plan had not been possible earlier because he had to pay primary attention to China's external enemies. Mao was now in a position to encourage the Chinese to "gird themselves to build our country [...] into a great industrialized nation with a high standard of modern culture in the course of several five-year plans".[45] Characteristic of Mao's four modernizations scheme was his "walking on two legs" strategy to stimulate "the mass upsurge". Much of this section draws from my published work *Mao Tse-tung's Ch'i and the Chinese Political Economy with Special Reference to the Post-Mao Modernization Revolution.*[46] Mao also called for the general line of "going all out, aiming high and achieving greater, faster, better and more economical results in building socialism". Introduced in his celebrated thesis "On the Correct Handling of Contradictions Among the People" delivered in February 1957, the Plan emphasized the implementation of his policy of "taking grain as the key link and ensuring an all-out development".[47] Certainly Mao's very policy was based on the general principle to "take agriculture as the foundation and industry as the leading factor" and arrange the national economy in the order of agriculture – light industry – heavy industry, contrary to the Soviet- dictated requirement of emphasizing heavy industry to the neglect of agriculture in China's First Five-Year Plan.

The policy emphasized "the people's livelihood". First, making agriculture primary to the national economy was determined by its important role in the economy as the source of the people's livelihood.[48] Second, because light industry "occupied a very important position in the development of the entire national economy and very closely affected the people's lives, so production was "for meeting the people's ever increasing needs".[49] Seen from our perspective, the development of light industry not only would help improve people's livelihood, but also "raise the peasants' income and further promote agricultural growth by using more farm and sideline products as raw materials for light industry which has a short production period and a quick turnover of funds".[50] In addition, its growth can accumulate more funds for heavy industry and increase the supply of raw materials, machinery and equipment for heavy industry, thereby helping the latter to expand.[51] Therefore, the Maoist argument was that "without the development of light industry, it was difficult to supply the urban and rural population with a rich variety of industrial goods for daily use and develop heavy industry at a faster rate". As a result of improving the people's livelihood, their great power could be summoned to develop China's national economy more effectively. The Maoists further argued that "heavy industry, which produces the means of production, can provide agriculture with an ever-increasing amount of farm machinery, chemical fertilizers, insecticides, electric power, and building materials to speed up agricultural modernization.[52] Furthermore, without developing heavy industry, "it would be impossible to have a consolidated national defense".[53] This marked the implementation of Mao's principle of "taking agriculture as the foundation and industry as the leading factor" in relation to the "walking on two legs" strategy. This strategy emphasized the following:

(1) the initiative of both the central government and the localities,
(2) speeding up industrial construction in the interior, while making full use of industry in the coastal areas,
(3) simultaneously developing (i) industry and agriculture, (ii) light and heavy industries,
(4) modern and indigenous methods, and
(5) at the same time, building small, medium-sized and big enterprises.[54]

Mao's "walking on two legs" strategy was a "new" mass line method of "putting proletarian politics in command and integrating

Party leadership with the masses".[55] Thus the slogan "let the local authorities engage in more undertakings under the unified planning of the central authorities" meant that "the Party organizations in the localities were to do works effectively in accordance with actual conditions".[56] This was designed to make possible the "mass upsurge" through developing the PRC economy *throughout* the nation more effectively. It was meant to make the people "organize themselves and concentrate on places and branches of work where they can give full play to their energy, to concentrate on production in breadth and depth and create more and more undertakings".[57] In other words, this strategy was meant to advance Mao's ideal of astronomical power more effectively. It stood in contrast with Liu Shaoqi's "revisionist line" of developing production within "a single sphere" and "absolute division of labor", which could not "unite with all possible".[58] Rather, "the big-, small- and medium-sized enterprises, the national and local ones" were "all energetically to make comprehensive use of resources".[59]

Thus, after the beginning of the Cultural Revolution, the rate of the development of mechanized agriculture accelerated. The number of tractors in 1970 was doubled that in 1965. There were big increases also in the number of drainage and irrigation machines, harvesters, threshers and other machines for processing farm and sideline products.[60]

Soon after the establishment of the people's communes in 1958, Mao introduced mechanization in agriculture where large-scale co-operative farming prevailed. He argued that "the fundamental way out now for agriculture lies in mechanization".[61] According to Mao, "co-operation therefore consolidation of the people must precede the use of big machinery". Understandably, the formation of the people's communes (that is, cooperativization) "not only created extremely favorable conditions for developing mechanization in farming, but also made it more pressing than ever".[62] Thus, alongside his mass line strategy, Mao now launched the mass movements to promote mechanized farming. The emphasis was on making small types of farm machines by relying primarily on *local* industries, but buying farm machinery depended on the collective economy.[63]

After 1969, Gurley observes, the Chinese economy had made large gains on a broad front through a balanced development program that emphasized both agriculture and industry, large and small enterprises, self-reliance, and individualist and collective incentives, among others.[64] Gurley also writes that "substantial progress has also been made in the urban areas in both heavy and light industry, high levels of employment, reasonably good rates of output growth" and that the country experienced no recession, inflation, or energy crisis in the first half of the 1970s.[65]

The Maoist economic model during the Fourth FYP period stressed the following relaxed characteristics, adhering to the mass line strategy for the purpose of uniting the entire population against possible external enemies:

(1) Foreign capital inflow was now allowed. This meant the opening up of the country to the outside world.
(2) For the first time, the Maoist leadership gave priority to the livelihood of the people allowing individual farming plots and individual labor. Dictated by international politics, this strategy was considered in tune with the US-led Western economic model and was allowed, provided that self-interest did not lead to exploitation.
(3) Economic development of rural areas featured communes and small industries.
(4) Decentralized development encouraged local self-reliance.
(5) Egalitarian characteristics still dominated in the short-run. The policy was to raise the living standard of the people overall avoiding the exploitation of the majority by the minority.

Clearly these characteristics of the FFYP demonstrated the typical Maoist approach for encouraging the growth of astronomical power from the very participation of the whole population in developing the national economy, while still paying attention to defense. However, the relaxed policy regarding individual and material incentives was meant to be in tune with the Western economic model. Although the mass line strategy and egalitarian characteristics were still intact, they were eventually to give way to the Western economic approach in terms of self-interest which will be elaborated later. The importance of the 4th FYP was that the time was ripe for Mao to introduce the vital Western capital, science and technology as elements of his modernization initiatives.

In 1973, with the implementation of the balanced National Economic Plan in which the new pro-Western Maoist economic strategy was introduced, the Chinese economy made large gains on many fronts.[66] This program emphasized agriculture and industry, large and small enterprises, self-reliance, individual and collective incentives, among other elements. As Liu and Wu observe, with the import of complete sets of equipment and new technology, industrial production began to pick up. The total output value of industry and agriculture in 1973 was 9.2 per cent higher than the previous year, while foreign trade increased dramatically. The total volume of imports and exports amounted to US$10.98 billion, an increase of 34 per cent over the same period.[67] This rate of growth, Liu and Wu posit, was the highest since the First FYP. I would attribute this increase for the most part to the favorable new international political situation, which made Mao's new economic efforts possible. In the following section, I will deal with the above two points in more detail.

The Watershed

Given Mao's open-door policy, foreign capital inflow was now possible, one of the primary economic characteristics of the Fourth FYP. In the newly relaxed international political arena, the Maoist leadership was in a position to give priority to the livelihood of the people for the first time through the application of principles of the US-led Western economic model. Mao's new strategy of opening China to the outside world was meant to enhance trade and attract foreign investment, which was to make national construction and infrastructure program possible.

First, given the relaxed international political situation, Mao needed to adopt the major principles of the US-led Western economic model to further the country's economic development. Mao realized that the concept of liberal individualism in the Western economic system could be a vital tool for "improving the livelihood of the people". Under this pretext, Mao announced his new economic strategy in 1971.

This new model featured small industries in the communes, while also encouraging local reliance in decentralized development. This paved the way for the application of the principle of Western principles, not only of individualism, but of material incentives as well. Mao was well aware that this would eventually lead to the abolition of his communes, with the spirit of individualism injected into his new economic endeavor. He certainly realized that this was logically practical. This was because in the changing international political environment, the capitalist Western world was now no longer a menace to China's survival.

Thus Mao's previously sacrosanct tenet of selflessly serving and uniting with the collective had to begin to incorporate the Western capitalist concepts of liberal individualism and material incentives. This would eventually make his egalitarian objectives redundant. Marxist "class struggle", which had made "selflessness" effective in unifying "98 per cent plus" of his people to weed out "class enemies", had to eventually die a natural death. Selflessness as a mass line strategy, which was devised to unite the masses effectively against imperialism, would also eventually and unavoidably become redundant. The economic-political-social change was that *collective* farms were to eventually give peasants individual family holdings, linking output to remuneration. The new economic conditions would inspire the appearance of a kind of "market economy" that would integrate with the world economy dominated by the US-led West. This meant that the ideological polarization of the capitalist and communist systems that had existed previously in China would be phased out over time. This was necessary with the occurrence of the new international political order.

Second, Mao understood that the means of generating growth would be to open up the country to foreign investment, which include the introduction of foreign management practices and innovative technologies especially those related to information and communication. His new foreign investment policy would encourage not only inflows of foreign direct investment into every industrial and service sector, but eventually the establishment of foreign invested enterprises in China. The key to successful industrial undertakings in this regard was primarily low wages, which can be paid in developing economies like China along with the application of new technology. But, more importantly, it involved the raising of (foreign) capital, the correct application of it and the judicious control of how it was invested and good returns on investment of capital. Mao understood that a financial system that operated on the market principles was needed. If this financial system could not operate in the Chinese market, foreign investors would be discouraged from entering the market. Therefore, it can be seen, in the long run, that foreign enterprises in Dengist China indeed played a very important role in enhancing Chinese foreign trade.[68]

Third, with the completion of the Great Proletarian Cultural Revolution, Mao obviously considered that the "proletarian" element now had no relevance to his modernization revolution. As discussed above, Mao's rectification campaigns and movements over a period of forty years were launched virtually one after another to combat primarily bourgeois attitudes and approaches, demonstrating Mao's determination to make a selfless communist man. The primary objective was to cement selfless communism against China's external enemies. These campaigns showed that he had an obsessive determination to "wipe out" capitalist thought at any price, as bourgeois culture and approaches were detrimental to his strategy of "uniting with all possible" and generating the astronomical power essential for his anti-imperialist fight. Mao believed that in uniting the people, bourgeois ill-effects must be neutralized.

Mao's rectification campaigns and movements to "wipe out capitalism from the face of the earth" were initiated on this basis and aimed at changing man's nature beginning with the leadership at the basic levels. As a result, his rectification campaigns were developed to promote inner Party discipline and for non-Party cadres and other non-Party elite. His anti-bureaucratism with respect to cadre work style demonstrated "his disgust of the bourgeois work approach", which not only could not win over the masses, but also would separate the Party from the masses. In ridding cadres of bourgeois ideas, these rectification campaigns and movements were aimed at transforming and winning over the masses to unify them as one in defense against external enemies. These external enemies were the US primary enemy during the 1950–1958 and 1959–1968 periods, the USSR as the "No.1 accomplice of the US" during the 1959–1968, and the Soviet Union as the primary enemy during the 1969–1976 period.

While the 1942–1944 inner party rectification campaign aimed at eradicating non-proletarian culture, the Rectification and Land Reform of 1947–1948 was initiated to encourage mass participation in rectification of rural basic Party leadership. The commandist methods of cadre work were singled out for attack in the 1950 rectification campaign. The Party Rectification and Party Building of 1951–1954 was primarily designed to deal with the capitalist "rich peasant thought" and rural cadre corruption, while the "Three- and Five-Antis" campaigns began an unending series of initiatives to enforce total subservience to the state of the bourgeoisie and to eliminate corrupt officials. The 1953 Anti-Bureaucratism-Commandism Movement in rural areas was a continuation of the Three Antis campaign. Even Mao's literary rectification campaigns of 1951–1956 were meant to serve as anti-bourgeois tools. The Anti-Rightist Struggle of 1957–1958 was directed against members of democratic parties as well as the bourgeois class in society at large. The Rectification Campaign of 1957–58 stressed criticism of "right conservatism" and the rectification campaign against "right opportunism" in 1959 was meant to stop the threat of "right opportunist ideology" from spreading throughout the whole nation. The Rectification Campaign of 1960–1961 was initiated to combat "landlord restoration and counter-revolutionaries" and improve cadre work style in urban and rural areas. In curbing excessive emphasis on material incentives during the three-year difficult period and thus dealing a blow to "capitalist restoration", the Socialist Education Movement of 1962–1966 was a prelude to the Great Proletarian Cultural Revolution of 1966–1969, the culmination of all Mao's rectification campaigns. The Cultural Revolution, which witnessed the displacement of the "leading persons in authority taking the capitalist road", reinstated the "proletarian" way of life to unite the populace against the external enemies.

All these campaigns and movements were meant to set the example of making a consolidated mankind emphasizing selflessness, to resist its enemies as mentioned above.

As discussed above, in the realm of international relations, the Chinese perception of the Soviet Union as the primary enemy and the United States relegated to the secondary position began in 1969 but was not officially acknowledged until October 1, 1972. The 9th CCP National Congress in April resolved to contend primarily with "Soviet revisionism by establishing the broadest possible international united front", which importantly was to include the United States. In addition to China's new UN membership in October 1971, the normalization of Sino–US relations was considered vital.

Along these lines at the Sixth Special Session of the United Nations General Assembly studying problems concerning raw materials and development in April 1974, Deng Xiaoping referred to "the important question of opposing imperialist exploitation and plunder" and announced China's new international economic policy. Deng's speech, first, emphasized that the Soviet Union was considered China's primary enemy, while the United States had been relegated to the secondary enemy. Next, it announced China's new development policy. Through relegating the United States to the secondary enemy status, China was now in a position to normalize Sino–US relations and to seek viable Sino–Western economic relations. The Chinese initiative was meant to appease the United States, the European powers and Japan, through the application of the market principles. In particular, the PRC aimed to acquire Western capital and modern technology through modernization.[69] China's new international economic policy was as follows:

First, encouraging the developing countries to develop their national economy through "individual and collective self-reliance", China aimed at winning their support for its new international economic initiative.[70] Second, more importantly, "self-reliance" in no way meant "self-seclusion and rejection of foreign aid" and "the Chinese always considered economic and technical exchanges beneficial and necessary for the development of the national economy and the exchange of needed goods ideal to make up for each other's deficiencies".[71] This shed new light on Mao's open door policy. Third, by virtue of spelling out China's position on international trade to be based on the principles of equality, mutual benefit and the exchange of needed goods, the PRC's new role in international trade was confirmed.[72]

Certainly Deng's announcement in the UN concerning China's new external policy was made under Mao's instructions. Deng's announcement encouraged Sino-Western economic relations and marked the permission of foreign capital inflow associated with advanced Western science and technology needed for the PRC's economic development. These developments signaled Mao's new external policy considered vital for his four modernizations scheme. Clearly the post-Mao opening up of the country to the outside world also originated from this very policy.

The "individual" factor being incorporated into Mao's new economic strategy was to guarantee the workability of the PRC's economic development. More specifically, the Chinese government made clear its position in the UN that through "individual and collective self-reliance", commune members were now allowed to farm small plots for their personal needs, engage in limited household sideline production, and keep a small number of livestock for their personal needs in pastoral areas. The requirement that "the development and absolute predominance of the collective economy of the people's communes were ensured" was only symbolic. In addition, the Chinese wanted the world to know that non-agricultural individual laborers were also allowed to engage in individual labor, provided it involved no exploitation of others within the limits permitted by law.

Under his theory of continued revolution, Mao's Cultural Revolution of 1966–1969 was extended to the Fourth FYP period, during which the Chinese were constantly reminded to "grasp firmly the task of criticism of the Liuist revisionism" and "prevent capitalist restoration".[73] Ideologically Mao's Cultural Revolution to rid the Party and the rest of the superstructure of bourgeois values and institutions, was meant to continue indefinitely for the purpose of preventing (Soviet) "revisionism". Liu Shaoqi and associates, for example, were considered "capitulationists of the Soviet revisionists", and "the Soviet revisionists" were considered as China's "primary enemies".[74]

International politics was clearly the determining factor in China's economic development. Therefore, the Liuist "revisionist" approach was condemned as "treasonous" at the height of China's anti-Soviet struggle, while the term "revisionism" was typically applied to Mao's Soviet enemies, both international and internal.

In short, an international political situation favorable to China allowed the Maoist leadership to prioritize the people's livelihood along with China's critical need for foreign capital inflow to help develop its economy based on Western economic principles. Mao's relaxed policies that provided individual (family) and material incentives were meant not only to improve the livelihood of the people, but also to avoid exploitation of the majority by the minority. All were written in the new Constitution promulgated at the First Session of the Fourth NPC in January 1975. The 1975 Constitution contained provisions regarding non-agricultural individual laborers and people's commune members, allowing them to farm small plots for their personal needs and to engage in limited household sideline production. This was demarcated from Liu's recommended "fixing of farm output quotas for individual households with each on its own and the abolition of farm plots for personal needs".[75] Though the spirit of dedicated selflessness still prevailed, it was not considered the most critical element. This contradicts Gurley's argument that the Maoist leadership was "persistent in encouraging collective endeavors that return benefits to the group and in promoting hard work partly through revolutionary fervor rather than entirely through promises of material gains".[76]

While the collective and the individual looked after their own interests, the Party provided rules and regulations to check abuses and abnormalities and avoid exploitation as spelled out in Article 5 of the 1975 Constitution. This was to ensure that social coherence was intact. This had been Mao's policy for realizing consolidation of the great majority of the people. Social coherence originally *had been* guaranteed with the establishment of the commune system for the purpose of military defense during the pre-1971 period when the PRC's primary enemy was US imperialism.

Conclusion

In the early 1970s, China began to view the Soviet Union as its primary enemy and the United States as a non-antagonistic secondary enemy. With the international environment now conducive to his plan of opening up China to the outside world, Mao began to adopt a more relaxed economic policy in 1971. This was to improve the livelihood of the people overall. His four modernizations scheme was initiated to promote the acquisition of US-led Western capital and modern technology along with the capitalist economic principles. With this context in mind, the post-Mao modernization revolution will be the subject of the following chapters.

Chapter Five
Mao's Legacy: Deng Xiaoping's Economic Reform and Open-Door Policy

In the earlier chapters, it was proposed that the hostile international political environment crucially dictated Mao Zedong's economic policy of the period 1950–1970, which was purely defense-oriented to counter the US imperialist threat or the "US–USSR collusion against China". Characteristic of the following period 1970–1976, however, was that the US-led Western powers became Mao's secondary enemies. The relatively more stable international environment became favorable to his planned modernization program for which opening up China to the outside world was of utmost importance. Firstly, as China's secondary enemy, the United States became the target in Mao's scheme to be a partner in collusion against Soviet "hegemonism", which was seen as hindering China's modernization endeavors. Secondly, the PRC now wanted to secure badly needed Western capital and science and technology for its economic reform. With the favorable international environment, and having inherited Mao's second model of development and his "three worlds" theory, in which the Soviet Union was treated as the primary enemy, Deng Xiaoping began to open up the country to the Western world, starting from the late 1970s.

The Period 1976–1980 and the Party Decision on the Four Modernizations

The New Year message of 1976 emphasized Mao's slogan "go all out, aim high and achieve greater, faster, better and more economical results in building socialism", and "push the national economy forward by speeding up the four modernizations".[1] The Fifth Five-Year Plan

(FFYP) aimed to continue to carry out Mao's development strategy, with "agriculture as the foundation and industry as the leading factor". Thus the order of priority was agriculture, light industry and heavy industry.

Although the *People's Daily* announced on the New Year's Day of 1976 that it was the first year of the Fifth FYP for developing the national economy, it published no details of the Plan. This was probably not the right time to formally announce Mao's fundamental change in his economic policy. The situation was aggravated by uncertainties arising from the following important events particularly in the second half of the year: (1) the death of Zhou Enlai in January 1976, (2) the continued struggle against Deng Xiaoping, "the unrependant capitalist-roader" against whom Mao had initiated the struggle for the second time in April 1976 against Deng because of his "right deviationist attempt to reverse correct verdicts", (3) the death of Chu De in July 1976, (4) the Tangshan earthquake near Beijing in July 1976, which reportedly killed one-third of a million people, (5) the death of Mao in September 1976, (6) the arrest of the "Gang of Four" in October 1976, and (7) "a standstill under the wrong ideological guideline of Party Chief Hua Kuofeng's 'two what-evers'", which first appeared in the editorial of the *People's Daily* and *Liberation Army Daily* on February 7, 1977, and Hua's subsequent ousting.[2]

However, in 1976 the "Outline of the Ten-Years Plan for the Development of the National Economy, 1976–85" was put forward by the State Council, as "envisaged" by Mao, in Premier Zhou's report to the Fourth NPC on the work of the government in January 1975. The Outline referred to the four modernizations in particular stressing agriculture and industry "to further improve the people's livelihood".[3]

In December 1978, two years after Mao's death, the Third Plenary Session of the Eleventh Central Committee of the Chinese Communist Party adopted Vice-Premier Deng Xiaoping's proposal to shift the focus of the entire Party's work to "socialist modernization" starting from the year 1979. With "the essence of holding high the great banner of Mao Zedong Thought", the so-called "socialist modernization" was translated into the "four modernizations of agriculture, industry, defense and science and technology". The Chinese claimed that this Herculean national task was based on "the theory of building socialism", which Party Chief Jiang Zemin attributed to Deng Xiao- ping as its principal founder and called the "Deng Xiaoping Theory". Jiang, however, declared that "Deng Xiaoping Theory is a continuation and development of Mao Zedong Thought".[4]

Origins and Methodologies of Mao's Four Modernizations Scheme

This section will substantiate the argument that the presently ongoing four modernizations plan is an integral part of Mao Zedong Thought. Deng Xiaoping affirmed that the origins of the plan could be found in Mao's theses of the "Ten Major Relationships", "Correct Handling of Contradictions Among the People", "The Situation in the Summer of 1957" and so forth. Deng went on to say that Mao's articles and speeches during the socialist revolution and construction "contain the ideas which we must continue to adhere to and develop today" and that "we must give the people a clear understanding of what specific ideas we have in mind when we say we will hold high the banner of Mao Zedong Thought and adhere to Mao Zedong Thought".[5]

In other words, Mao's theses emphasized the "proper relationships" among agriculture, light industry and heavy industry. Deng Xiaoping adopted Mao's ideas on the four modernizations plan, saying that "heavy industry is the core of China's economic construction and at the same time, full attention must be paid to the development of agriculture and light industry".[6] In April 1980, referring to Mao's article "The Situation in the Summer of 1957", Deng talked with some leading members of the Central Committee concerning the importance of Mao's ideas on building an adequate foundation for modern industry and agriculture in the four modernizations scheme.[7] More importantly, Mao's modernization plan was based on his theses regarding the relationship between industry in the coastal regions and industry in the interior, as well as the relationship between economic construction and defense construction.[8]

Deng emphasized that the "methodologies" for the four modernizations scheme were adopted from Mao. These were "the mass line" and "seeking truth from facts" – "the quintessence of Mao Zedong Thought".[9] In adopting Mao's motto of "seeking truth from facts" as the CCP ideological line, Deng wrote:

> Marx and Engels propounded the ideological line of dialectical and historical materialism, a line, which Comrade Mao Zedong summarized in the four Chinese characters "seek truth from facts". To seek truth from facts, we must proceed from reality in all things, link theory with practice and hold practice to be the touchstone of truth – that is the ideological line of our Party.[10]

Therefore Bernstein was mistaken in his claim that "practice is the sole criterion of truth" and "truth through facts" were "the precepts of Deng Xiaoping".[11]

Calling for the Chinese masses to "strive for Four Modernizations with one mind", the *People's Daily*, in its February 9, 1979 editorial, emphasized "the importance of determination and unity of purpose: When people are of one mind, they can move Mount Tai". This is a reflection of Mao Zedong's spirit of "concentrating the astronomical forces to remove the three big mountains – imperialism, feudalism and bureaucrat-capitalism that had lain like a dead weight on the people". Deng called this spirit "ning ju li of the people" (凝聚力).[12] With Mao's spirit of driving "the concerted efforts of the nation", the Dengists aimed at removing China's "two mountains of economic and technological backwardness".[13]

Harnessing the people's power was very important to the post-Mao leadership, because, like Mao's "astronomical power", it not only spurred them to realize their modernization plans, but also provided the theoretical base for acquiring this power to implement the scheme. However, only in a peaceful and stable international environment can China's "mountains of economic and technological backwardness" be uplifted through capitalist economic principles and the application of advanced science and technology, particularly those of the US-led Western countries. It seems therefore that the vision of the Dengist and subsequently the Jiangist leadership was stimulated by Mao's ideal of realizing the four-modernizations scheme for "ten thousand generations".[14] The Dengists claimed that "making the four modernizations the focus of our work was the will that Comrade Mao Zedong bequeathed us".[15]

The International Political Environment in 1979–1985

The post-1979 international environment continued to be favorable to Deng Xiaoping, enabling him to carry out Mao's four modernizations revolution. By opening up the PRC to the outside world, the Dengists aimed at tapping science and technology as well as foreign capital from the US-led West for their economic reform.

Inheriting Mao's modernization initiatives, the post-Mao global strategy focused on the *maintenance* of normalized relations with the United States, Japan, and other advanced Western industrialized countries within a peaceful and stable international environment.[16] Without the direct foreign investments and sophisticated technology of the advanced Western world, it would be difficult for China to carry out its modernization program. The argument here is a sharp contrast to the thesis of Kau and Marsh as follows:

> While Deng's ideas for changing China's basic domestic policy were unmistakably clear throughout the 1980s, the direction of Beijing's foreign policy and security strategy remained somewhat ambiguous and uncertain. China's strategic and economic ties with the West had developed in the past decade to the point where Beijing could not afford to make any major shifts without jeopardizing the nation's central commitment to the "Four Modernizations" and reform. [...] As the world witnessed the emergence of a new international order, China declared its pursuit of an "independent" foreign policy of peace and of opening up. Yet at the same time, China's concrete regional and global roles remained undefined.[17]

It was clear that Deng's foreign policy was primarily based on Mao's "three worlds" strategic concept against "Soviet hegemonism". This was because any sort of "hegemonism" would impede China's quest for the four modernizations.

> Comrade Mao Zedong formulated the strategy of differentiating the three worlds and personally ushered in a new stage in Sino–American and Sino–Japanese relations. By so doing he created new conditions for the development of the worldwide struggle against hegemonism and for the future of world politics. (Comrade Mao's aim was to) try to win over the second world countries for a concerted effort against hegemonism, and establish normal diplomatic relations with the United States and Japan.[18]

Therefore, in the first half of the 1980s, based on the international reality of the time, Deng continued to treat the Soviet Union as the primary enemy of the First World, while the United States was its secondary enemy.[19] The Sino–US Normalization Communique was signed in 1978. This perception placed Japan and other US-led advanced Western industrialized nations in the Second World. China now aimed at "colluding with its secondary enemies" against "hegemonism" of its "primary enemy".

Soviet expansionism and hostility toward China was the main external threat during the period. Chinese propaganda asserted that the Soviet Union was the source of the next world war. Moscow had deployed up to a third of its total strategic nuclear forces, including more than 160 SS-20 medium-range, triple warhead missiles, in the Far East over the decade 1977–1986.[20] The Chinese were satisfied that Soviet backing for Vietnam was being viewed with growing unease by the non-communist neighbors of Southeast Asia. The Soviets invaded Afghanistan in 1979. A year earlier, the Soviet-supported Vietnam had invaded Cambodia to overthrow the Chinese-backed regime.

The Dengist "independent" foreign policy based on the principle of "flexible pragmatism" ruled out the establishment of a strategic or military alliance with Washington. However, gravely concerned about its border security, China tacitly agreed to act in a sort of loose but potentially hostile anti-Soviet collusion with the United States in mid-1984. In July that year, US Under-Secretary of State for Political Affairs, Michael Armacost, claimed that the US sale of weapons to China was intended for defense against the Russians, and that a China which could secure its northern border was "important" to the US.[21] Thus, although Soviet expansionism and hostility towards the PRC posed the main external threat during this period, the international environment remained relatively stable for the PRC's economic reform and open-door policy. This was in contrast with the period 1959–1972 when the United States was China's primary enemy, and the Soviet Union was the "the No. 1 accomplice of the United States".[22]

Understandably, therefore, on many occasions, Deng had stressed that stable and peaceful domestic and international environments were crucial to China's economic reform and open-door policy.

> We really need a peaceful environment [...] for the interest of our own country [...]. The goal of our foreign policy is a peaceful environment for achieving the four modernizations. These are sincere words, not just empty rhetoric.[23]

> Without a peaceful environment, how much (national) construction could there be? [24]

In adopting the Maoist foreign policy strategy, in August 1985 Deng Xiaoping aimed to create a "peaceful international environment [...] to absorb as many things as possible from other countries".[25] The Dengists were eyeing the US foreign direct investment and sophisticated technology. Kungchia Yeh wrote:

> The United States has the largest technical-industrial complex in the world and is at the forefront in a number of fields of great interest to the Chinese, such as super-computers, microbiology, and materials sciences. In the last two decades (that is, 1972–92), the United States has attracted many high-powered scientists from all over the world to settle in the country.[26]

Yeh went on to argue that most American businessmen were eager to sell technology to China.[27]

Deng's principle of "flexible pragmatism" only paid lip service to China's pledge of "continued support for the developing and underdeveloped countries against the imperialist superpowers", except in the cases of the neighboring Afghanistan and regional Cambodia, where support of both were directed at the Soviet Union. In the early 1980s, while repeatedly claiming China's leadership of the Third World, Deng initiated his original "good neighborliness" diplomacy. Spelling out this policy in December 1982, Deng promised that China would continue its efforts to develop relations with Southeast Asian nations "on a long-term basis".[28] Beijing now began to scale down its military support for Southeast Asian insurgents. With China playing a crucial role, a political settlement of the thirteen-year-old Cambodian problem was worked out in December 1991.[29] The object was to win over not only the Little Economic Dragons, but also the wealthy Chinese in Southeast Asia to invest in the PRC with much needed technology transfers.

Mao's Modernization Revolution in Phases

As mentioned above, in 1979 the Dengists claimed that "making the four modernizations the focus of our work [...] was the will Comrade Mao Zedong bequeathed us". In the following, Mao's legacy will be discussed in terms of the ongoing four modernizations starting in December 1978 in the continued stable and peaceful international environment.

Firstly, Mao's "methodology of thinking" was "to make the universe my greater self who is concerned with the affairs of the whole world and ten thousand future generations".[30] The important tasks of "uprooting the mountain of feudalism", "wiping out capitalism", and "annihilating imperialism", were initiated to achieve the objective of making the whole world an "ideal place" for "ten thousand future generations". Thus, he "exerted the strength to uproot these three big mountains".[31] Mao's method was by "digging together" with the great masses of the people, his "Almighty God" and with the iron will of the "Foolish Old Man who removed the mountains". Adopting Mao's spirit, Deng Xiaoping believed that Mao's plan for the four modernizations "will affect thousands of years to come and is a cause for ten thousand generations to come" (千秋万代的事业).[32] In carrying out this gigantic task, Deng was determined "not to rely on the help of God [...] but to rely on our own efforts, learning from experience and pushing resolutely ahead".[33] He declared that "we are doing something that China has never done before, not in thousands of years" and that "the current reform will have an impact not only domestically but also internationally.[34] Thus Mao's spirit stimulated Deng's vision of realizing the four modernizations for "ten thousand future generations" and this spirit was aimed at inspiring "the future generations" to continue his modernization revolution. It is thus important to acknowledge that Mao had provided Deng and the successive Chinese leaderships with the theoretical foundation for this gigantic task.

I have argued that in his tasks of "wiping capitalism from the face of the earth", "annihilating imperialism" and carrying out the four modernizations scheme, Mao needed "astronomical power" (大力).[35] This, Mao himself said, was "the strongest power in the world and can be generated when all people unite".[36] The precondition of the Herculean task of realizing the four modernizations was to "improve the people's livelihood", while modernizing agriculture was "basic", and modernizing light industry was "the leading factor". With the people's livelihood improved, the people's power can be tapped for tackling the four modernizations task more effectively. This study will argue that Deng and subsequently Jiang led the whole population to carry out Mao's modernization revolution in phases. By improving the people's livelihood first, the post-Mao leadership aims to tap astronomical power for the modernization tasks.

The Productive Forces

As discussed above, it was Mao's perception that astronomical power could be harnessed through science and technology. Deng also referred to Mao's statement on making "greater contribution to humanity" in the sphere of science and technology and to Mao's emphasis on "the battle", which "had to be won for science and technology to further develop China's productive forces".

Inspired by Marx's view that "science and technology are part of the productive forces" and by Mao's speech in the Sixth Supreme State Council Meeting in November 1956 that "the purpose of the socialist revolution is to emancipate the productive forces". Deng Xiaoping argued that Marx's statement was "incomplete".[37] According to him, "the complete statement should be that science and technology constitute a *primary* productive force" (Emphasis added).[38] Quoting Mao, Deng contended that "the basic task (of our four modernizations) is to maintain socialist convictions and principles, expand the productive forces and *raise the people's living standards*" (Emphasis added).[39] Deng maintained that "the reform of the system for managing science and technology was designed to liberate the productive forces".[40]

Emphasizing the importance of education to the development of science and technology, he stated that "all trades and professions should promote science, technology and education. Large enterprises should all have their own scientific and technological research organs and personnel. Every professional department should conduct scientific research".[41] On the importance of education, Deng declared that "education should be geared to the needs of modernization of the world and of the future".[42]

It seems that Mao effectively created a legacy of modernization spirit for China's future generations. Therefore, it is safe to claim that Mao's spirit has now been institutionalized through the country's ongoing modernization revolution.

In building socialism with Chinese characteristics through implementing China's four modernizations scheme and economic reform, Deng Xiaoping gave first priority to developing the productive forces among the peasantry. He argued that "eighty per cent of the population lives in rural areas and China's stability depends on the stability of those areas".[43] He concluded that the policy should "invigorate the economy by adopting an open-door policy to bring the initiative of 80 per cent of the population into full play".[44] It was noted earlier that Mao's "class struggle" to make "selflessness" effective in uniting the majority (98 per cent plus) of the people to weed out the "class enemies" now had to be phased out.

Deng's next step was economic reform in the urban areas as decided by the Second Session of the Sixth National People's Congress. The urban reform involved not only industry and commerce, but also science and technology, education and all other fields. The

Chinese aimed to carry out reform at home and to open up the country wider to the outside world to bring in foreign investments, the indispensable supplement, and advanced technology.[45]

Deng's Style of "Socialist Orientation"

Deng attributed the initiative of the modernization revolution to Mao "who blazed a Chinese road by integrating Marxism-Leninism with Chinese realities".[46] He emphasized that in the course of carrying out the economic reform and the four modernizations, it is important to maintain their "socialist orientation".[47] By "socialism", he meant, "the Chinese economy must be dominated by public ownership and there must be of no polarization".[48] Deng's staunch non-capitalist stance was decisive: "Our experience has shown that we cannot take (the capitalist) road".[49] In terms of the Maoist language, he argued: "If we took the capitalist road, a small number of people in certain areas would quickly go rich; and a new bourgeoisie would emerge along with a number of millionaires, while the overwhelming majority of the people would remain in poverty, scarcely able to feed and clothe themselves".[50] Thus, according to Deng, raising the standard of living of *all the people overall* was the first priority of socialism. As productive forces develop, the people's material and cultural life would constantly improve. He therefore argued that the fundamental task for the socialist stage was to develop the productive forces.[51] The Maoist socialist modernization, according to Deng, was to unite the people together and prevent the growth of capitalism or polarization of wealth so as to bring about common prosperity.[52]

Deng elaborated on his Maoist way of tapping the people's power as follows:

> Over the past several decades, the Chinese Communists had united the people on the basis of firm convictions that enabled them to struggle for their own interests – the interests of the overwhelming majority of the people. Without such convictions, there would have been no cohesion among the people, and

> they would have accomplished nothing. That is why we have been able to unite the masses and mobilize them to act with one heart and one mind.[53]

In April 1990, Deng concluded his speech "We Are Working to Revitalize the Chinese Nation" in the Maoist style of power consolidation because "when the Chinese people are disunited, they are weak, but "when they join together, they have enormous strength".[54]

Why did the Maoists brand Deng Xiaoping as "the No. 2 capitalist roader" during the Cultural Revolution and "the unrepentant capitalist roader"?

It is the author's belief that Deng honestly disagreed with Mao's Great Leap Forward (GLF) and the commune, which could not effectively develop or could undermine the productive forces.[55] His disagreement might not have taken into consideration the international perspective as the primary issue. All this could not be considered as "treasonous". He was "treated differently" compared with Liu Shaoqi, "the Chinese Khrushchev" or with Peng Dehuai who was opposed to Mao's GLF with "Khrushchev's encouragement". Even Deng Xiaoping's "attempt to reverse correct verdicts" of the Cultural Revolution obviously could not be regarded as treasonous.

Deng's staunch Marxist stance was well known even long after the Cultural Revolution. For instance, he persistently emphasized the domination of public ownership in the national economy, which was integrated with the post-1971 budding market economy. Deng adopted Mao's mass line strategy for the four modernizations scheme. Furthermore, in his attempt to raise the living standard of the people, Deng consistently promoted a "non-capitalist" stance to prevent the growth of capitalism. This was because, according to him, capitalism would lead to the polarization of wealth. However, why was he "capped with" the stigma of "the No. 2 capitalist roader" during the Cultural Revolution? To accept the term "capitalist roader" at face value is misleading. Although given the "cap of a capitalist roader", Deng was actually branded as a "Soviet revisionist". This was not because he agreed with Liu Shaoqi's Soviet-oriented economic strategy as a result of the "three bad years" following the GLF, but because he saw it a solution to the mass famine, as shown in his statement: "What did it matter", asked Deng once, "whether the cat was black or white – as long as it caught the mouse?" Although the capitalist economic measures of Liu Shaoqi enabled the Chinese economy to recover from the disastrous conditions partly created by the GLF, Liu's Soviet approach with his emphasis on the primacy of the Party as organization implicitly denied Mao's "redness", his revolutionary cadre policy and so forth. This Liuist approach, in the long run, had detrimental effects on Mao's basic policy for "uniting all who could unite". The crux of the matter was that in 1954 the Soviet "revisionists" were beginning to collude with the United States against China, threatening its survival. "Revisionism" means the "liberalization" of economic policies and the application of capitalist methods such as over-emphasis on "expertise" and material incentives to run the economy.[56] On the surface, Mao considered the Soviet approach to be a betrayal of the Marxist principles. However, more importantly, Mao's real concern was the implication of this "revisionist" approach. This was because the Soviet Union "coexisted with the US-led West" and was the "No. 1 accomplice of the US" against China. Understandably, Deng, who had never been considered "treasonous", was "capped" with the name of "capitalist roader", and banished to Nanchang in Jiangxi province but he was rehabilitated after the Cultural Revolution. On the other hand, as "China's Khrushchev", the "treasonous" Liu was critically different.

From Theory to Praxis

It has been shown earlier that only in a peaceful and stable international environment can the "two mountains of economic and technological backwardness" of China be uplifted through the application of capitalist economic principles and advanced science and technology from the outside world particularly the US-led Western countries. To reiterate, stimulated with the Maoist spirit, this post-Mao vision was to realize the four modernizations scheme for "ten thousand generations". It has also been shown that Mao could perceive the power that science and technology could generate, a perception which paralleled Marx's view of these two elements. Deng went further by saying that China's productive forces could only be effectively developed with advanced science and technology. In addition, Deng made his "non-capitalist" stance by emphasizing that the public sector was to play "a predominant role in the economy" to ensure social cohesion as put forward in the 1975 Maoist Constitution. This "socialist orientation", however, eventually proved inefficient in his attempt at economic reform. This point will be discussed later.

By effectively "improving the people's livelihood", the post-Mao leadership was able to rationalize Mao's strategy of long-term economic development with material incentives. As discussed above, Mao was able to realize astronomical power for his great task through his mass line strategy of organizing the whole population. In the same way, the post-Mao leaders stimulated a quarter of the world's population to "uproot the mountains of economic and technological backwardness". Thus, according to Deng, the aim of Mao's mass line strategy in "raising their living standard was to get the support of the population".[57] Deng and subsequently Jiang displayed Mao's spirit by inspiring the people to acquire astronomical power for social change. As noted above, an important factor was phasing out the Maoist "class struggle".

By opening up the country to the outside world, the post-Mao leadership aimed to attract science and technology as well as foreign capital, especially from the US-led West. Furthermore, Deng's "good neighborliness" policy, which was compatible with the peaceful and stable international environment, was aimed at creating a new Asian economic miracle. This policy was subsequently extended to include Western Europe and elsewhere. The post-Mao leadership can therefore be said to have inherited Mao's spirit through its open-door policy aimed at inducing the whole world to modernize China. It was to lead a quarter of mankind to "uproot the mountains of economic and technological backwardness". This point will be discussed in the next chapter.

In the early 1980s, Deng initiated the "one country, two systems" strategy for the gradual resumption of sovereignty over Hong Kong, Macao and Taiwan. This was contrary to Mao's strategy, and became Deng's second front. This principle, as will be seen, was not compatible with the peaceful and stable Asia-Pacific environment. This issue will be discussed in the next two chapters.

Deng Xiaoping's Open-Door Policy and Reform Strategy

As discussed above, in the historic Third Plenary Session held in December 1978, the PRC adopted Vice-Premier Deng's policy of economic reforms and formally opened up China's economy to market forces and foreign investment. Since then, the Chinese government has committed itself to moving away from a rigid centrally planned economy to a relaxed planned-cum-market economy initiated by Mao in 1971. Deng called it "socialism with Chinese characteristics".[58] Along with Western economic principles, the post-Mao modernization revolution has naturally brought about political change, thus rendering irrelevant the ideological fervor, class struggle and mass political campaigns of the Maoist era.

Capital Inflows and Technology Transfer

China's development of science and technology has been and still is far behind that of the advanced nations. Therefore, in adopting Mao's new economic strategy, the Dengist policy of attracting foreign investment and funds was associated with its need for foreign technology. Achieving its goals of quadrupling its 1980 GNP by the end of the twentieth century depended on increasing capital and labor inputs, but more importantly, on advanced science and technology to enhance productivity. Thus, technology transfer was crucial to upgrading its technological levels and eventually to improving its competitiveness in the global markets. Or, in Deng's words:

> Our experience shows that China cannot rebuild itself behind closed doors and that it cannot develop in isolation from the rest of the world. It goes without

saying that a large country like China cannot depend on others for its development; it must depend mainly on itself, on its own efforts. Nevertheless, while holding to self-reliance, we should open our country to the outside world to obtain such aid as foreign investment capital and technology.[59]

With the Maoist strategy of opening up the PRC's economy to the outside world, the Dengists set out to acquire not only foreign investment funds, but also modern technology from the advanced Western countries especially the United States, West Germany, Britain, France, Japan as well as the Four Little Dragons. In addition, China began to send students abroad to accelerate the process of technology transfer.

As mentioned above, Deng's open-door policy was to facilitate technology transfer through international trade. Thus, special economic and technology zones were initiated along the PRC's coastal regions not only to facilitate its foreign trade, but also to attract joint ventures and foreign investments. A joint venture law was also promulgated in 1980. Initial contact with world markets was mainly through the four special economic zones of Shenzhen, Zhuhai, Shantou, and Xiamen. Deng's concept of the Special Economic Zones (SEZ) was so successful that the central government in 1984 extended this scheme to fourteen coastal cities and Hainan Island for foreign investments. The fourteen coastal cities are: Dalian, Qinhuangdao, Tianjin, Yantai, Qingtao, Lianyungang, Nantong, Shanghai, Ningbo, Wenzhou, Zhangjiang, Fuzhou, Guangzhou, and Beihai. In 1985, it further opened up three special regions of the Zhujiang Delta, the Changjiang Delta and the Minnan Delta, which included Xianmen, Quangzhou and Zhangzhou as special areas. The government also accelerated the development of Shanghai's Pudong New Area.

Starting from the early 1980s, foreign investors were invited to these special economic zones. The most successful part of the initiative was attracting wealthy overseas Chinese investors, particularly from Hong Kong through whom massive capital was transferred to the cities in the Zhujiang Delta laying the foundation for the PRC's successful export policies. In the Delta, by far the most successful was Shenzhen, which grew within ten years from a village of 20,000 to an industrial metropolis of two million people.[60]

Starting in 1979, Deng broadened Mao's Western-oriented "individual" economic principle by breaking up the collective farms in order to give farmers individual family holdings and linking output to remuneration. Based on Mao's relaxed economic strategy of 1971, this scheme, called the household responsibility system, was implemented among the Chinese peasantry. The restructuring of the rural economy understandably saw the modification of Mao's defense-oriented and highly centralized people's commune system. Under the new system, the lowest level of the former commune system, i.e., the production team, was abolished, and the former brigade became the village committee. This meant that ownership of the land remained with the village or township thus featuring both centralized and decentralized management. The function of the village committee was now to contract land out to families, collect tax and effect payment to finance collective undertakings such as irrigation, and to administer sales of produce to the state.[61] With Mao's new material incentives and the Western-oriented principle of self-interest serving as catalysts, Deng's new strategy aimed to "invigorate our domestic economy".[62] Mao's new relaxed economic strategy of this socialist planned market economy would increase output and incomes, particularly for the peasantry, who made up about 80 per cent of China's labor force. The reform effort transformed the majority of individual households into basic productive establishments. Deng's incentive policy led to the following important market features. After selling a compulsory fixed quantity of grain output to the state and paying fixed land rents and taxes, individual farmers were given greater freedom in marketing their surplus products, both agricultural and industrial, and in developing sidelines. While the government increased the purchasing prices of farm products, the pricing of these products became increasingly regulated by the market rather than by the state. The farmers were given rights to engage in rural and township industries, commerce, transport, and so forth.[63] This scheme would allow them to diversify their household sources to increase their incomes. To Deng, "planning and the market are both means of developing the productive forces".[64] This economic feature aimed at improving "the livelihood of the whole population".

Structural changes that came about in the Chinese economy were attributed to the fundamental changes in Deng's economic-social development strategy. Reforms in agriculture were first implemented by liberating the peasants from the collective sector. This achieved immediate success. Cheng has recorded the increased productivity in the peasantry for the period 1978–1984 as follows:

> During the period 1978–1984, grain production increased by an average of 4.8% a year and reached a record harvest of 407 million tons in 1984; agricultural production too expanded by 50% in the same period.[65]

It should be noted that the foundation for this agricultural success was laid by Mao's new economic policy, under which the economic performance in the period 1977–1978 was reasonable in terms of growth rate led by the Maoist Hua Guofeng leadership. By encouraging the peasantry to set up their own enterprises, about 160 million people were lifted out of poverty by 1984, and rising rural incomes brought much new housing construction and saw the emergence of rural industries.[66]

The Scheme of Urban Restructuring

Building on the success of the rural reform, a comprehensive urban restructuring scheme was initiated in May 1984. With Mao's 1971 new strategy emphasizing local control, the post-Mao era witnessed a broad range of structural economic reforms to free enterprises from state and Party control. The separation of government administration from enterprise management was to reduce the political and administrative interference from the Party.[67] Thus a gradual transformation of existing industrial enterprises occurred with the simplification of administrative procedures, while structurally market forces were introduced to direct and regulate economic activities. This meant that greater autonomy was given to individual enterprises to introduce their own production plans, scheduling their daily operation processes as well as setting their own prices.[68] All this was based on the principles of Deng's new self-responsibility system. It served to revitalize the Chinese industrial enterprises by giving them decision-making powers, while promoting technological transformation of the enterprises. This was a new "enterprise responsibility system" in which "township and village industrial enterprises" were set up as joint ventures (with foreigners) and wholly owned foreign and private enterprises. They were given the responsibility for their own profits or losses, and managers of these enterprises were given greater decision-making authority. Furthermore, small-scale private businesses were promoted to stimulate production and absorb unemployed labor.[69] "Expertise" and "professional" elements were adopted to "invigorate the industries".[70] Using Mao's new economic model, the government, at both the national and local levels, reduced its direct management role concerning enterprises and began to assume a more regulatory and supervisory role.

Another change was the rehabilitation of experts and intellectuals, whom Deng regarded as an integral part of the "productive forces". Universities and colleges were restored and expanded. China now recruited technocrats to the political leadership, while older politicians, who resisted these changes, were asked to retire. Mass support increased with major improvements in living standards.

In terms of ownership, the Chinese economy was now generally classified into (1) the state sector, (2) the private sector and (3) the collective sector.

An important Dengist "non-capitalist" policy feature was the state sector, which "plays a predominant role in the economy". This was in essence the Maoist strategy of "developing the collective economy" to ensure social cohesion as put forward in the 1975 Constitution.[71] The Dengists announced that "exploitation of others can be avoided by law" as stipulated in Article 5 of the Constitution.

Developed from Mao's relaxed economic strategy, Deng's private ownership policy was extended to form the private sector in the Chinese economy. Deng argued that his policy of allowing the private sector to expand would not weaken the predominant position of the public sector, which was a basic feature of the Dengist model as a whole. Further, his policy was to develop the productive forces more effectively and strengthen the public sector, which was meant to play a predominant role in preventing "polarization".[72] In Deng's own words:

> Does this run counter to the principles of socialism? No, because in the course of reform, we shall make sure of two things: one is that the public sector of the economy is always predominant; the other is that in developing the economy we seek common prosperity, always trying to avoid polarization.[73]

The collective sector is made up of units in both rural and urban areas. In the rural areas, the collective units, which mainly consist of the small-sized township and village enterprises, were successful under the prevailing market conditions particularly with its lower cost structures, for instance, its lower wage scale. Starting from 1979, its annual growth rate of more than 20 per cent was impressive, compared with the overall annual industrial growth rate of about 13 per cent.[74] The collective sector in the rural areas accounted for about 35 per cent of China's total industrial output. Owned by its 135 million workers, it was about 29 per cent of the country's total rural labor force.[75]

The resultant growth in the Chinese economy in the years 1985 and 1986 was at 12.3 per cent and 9.2 per cent respectively, while its industrial output expanded by 18 per cent and 11.1 per cent.[76] With regard to industrial output, while the state sector increased only 12.9 per cent and 6.2 per cent respectively in these two years, the collective sector grew by 30.9 per cent and 16.7 per cent and the private sector improved by a remarkable 60 per cent in 1986.[77] Though the public sector was given a "predominant role to avoid polarization", the public ownership, which was not fully integrated with the market mechanism, eventually led to huge losses which hindered the banking reform. This will be elaborated later.

The Five-Year Plans of the Post-Mao Era

As mentioned above, in the historic Third Plenary Session held in December 1978, the PRC adopted Vice-Premier Deng's policy of economic reforms and *further* opened up China's economy to foreign investment and market forces. The Chinese government committed to moving away from a rigid centrally planned economy to the new Maoist planned-cum-market economy. The origins of this new strategy can be linked to the change in US policy regarding the Far East. Responding to the Kissinger–Nixon Doctrine conceived in the early 1970s for the US gradual withdrawal of US troops from Southeast and Northeast Asia, Mao saw that normalization of Sino–US relations was possible in the face of the Soviet threat. Both China and the United States viewed Soviet expansionism as their principal concern and the USSR was now treated as China's primary enemy. Thus, the table-tennis diplomacy staged in 1971 led to a decisive change of the PRC's relations with the superpowers, enhanced by President Nixon's visit to China in 1972. In addition, with China's new membership in the United Nations in October 1971, normalization of Sino–US relations was seen as necessary.

In the sphere of economic development, this initiative was not only to establish trade relations with the United States, Japan and Europe, but also to adopt the principles of the Western liberal economic model. The Chinese were also eager to acquire Western capital and modern technology for their modernization initiatives. For example, huge construction and infrastructure programs were designed to stimulate domestic growth to spur such imports. Therefore, the Fourth FYP witnessed Mao's new power harnessed from the liberal development policy among the peasantry. This Maoist planned-cum-market economy and the Dengist economic system "adhered to Marxism and Mao Zedong Thought", which Deng called "socialism with Chinese characteristics".[78] In the following section and the next two chapters, the various post-Mao modernization-related five year plans will be examined in the context of Mao's Fourth FYP, with the needed modifications.

In his report, Hu Yaobang called for the continuation of the policy of giving a leading position to the state sector in the economy and the development of diverse economic forms. Problems of the state-owned enterprises (SOE) had already appeared during the modernization drive under the conditions of the new socialist market economy. The state sector, comprising the "sunset industries" of coal, steel, and textiles, remained the largest employer with more than 100 million workers. As noted above, the sector had been making huge losses. Its share of industrial output declined from 76 per cent in 1980 to 50 per cent in 1991. Therefore, a significant transformation of the ailing SOEs was needed.

Hu Yaobang also promoted the policy of giving the leading role to the planned economy based on public partnership, and a supplementary role for market regulation. This witnessed the emergence of market mechanisms in the Chinese economy. In addition, Hu stressed the expansion of economic and technological exchanges with foreign countries, whilst urging the maintenance of self-reliance. However, the tenet of "self-reliance" was kept in name only.

Deng's thought on education related to the four modernizations scheme was crucial. In May 1977, he had pointed out that China was at least twenty years behind the developed countries in science and technology.[79] He called for the upgrading of science and technology education at every level, from primary to secondary, and higher education in key colleges and universities. He urged the Party to have "respect for knowledge and respect for trained personnel" and to develop more institutions of higher education.[80] In late 1977, Deng urged the Party to restore the education system that had been ruined during the Cultural Revolution and recommended them "to enhance the intellectuals' material well-being".[81] To Deng Xiaoping, expanding education was of paramount importance "even if it means slowing down in other fields".[82] In 1978, with his position secured, he announced new policies regarding intellectuals and education.[83] As a result, China began to send students abroad to accelerate the process of technology transfer. This initiative was only possible with the prevailing favorable international environment brought about by Deng's new "good neighborliness" diplomacy.

In December 1978, China began to send scholars overseas for research in disciplines badly needed in the national economic construction.[84] In the same year, the country sent more than 800 students to over twenty Western countries, including the United States, Britain, France, Germany, Canada and Japan.[85] During the period 1978–1998, it sent about 300,000 scholars and students to 103 countries, 47,000 of them supported by the government and 92,000 by their work units, while 154,000 were private students.[86] With a booming economy, Chinese families could afford premium education.

On the other hand, China's institutes of higher learning began inviting foreign experts to give lectures and conduct cooperative research and joint training for graduates.[87] Furthermore, from the early 1980s, the PRC cooperated with the United Nations for the international transfer of knowledge concerning high-tech and advanced educational managerial expertise.[88] The World Bank has been the largest cooperative partner of China's education sector with projects covering various fields, such as higher education, teacher training, vocational education, adult, basic and audio-visual education.[89]

Other fundamental tasks of the Sixth FYP included a review and adjustment of the direction for heavy industry, technical transformation in existing enterprises based on technical renovation, intensified construction of national defense and the national defense industry, population control and greater environmental protection. In addition, in accordance with Mao's plan as spelled out in his "Ten Major Relationships" of April 1956, the Sixth FYP was "to make the most of the coastal areas and take full advantage of their special favorable conditions to help stimulate economic development in the interior". The Plan aimed "to intensify the development of energy resources and energy saving, speed up the construction of harbors and railways and intensify their technical transformation".

This FYP was to carry on the policy of readjusting, restructuring, consolidating and improving the national economy,[90] and the general guiding principle was to lay a solid foundation for economic development in the future.[91] Understandably, with the favorable international environment, this aimed at "continuing to improve the people's livelihood" in general.[92] This meant an increased output of agricultural produce, textiles and other light industrial goods as well as other consumer goods industries to raise the per-capita consumption level. In his report to the National Congress of the CCP on September 1, 1982, Hu Yaobang, Deng's Party Secretary, emphasized that the most important objective in China's economic growth was to "properly solve the problems of agriculture, energy and transport and of education and science". Agriculture was the foundation of the national economy and, needless to say, if it grew, the Chinese would be able to handle other problems more easily. In his speech "We Shall Concentrate On Economic Development" on September 18, 1982, Deng put energy resources and communications as the second national strategic priority for the four modernizations scheme after agriculture.[93] This was because "energy shortage and the strain on transport were major checks on the country's economic development. Transport capacity lagged far behind the increasing volume of freight".[94]

The success of China's modernization plan depends, to a large extent, on whether it can meet its energy needs. By the end of the century, if its total output value of industry and agriculture was to be quadrupled as planned, the required production volume of oil, for instance, should be at least doubled. However, its plan to expand the energy program has been impeded by a severe shortage of funds. In addition, poor transport infrastructure has caused bottlenecks and uneven distribution of energy commodities, especially oil and coal.

In December 1981, Premier Zhao Ziyang stated in the Fifth NPC that more coal was to be used during the 1990s to save oil for export. This certainly contributed to the increase of domestic demand for coal. The Chinese government's policy was shifting the country's inefficient oil-burning industries over to coal in an effort to conserve oil.

Investments in the country's transport and communications infrastructure had lagged behind other sectors of the economy. Its railway system was very inadequate, despite massive track-laying work over the years. China urgently needed to expand its rail network to meet the increasing demand for energy and raw material transport, as some northern refineries were largely sitting idle because they could not move oil products fast enough.

In sum, the first priority of the Plan was to "improve the people's livelihood" with the aim of furthering the modernization process. This was possible because of the relatively favorable international environment brought about by China's peace-making efforts.

Conclusion

In attracting advanced technology and capital from the West for their modernization revolution, the Dengists continued to apply Mao's strategy of opening up the country to the outside world and carry out his Western-oriented economic reform. This was feasible with Deng's global strategy based on maintaining normalized relations with the international community, particularly the US-led West, and his new "good neighborliness" policy in helping create a peaceful and stable international environment. However, internally, Deng's staunch "non-capitalist" stance was not bold enough to reform the state-owned enterprises, which led to great losses. In the following two chapters, attention will focus on Deng Xiaoping's and subsequently Jiang Zemin's approaches with regard to the SOEs.

Chapter Six
The Transformation of the Bipolarity: From "Good-Neighborliness" to Inducing the Whole World to Help Modernize China

Characteristic of the period 1986–1991 was China's vigorous efforts to promote regional and global peace and stability conducive to its economic modernization endeavors. In this chapter, I will argue that the transformation of the bipolarity made the international environment even more favorable to China's modernization drive. The transformation of the bipolarity began in the mid-1980s when Deng Xiaoping launched the second stage of his modernization program through China's Seventh Five-Year Plan (1986–1991). I will also consider how Deng's "good-neighborliness" strategy in action induced the whole world to help modernize China.

The Transformation of the Bipolarity

With the accession to power of the Soviet leader Mikhail Gorbachev in March 1985, the international order of bipolarity began to transform. This had important implications for Deng's global strategy of maintaining China's normalization of relations with the West favorable to its four modernizations program. First, the expensive arms race with the US and the enormous foreign aid program had been a drain on the Soviet power. The rigid Soviet economic policy inevitably led to severe economic recession and material shortages. As a result, the Soviet leader began to carry out a program of significant changes. By adopting Western economic principles, his new strategy aimed at attracting foreign capital to enhance productivity and efficiency.

Gorbachev also made a radical shift in Soviet military and defense policy by adopting the so-called "reasonable sufficiency" strategy. In essence, his new approach called for a reduction in the size of the army and defense expenditure, while keeping reliable security. Furthermore, discarding the self-serving and coercive foreign policy, he formulated a new strategy, which stressed global security, non-interference in the internal affairs of other nations and a curtailment of foreign aid. Gorbachev's new foreign policy called for withdrawal of Soviet troops deployed in foreign nations. In dealing with the West, clearly the Soviet leader pursued detente, which emphasized disarmament, the avoidance of military confrontation, and the resolution of existing problems through political means. As a result, a new situation evolved in which security issues between the Soviet Union and the United States had come to focus on arms control rather than on military competition.

In December 1987 Gorbachev and Reagan signed the first major disarmament pact of the nuclear age in Washington, that is, the Intermediate-Range Nuclear Force Treaty. This was an important step to ease the threat of nuclear war.[1] In February 1988, Gorbachev announced the Soviet unilateral withdrawal of all the troops from Afghanistan. In that year, he announced the abandonment of the Brezhnev Doctrine of limited sovereignty that the Soviet Union was ready to use military force to stop undesirable political developments in the Socialist bloc. In his speech in the United Nations General Assembly in December that year, Gorbachev proposed a cut of the Soviet armed forces by 500,000 troops in two years, and the withdrawal of 10,000 tanks, 8,500 artillery pieces and 800 combat aircraft from East and Soviet Europe. He also decided to withdraw the forces deployed in Mongolia and Soviet Asia.[2] This would reduce Soviet conventional superiority in Europe.

Soviet and US Foreign Policies Regarding Asia

In his Vladivostok speech on July 28, 1986, Gorbachev announced the Soviet initiative of establishing a new international order in the Asia-Pacific region through cooperation. Evidently he was convinced that the peace and stability of Asia should be based on economic rather than military terms. Understanding that economic strength can produce political and strategic power, the Soviet leader strove to find a viably peaceful international environment in which to build Soviet economic and hence strategic strength. In another speech at Krasnoyarsk in September 1988, Gorbachev attached great importance to the economic development of Eastern Siberia. Certainly the Soviets were eyeing the technology and capital of Japan and the newly industrialized countries in the Far East.

The shift in Soviet foreign policy led to its application of pressure to Vietnam to withdraw its troops from Cambodia. The mammoth military aid to Vietnam had been a drain on the Soviet strategic capability; and about two-thirds of this aid was to be curtailed. The withdrawal of Soviet troops from Afghanistan and Soviet pressure on Vietnam led to a cessation of hostilities in the Indian Ocean and the Asia-Pacific region. In 1988 Mikhail Gorbachev offered to close down the Soviet bases in Vietnam in exchange for the US withdrawal from Clark Air Base and Subic Naval Base in the Philippines.

However, the US Asian policy emphasizes Asia's importance to itself, and the cooperation and shared leadership with all Asian countries in the pursuit of common interests there. Thus the United States continual military presence in Asia aimed at maintaining peace and stability of the region as vital for business investment and economic growth, although its presence there was to be eventually reduced. Major US economic interests had been and still are at stake in the Far East. For instance, its 1988 annual trade turnover in the Asia-Pacific region alone was about 37 per cent of the total worldwide, that is, about US$300 billion, and this was far more than that for the Trans-Atlantic trade for the same year which was about US$186 billion.[3] The US overseas investment shifted to the region with an average annual growth of about 12 per cent, surpassing that of other regions.[4] The United States was the second largest trader and investor in ASEAN after Japan. It was understandable that Gorbachev's proposal was not accepted. Nevertheless, the United States had already felt the Soviet leader's sincerity. The Soviets began to withdraw from Cam Ranh Bay at the end of 1990.

Sino–Soviet Relations

Calling for closer ties with the PRC and announcing the Soviet troop withdrawals from Afghanistan and Mongolia on China's northern border, Mikhail Gorbachev's speech of July 1986 foreshadowed the prospect of a detente of the two communist giants. In February 1989 Foreign Minister Eduard Shevardnadze announced the Soviet reduction of 250,000 soldiers deployed along the Sino–Soviet border including 120,000 men stationed along the Mongolian and Manchurian borders. This pullout reduced the Soviet threat to China. Gorbachev's efforts including the Soviet troop withdrawal from Afghanistan and Soviet pressure on Vietnam to withdraw its troops from Cambodia led to Deng's acceptance of a Sino–Soviet summit meeting in Beijing in May 1989. This meeting, which symbolized the beginning of the Sino–Soviet normalization of relations, marked the end of their 30-year-old military confrontation. In October that year, both parties discussed the establishment of a "non-military zone" along their border, where troop withdrawal had already begun. In May 1991 the PRC's Party Secretary Jiang Zemin reciprocated Soviet leader Gorbachev's visit to Beijing, and this marked the first visit to the USSR by a party chief of the People's Republic of China since 1957. Prior to Jiang's departure to Moscow, both sides had declared that they no longer posed a threat to each other. During his visit, the Sino–Soviet eastern border accord was signed.

China's Role in the Quest for a Cambodian Solution

Soviet and Vietnamese hegemony in Indochina was a major cause of China's punitive attack on Vietnam in February 1979. Its stance on Indochina was clear: with the ending of Soviet support to Vietnam's Cambodian policy and with unconditional withdrawal of Vietnamese troops from Cambodia, a political settlement of the Cambodian problem would be possible. The United States, the Soviet Union, the ASEAN states, and China all believed that peace and stability in Southeast Asia was crucially based on the political settlement of the 12-year-old Cambodian problem. All these parties also realized that in finding a political solution to this problem, tripartite cooperation between the US, the USSR and the PRC was crucial. As discussed above, the Soviet initiative to establish a new international order in the Asia-Pacific region was based on cooperation, hence the Soviet pressure on Vietnam to withdraw its troops from Cambodia was inevitable.

In September 1990, the Chinese and Soviet foreign ministers agreed in Harbin to suspend military aid to all the warring factions in the Cambodian conflict. The Chinese leadership guaranteed the members of the ASEAN group that it would not support the Khmer Rouge's aim of monopolization of power, in addition to announcing its direct talks with the Phnom Penh government. Furthermore, encouraged by the PRC, the three factions in the Cambodian resistance coalition reached an accord in Beijing to take part in working out the highest-level central committee for the Jakarta conference on troop withdrawal of the warring factions under direct UN supervision.

During his visit to Moscow in May 1991, China's Party Secretary Jiang Zemin talked with Soviet President Gorbachev on the security of the Asia-Pacific region and the political settlement of the Cambodian problem. In the joint communiqué issued at the end of Jiang Zemin's trip, both parties "support the political settlement stipulated by the United Nations Security Council".[5] With China's crucial role, a political settlement of the Cambodian problem was eventually worked out. In October 1991, the UN-sponsored peace accord was signed in Paris between the Vietnam-backed Phnom Penh government and the three guerrilla factions, thus bringing a formal end to 13 years of civil war in Cambodia.

The withdrawal of Soviet troops from Afghanistan and Mongolia on China's northern border and Soviet pressure on Vietnam to withdraw its troops from Cambodia confirmed Gorbachev's genuine peace initiatives. As a result, the Soviet Union in the Dengist worldview was relegated to the position of secondary enemy and quickly transformed into a "friend", following Jiang Zemin's visit to Moscow.

The unprecedented international changes since the autumn of 1989 had been the transformation of Eastern Europe, the significant reduction of Soviet conventional forces in Europe, the disintegration of the Warsaw Pact, the re-unification of East and West Germany, which the Soviet Union sanctioned, and finally the collapse of the

Soviet Union itself. These changes represented the most dramatic developments in international politics since the end of the Second World War.

The Sino-US Economic and Trade Relations: 1979–1990

With the normalization of Sino–US diplomatic relations in January 1979, Deng Xiaoping visited the United States and signed agreements on cooperation in science and technology, education, commerce and other exchanges. China aimed at introducing capital, technology and management skills from the United States, which were conducive to its economic modernization program.

During the period 1979–1982 the volume of the Sino-US trade reportedly grew at an annual average rate of 45 per cent.[6] Their two-way trade in 1984 was a record of about US$6.1 billion, an increase of 50 percent over 1983.[7] In 1987, China exported commodities to the United States totalling US$3.04 billion and imported US$4.835 billion worth of goods from that country.[8] In 1988, the United States was China's third major trade partner.

China attached great importance to developing cooperation with foreign enterprises by integrating technology with trade. In January 1984, the Accord on Industrial and Technological Cooperation was signed during Premier Zhao Ziyang's US visit.[9] Paul Wolfowitz, US Assistant-Secretary of State in charge of East Asian and Pacific affairs, estimated high-tech exports to China to exceed US$1.5 billion in 1984.[10] In July that year, both countries signed a working program for cooperation in aviation and space industry.[11] During the period 1984–1987, China also imported machines and equipment valued at US$1.6 billion, an increase of 24.4 per cent to 42.2 per cent, from the United States.[12] Major commodities included planes for civilian use and of transport, vehicles, computers, oil, chemical equipment and power generating equipment.

The number of joint ventures with US companies operating wholly-owned enterprises outside China's special economic zones also increased.[13] The PRC promulgated its patent law to absorb advanced foreign particularly US technologies. In 1987, the US was China's biggest foreign investor, both in terms of total value and the number of projects involved.

Relations with the European Community Strengthened: 1979–1991

With the largest number of developed countries, Western Europe boasts abundant capital and advanced technology. Since 1979, China had aimed at close cooperation with the region particularly in the scientific and technological fields. During the period 1979–1991, China attracted a great amount of euro capital for direct investment, owing to its improved structure of foreign investment.

Immediately after the founding of the European Community (EC) in the 1950s, a small scale of trade between EC members and the PRC began. By September 1975, the further development of diplomatic relations between them had been accelerated. In 1978, their first trade agreements were signed.[14] Since then, Sino–EC cooperation had extended to areas such as energy, science and technology, assistance to underdeveloped areas in China and the training of skilled people.[15] In October 1983, Premier Zhao Ziyang pledged to give preferential treatment in trade to those European countries which helped provide the PRC with advanced technology.[16] For example, by 1987, China had already signed more than 50 technology transfer agreements with the German conglomerate the Siemens Company in Frankfurt including parts for large integrated circuits, programme-controlled exchanges, hydroelectric generators and medical equipment.[17]

The European Union was always a strong backer of the PRC's entry into the General Agreements on Tariffs and Trade and supported its entry into the World Trade Organization (WTO). Further, the European Community granted the general preferential treatment to China as early as January 1980. By 1987, the volume of Sino–EC bilateral trade valued at about US$11 billion was four times that of 1978.[18] This made the EC China's third largest trade partner after Hong Kong and Japan.[19]

Since the late 1970s, shifting away from the Maoist policy of world revolution, Deng Xiaoping's global strategy had been based on "flexible pragmatism" to maintain normalization of relations with the United States, Japan, and other advanced Western industrialized countries. It had particularly created a peaceful and stable regional environment vital to China's open-door policy of attracting foreign capital and advanced technology for its economic reforms and four modernizations program.

However, the 1989 Tiananmen Square military crackdown of the pro-democracy protests adversely affected Sino–US relations. The military crackdown led to a series of sanctions against the PRC in the US House of Representatives. In addition, the Summit of Seven (G-7) of the leading Western industrialized nations in Paris in July 1989 denounced the PRC's "violent suppression in violation of human rights". Foreigners cut investment funds in the country and the United States, Europe and Japan took economic sanctions against the PRC.

However, Western European sanctions against China lasted only one and a half years, with the EC foreign ministers restoring their relations with the PRC particularly in trade, economic matters, science and technology in October 1990.[20] In 1991, reportedly, China's trade with the United States was US$14.2 billion, with Western Europe reaching US$17.32 billion and with Japan totalling a record US$22.8 billion.[21] Its foreign trade reached US$135.7 billion in 1991 compared with US$38.1 billion in 1980, an increase of 350 per cent.[22] The impact of Western economic sanctions against the PRC was softened up. In the next section, we will consider Deng's "good-neighborliness" policy and how it was extended to the whole of the world.

Deng's Development-Oriented Strategy: From "Good Neighborliness" to Inducing the Whole World to Help Modernize China

Since the late 1970s, Deng Xiaoping's strategy has been to continue maintain normalization of relations with the US-led advanced Western industrialized countries including Japan. This was certainly possible with a peaceful and stable global and regional environment conducive to the PRC's open-door policy of attracting foreign capital and advanced technology for its economic reforms and four modernizations program. Stimulated by the Asian economic miracle, which had swept across the continent, Deng formulated the "good-neighborliness" policy. As a result of the collapse of the Soviet Union, Deng's "good-neighborliness" policy was extended to Russia. In short, his global strategy was aimed at attracting foreign capital and advanced technology not only from the US-led Western world, but also from the world at large. In this section, I will discuss how investment from its economically advanced neighbors helped China to create a new Asian economic miracle.

The "Good Neighborliness" Policy in Action: 1979–1991

From the beginning, China's modernization efforts had been stimulated by the Asian economic miracle, which swept across Asia. This miracle began with Japan, which subsequently inspired the remarkable economic development of the four Newly Industrialized Economies (NIEs) of South Korea, Taiwan, Hong Kong and Singapore, which enjoyed the fastest rise in incomes ever seen in history. Their real GDP growth averaged 8.5 per cent per year during the period 1960–1990, compared to average economic growth in the developing world of 4.8 per cent per annum. Since 1979, the Chinese government had played a crucial role in its modernization revolution, with the aim to be part of the development miracle of the NIEs. In that year, its "good-neighborliness" policy was initiated to strengthen Western Pacific economic cooperation in particular with its economically advanced neighbors.

By adopting the export-led growth policy, the so-called "five little economic dragons" stressed the enhancement of labor productivity, technology transfers, work ethic, organizational discipline and management skills. However, unlike Japan and the Newly Industrialized Economies, which all lack natural resources, China embarked on a major program of export-oriented industrialization based on its open-door policy. Emerging from the effective implementation of this new policy was associated with its import-substitution strategy for manufactured exports. And its trends of growth and industrialization required high rates of investment. The PRC's level of investment boiled down to the rate of foreign direct investment (FDI). The rapid growth of FDI in the export-oriented, labor-intensive manufacturing was a marked feature of growth in the PRC and Asia's "dragons" over the past twenty years.

The growth in intra-regional trade with China at its center was associated with a dramatic increase in intra-Asia direct investment with most of the investment flowing to China, according to Hong Kong's Economic Risk Consultancy. Japan and South Korea were big investors, but the biggest were ethnic Chinese. "Most of this investment came from Taiwan and Hong Kong, but significant amounts also came from the Chinese in Indonesia, Singapore, Malaysia, and Thailand", the Consultancy argued. It went on to say that this helped bind their economies more closely with China. The report described cross-border business interests of ethnic Chinese as the "glue linking China to other Asian countries".

As development economists observed, the higher the quality of growth is, the more it contributes to better employment level, rising wages, reduced poverty, better income distribution, improved standards of living and greater opportunities for personal fulfillment. By 2000, they predicted, Asia would be the world's largest market with purchasing power exceeding North America or Western Europe. In the following section, I will consider the influence of the economic development of the five "dragons" on post-Mao China, their economic and trade relations.

Since the end of World War II, Japan has become an important ally of the Western powers headed by the United States, which played a crucial role in the Japanese economic development by supplying the needed capital equipment, foreign direct investment, financial loans, technology and management skills. Following the US occupation, the period 1945–1954 saw Japan's rapid economic growth. The 1955–1960 GNP even increased phenomenally at an average 8.7 per cent per annum.[23] The US aid and support with respect to technology transfer were crucially related to the United States using Japan as a military base for the Korean and later the Vietnam Wars.

Initially Japan developed its labor-intensive light industries and subsequently increased productivity and exported the products.[24] Its next stage was to use the foreign exchange earned to import capital equipment to invest in infrastructure and additional export industries.[25] Its exports were further expanded and higher levels of industrialization were achieved.[26] Government encouragement in various forms of subsidies played a crucial role in the early stages of Japanese industrialization.

During the period 1979–1991, Japan's economic development certainly stimulated China's modernization scheme. Since its occupation of Japan in 1945, the United States had played a crucial role in Sino–Japanese relations, which were the basic features of the Sino–Japanese ties. Understandably, since their diplomatic ties established in 1972, Sino-Japanese economic and trade relations had grown steadily. In 1978, an eight-year Sino–Japanese non-governmental trade agreement was signed for China to import Japanese technology and equipment from Japan and export crude oil and coal to Japan.[27] In 1979, the agreement was extended to cover a period of 13 years for both countries to export to each other between US$20 billion and US$30 billion of goods.[28] In 1981, their trade volume was worth US$10 billion.[29] Despite the world trade slump in 1991, Sino–Japanese trade reached US$20.2 billion.[30]

Since 1979, a large number of labor-intensive, foreign-industrial enterprises had been set up in China's coastal areas. Japanese investment in China increased continuously.[31] By June 1991, Japan's investment in China had been worth US$2.6 billion, next only to Hong Kong, Macao, Taiwan and the United States.[32] In 1990, reportedly, four of the ten major hard-currency-earning foreign-invested enterprises in China were Japanese.[33] Japan's crucial stages of economic development should have served as a viable model to inspire China's modernization program.

Taiwan

With Deng Xiaoping's "good neighborliness" initiative, inviting the Taiwanese business community to invest in the mainland was considered necessary. With the "Message to Taiwan Compatriots by the Standing Committee of the National People's Congress" on New Year's Day of 1979, establishing better economic and trade ties between the two sides were initiated.

Since the early 1960s, Taiwan had pursued a government-led program of export-oriented industrialization. About 52 per cent of the industrial growth in the 1961–1971 period resulted from increased exports of manufactured goods. In the late 1960s, its new strata of industrialization dominated by transnational corporations began to produce consumer electronics and related components. In the 1971–1976 period, 81 per cent of the growth was related directly or indirectly to manufacturing export activities. Characteristic of the period 1973–1979 was the development of a new set of heavy industry such as steelworks, petrochemical complexes and shipyards. With part of the production of these industries designated to the world market, the post-1979 period witnessed Taiwan's transformation of its industrial structure into a higher technology type of production. Taiwan's economic program of export-oriented industrialization stimulated China's development.

Beginning in the late 1970s, the world market was no longer expansive and new protectionism appeared all over the North especially in the United States, which took about 48 per cent of total exports from Taiwan in 1986. Technological development in the core countries eroded the worldwide micro-electronic production. Cheap labor lost its importance. The Asian NIEs were confronted with competition from a new generation of exports of light manufactured goods. Many of these came from China, which was an important determinant of Taiwan's economic policy.

During the period 1979–1989, the value of the two-way transit trade across the Taiwan Straits amounted to 11.8 billion yuan (US$1.47 billion). The first half of 1990 witnessed the craze of investment of more than 1,000 Taiwanese businesses in the mainland totaling US$1.5 billion.[34] The goods imported from Taiwan, reportedly, were all industrial raw materials. By the end of 1991, their entrepot trade value had amounted to US$5.79 billion with the total investment of US$2.5 billion by Taiwanese businessmen.[35] The mainland became Taiwan's fifth largest trade market while Taiwan was the sixth largest trading partner of the mainland.[36]

South Korea

South Korea became a NIE in a relatively short time, with a literate and motivated work force and an entrepreneurial spirit enhanced by the government-led economic development policy. Pursuing a growth-first strategy in its initial stage of import-substitution in investment, South Korea was successful in diversifying manufactured commodities with its outward-oriented approach.

During the 1962–1991 period, the remarkable South Korean economy expanded at an average annual rate of about 9 per cent, with the growth of nominal per capita GNP from US$87 to US$6,498.[37] Commodity exports rose from US$54.8 million in 1962 to US$71.9 billion in 1991 making the country one of the world's major trading partners.[38] While its exports of manufacturing goods dominated the national economy, heavy industrial products also increased steadily demonstrating South Korea's industrial transformation.

Imported technology made great contributions to the rapid growth of the economy. During its five successive Five-Year-Development Plans of 1962–1986, foreign technology and foreign capital were imported mainly from Japan, followed by the United States with Western European countries as minor suppliers.[39] The imported foreign technology was absorbed very rapidly, particularly during the 1970s and the first half of the 1980s.[40]

The government directly involved in public enterprises and provided incentives to the private sector, which carried about 65 per cent of the nation's total investment.

South Korea's government-led development strategies of export-oriented industrialization greatly inspired the PRC in the early 1980s. More importantly, its excellent export performance was crucial to the government's efforts in initiating trade relation with China, which has a different political ideology.

In 1986, Beijing–Seoul bilateral trade accounted for 2.3 per cent of the PRC's total trade. In 1992, South Korea became the seventh largest trading partner of the PRC, while the PRC became South Korea's fourth largest trading partner.[41] Eager to tap South Korean technology and investment, Beijing began warming toward Seoul in the late 1980s. Their diplomatic relations were established in August 1992.

Hong Kong

Inherited from the colonial British in July 1997, the economic policy of the Hong Kong Special Administrative Region has continuously adopted free-enterprise, market-oriented system with minimal government intervention in the private sector. The simple and low tax model provides good incentives not only for workers, but also for investors to promote its export-led industrialization. The government's role is to provide the needed infrastructure and a sound legal and administrative framework conducive to the territory's economic growth.

Since the beginning of its economic reform and open-door policy in 1979, the PRC's economic and trade relations with Hong Kong had been enhanced. Hong Kong more than before directly facilitated Guangdong province's trade expansion drive by serving as an important market for Guangdong's exports, as a middleman in handling entrepot trade and in the transshipment of China's trade products. A producer to supply goods of Hong Kong origin for consumption in the mainland, Hong Kong also acted as a consultant offering advice, fund management resources and administrative expertise for China's production works and trade activities. Furthermore, China's open-door policy encouraged not only Hong Kong enterprises to invest in the mainland, but also Chinese and foreign enterprises to invest in Hong Kong. Foreign enterprises set up branches in Hong Kong, for instance, trading houses and banks, to capitalize on the Chinese markets. Since the 1980s, the investment boom in Hong Kong enterprises in South China and its outward processing trade had replaced its traditional China trade.[42] From a traditional base of entrepot, Hong Kong SAR's role had been changed to a control base for the Guangdong province. In 1991, Hong Kong enterprises in this province employed 3,000,000 manufacturing workers; this number was four times that of Hong Kong itself.[43]

Benefitting from Hong Kong's important role, Guangdong, the first Chinese province to carry out market economy, was crucial to China's open-door policy. Its real economic growth reached an annual average of 12 per cent during the period 1979–1989, the highest among its 30 provinces and autonomous regions, and exceeded that of the mainland overall by more than 3 per cent annually.[44]

In 1980, China began to build its four Special Economic Zones (SEZ), which were crucial to its policy of opening to the outside world. Four SEZs were established in Shenzhen, Zhuhai and Shantou in Guangdong province and in Xiamen in Fujian province with the aim of strengthening international cooperation through processing-cum-exporting or free trade with preferential treatment. This plan was to attract foreign investors to set up enterprises for importing advanced technology, creating jobs, and bringing in foreign exchange.

Adjacent to Hong Kong, Shenzhen is an ideal SEZ. As a modern international metropolis, Hong Kong could provide large amounts of foreign investment, advanced technology and scientific techniques and as well as management skills China badly needed in its modernization drive. Through cooperation, Shenzhen conveniently learned modern urban construction and management methods and trained professionals and so on. Understandably the mainland government planned to turn Shenzhen into a high tech industrial base, a regional financial, information, trade, transportation center and a tourist resort, that is, a modern international metropolis like Hong Kong. In a word, Shenzhen and other Special Economic Zones were established to speed up the development of capitalism by implementing flexible marketizing policies.

These initiatives encouraged Hong Kong capitalists to relocate their labor-intensive manufacturing industries across the border to the Pearl River Delta to take advantage of the abundant but cheap labor supply, favorable geographical conditions, easy railway transportation and new highway system. Since 1979, these had brought in increased levels of investment and entrepot trade to Southern China. Further, rapid economic growth in the Asia-Pacific region over the 1980s provided an added stimulus.[45] The re-export trade demonstrated a significant increase, with an average annual growth rate of 26.6 per cent in real terms in the period 1984–1993.[46] By the early 1990s, 70 per cent of Hong Kong's leather, electronics and plastic industries had already been relocated to the Delta thus bringing into the Guangdong province both advanced technology and a sales network.[47]

Singapore

In the mid-1980s, China considered that Singapore, one of the "four little Asian dragons", was important for its modernization program with its remarkable economic experiences. And in his South China inspection trip in February 1992, Deng Xiaoping encouraged the Chinese to adopt the Singapore model of economic and social development and administrative efficiency. A year later, Singapore's Senior Minister Lee Kuan Yew proposed a Singapore-developed industrial park in Suzhou, with China's enormous market and cost advantages and the Singapore-style of estate management. Suzhou is 80 kilometers west of Shanghai and one of a number of cities in the Yangtze River Delta which was aimed to be an important pole of the world economy in the 21st century.[48]

In the 1960s and 1970s, Singapore's industries were primarily labor-intensive due to its need to create jobs for the large army of the unemployed population. However, since the beginning of the 1980s, its capital-intensive industries had begun to replace the labor-intensive types. Labor became short in supply as the island republic climbed up the education and skill ladder.[49]

Beginning in the early 1960s, Singapore's economy grew by an average of 8.4 per cent per annum. Its per capita income in 1995 was

US$31,200, which was in real terms seven times more than in 1960.[50] In per capita GNP at PPP (Purchasing Power Parity) terms, it was the ninth richest nation in the world in 1995. The Business Environment Risk Intelligence classified Singapore as a developed economy in its assessment of countries and workforces, while the OECD announced the graduation of the NIE to the developed country status in 1996.[51] *The World Competitiveness Report* ranked Singapore second among 44 economies, just behind the United States. It was in this context that Singapore's success inspired China to follow similar footsteps and made economic and trade relations with the island republic possible.

In view of Singapore's disadvantages of having a small domestic market, limited land and labor resources, the government encouraged the business community to upgrade their business and develop quality workforce, to capitalize on the strong Singapore dollar and to invest strategically overseas. The government began to eye the PRC in the late 1970s for bilateral business.

Singapore–China economic and trade relations had already been prominent at the time when their diplomatic relations were established in October 1990. Since then, the Singapore government had ceaselessly encouraged its businessmen to pioneer in the rising market of the PRC.

The PRC's rapid economic development provided a huge market for Singapore. With China's demand for products such as integrated circuits and microelectronics modules rising, Singapore increased exports of these goods to China.[52] Further, with more and more Chinese manufacturing enterprises taking Singapore as an export transshipment port, Singapore's imports from the PRC began to rise substantially.[53]

During the period 1979–1991, the island republic was already regional headquarters for MNCs, owing to its strategic position, transport infrastructure and well-developed supporting services of banking, accounting and management consultancy and others. Singapore had over 30 years of experience in promoting foreign investments there.

The Asia-Pacific region is where China reaches the outside world. The region's security bears directly on the PRC's economic development. The success of China's opening to the outside world and modernization scheme greatly depends on the region's long-term peace, stability and development. China cherishes the political stability and impressive economic development of the region. On this basis, Deng Xiaoping initiated the so-called "good neighborliness" diplomacy. In 1979, as noted above, the PRC began to scale down its military backing for Southeast Asian insurgents. Understandably in December 1982, Deng promised that China would continue its efforts to develop its relations with Southeast Asian nations "on a long-term basis".[54] As discussed above, with the PRC's crucial role in facilitating the signing of the UN-sponsored peace accord between the Vietnam-backed Phnom Penh government and the three guerrilla factions, a political settlement of the Cambodian problem was eventually worked out in the early 1990s. As a result, this brought a formal end to thirteen years of civil war in Cambodia.[55]

Thus, China and the Southeast Asian nations began to develop closer political and economic ties. In August 1990, China and Indonesia restored relations after a 23-year suspension. Two months later, Singapore established similar bilateral ties with the PRC. In November 1991, the Sino-Vietnamese summit marked their normalization of ties and brought to an end the antagonistic relations from the mid-1970s thus opening a new era. In 1991, China became a consultation partner of ASEAN.

Learning from the experiences of the NIEs, the ASEAN-4 (that is, Malaysia, Thailand, Indonesia and the Philippines) launched their economic development relatively late. Malaysia and Thailand began the export-oriented labor-intensive manufacturing strategy in the early 1970s, while the Philippines started in the late 1970s and Indonesia in the early 1980s. In the ASEAN-4, the average annual growth in the 1980s was about 6 per cent. The third tier of development pattern in the Asia-Pacific region, which emerged in the early 1980s, was exclusively the PRC. China's exports increased markedly as a result of its open-door policy. Sino–ASEAN trade and economic cooperation developed quickly, mutual investment expanded and financial cooperation strengthened. This pattern is known as the "flying geese development paradigm" in which Japan had traditionally taken the lead.

Deng's "Good-Neighborliness" Policy and Sino-Russian Relations: 1979–90

As discussed above, during the period 1979–89, increasing *detente* between the two communist giants gradually led to the restoration of party-to-party relationships. For instance, at the end of July 1986, Gorbachev expressed Soviet willingness to discuss the establishment of neighborly relations with the PRC; in 1987, Gorbachev agreed to press Vietnam to withdraw its occupying troops from Cambodia.[56] In May 1989, the Gorbachev-Deng summit meeting in Beijing heralded the complete normalization of the Sino-Soviet relationship. In April 1990, Li Peng signed a series of agreements with the Soviets in Moscow on cooperation in the fields of trade and the economy, science and technology.[57]

The Implications of the "Good neighborliness" Policy

With the introduction of its policy of opening to the world in 1979, China's "good neighborliness" policy induced not only Sino–Latin American bilateral cooperation, but also brought the existing Sino–African cooperation closer. In the following section, I will consider China's economic relations and trade with the countries of the South American and African continents.

Sino–Latin American Economic and Trade Relations: 1979–1990

With the restructuring of the economic system and the introduction of its policy of opening to the world since 1978, China's economic relations and trade with the Latin American countries had become active. Reportedly the value of their trade was US$1.64 billion in 1984.[58] During the period 1979–1990, two-way investment was also active. For instance, Brazil's Petrobras International S.A. drilled oil on the South China Sea together with the British BP Petroleum Development Ltd. The China International Forestry Corporation invested in the establishment of the CIFEC Madeiras Industria E. Comercio Ltda to make plywood in Manaus, Brazil.[59] In addition, the Bank of Brazil and several Brazilian companies set up offices in Beijing to expand business.[60] In the period 1980–1983, Sino–Latin American trade was worth US$6.1 billion.[61]

Sino–Latin American ties in scientific and technological cooperation were active particularly with Brazil, Mexico, Argentina, Venezuela, Chile and Colombia.[62] Sino-Brazilian links in computer technology, rubber production and patent laws were formalized in 1982.[63] The Sino-Argentine scientific and technological agreements were signed in 1980 and 1984.[64]

Sino–African Economic and Trade Relations: 1979–1990

For half a century, economic cooperation between China and the African continent developed from the PRC giving unilateral aid to the latter into bilateral cooperation in the fields of trade, investment and contracted engineering. Bilateral trade in 1975 was valued US$670 million. Over the past 30 years, Sino–African trade volume continued to increase. Towards the mid-1990s, China encouraged cooperation between Chinese and African enterprises. Today, Sino–African cooperation in trade, investment and contracted projects continues to flourish.

The Seventh Five-Year Plan Period (1986–1990)

With new confidence and experience gained from the Sixth FYP and a relatively stable and peaceful international environment conducive to its modernization program, China launched its Seventh FYP for national economic and social development in March 1986. This was Deng's second-stage modernization program. It was the first time ever since the founding of the PRC that this five-year plan had been adopted before it was promulgated and implemented by the Sixth NPC. The new Plan showed features similar to those of the Sixth FYP. However, in view of the losses incurred in the state sector, any further economic reform without effective transformation of the troubled state-owned enterprises would not be crucial.

Deng's basic idea was that China's enterprise reform was to secure a way for integrating public ownership with the market economy for its SOEs without leading to privatization of these enterprises. In the process of reforming the state sector, though injecting Western market principles in it, privatization was not meant to be a dominant factor. The Dengists now aimed to establish a new economic structure in the following fields:

(1) Making socialist commodity producers and management centers relatively *independent* so as to assume sole responsibility for their losses and profits.
(2) Further unclogging the channels of commodity circulation and perfecting *the market system*.
(3) Changing the state management of enterprises gradually from direct to indirect control and establishing a new system under which this control was to be exercised *indirectly* through economic, legal, and limited administrative means.

The new Seventh FYP also had features similar to the previous plan as follows:

(1) Further rationalizing the industrial structure to keep pace with the people's changing demand patterns and with the modernization of the national economy:

– Continuing to take agriculture as the foundation of the national economy,
– Continuing to promote the all-round development of the rural economy with regard to farming, forestry, animal husbandry, side-line production and fishery.

(2) Continuing to give priority to the expanding sectors of energy, communications and telecommunications as well as the production capacity of raw and semi-finished materials.
(3) Further developing science, technology and education.
(4) Increasing the nation's total industrial and agricultural output value at an average annual rate of 6.7 per cent and the GNP at an average annual rate of 7.5 per cent, but with slightly lower than the actual speed achieved during the 6th FYP.
(5) Further improving living standards by developing the consumer goods industry to raise the per-capita consumption level at an annual rate of between 4 and 5 per cent.
(6) Further implementing the policy of opening to the outside world to expand foreign trade and economic and technological exchanges.
(7) Promoting cultural and ideological advance while furthering material progress.
(8) During the Seventh FYP period and in the 1990s,
– speeding up the development of the east coast region and
– concentrating on building the energy and raw and semi-finished materials industries in the central region.

This Seventh FYP further aimed to raise the people's living standards overall.

To conclude, the Seventh FYP began with the continuation of the Maoist development strategy in agriculture, light industry and heavy industry, while the Outline of the Ten Years Plan continued to emphasize agriculture and industry to further improve the people's livelihood. With the Maoist material incentives and self-interest serving as catalysts, Deng Xiaoping's second-stage economic reform was announced. Deng's socialist planned market economy was to invigorate the economy and improve the people's livelihood so as to harness the people's power for carrying out the four modernizations more effectively. By raising the people's living standards overall, Deng rationalized Mao's strategy of long-term economic development. China's economic reform and open-door policy brought remarkable achievements, despite the 1989 Tiananmen pro-democracy military crackdown. The GDP average annual growth was more than 10 per cent for the period 1978–1991. With the international environment now conducive to Deng's and subsequently Jiang's open-door policy, the PRC aimed at acquiring the modern technology and foreign investment funds from the advanced Western countries and the four economic "dragons". This was compared with the hostile situation in the period 1949–1970, which Mao's China was impotent to hinder.

Deng's Non-Rational Strategy of the "One Country, Two Systems"

We surveyed Deng's strategy of inducing the whole world to help modernize China. However, in the following, we will argue that his "one country, two systems" policy contradicts this very strategy.

In the early 1980s, Deng initiated the "one country, two systems" formula under which nothing fundamental would be changed for 50 years. This led to the signing of the Sino–British joint declaration on the question of Hong Kong in mid-1984. With the anticipation of the resumption of sovereignty over Hong Kong in July 1997 and Macau in December 1999, Deng aimed at reunifying the entire nation through this formula which primarily includes Taiwan.[65]

Since its establishment in 1949, the PRC has never been in a position to announce a timetable for the reunification with Taiwan. With the unfavorable international environment, its most important task was to deal with the following:

(1) its US primary enemy during the period 1950–1958,
(2) its US primary enemy together with the USSR as the "No. 1 accomplice of the US" during the period 1959–1968 and
(3) its Soviet primary enemy during the period 1969–1976.

Understandably, in 1971 Mao told Henry Kissinger that China could wait for 100 years to reunify with Taiwan which had become the issue of secondary importance in Mao's worldview. Mao meant that at the right time when becoming the primary task, the question of reunification should be tackled.

However, in July 1983 Deng told Professor Winston Yang Liyu (杨力宇) of Seton Hall University, South Orange, New Jersey, USA that "it would not be true to say that we are in no hurry. People like us, who are advanced in years, wish to see reunification as soon as possible".[66] Deng's statement is not rational. It was not the right time for the reunification. With the four modernizations scheme as Deng's primary concern, his new policy of "peaceful reunification" dangerously created a new major task for the country. The PRC was determined to retain the use of force as an option to achieve the reunification.[67] A Taiwan declaration of independence would trigger war. This would certainly involve the US military action based on its Taiwan Relations Act. With its attention divided, China could not fully concentrate its efforts on dealing with either major task. Mao's strategy was that "through consolidation, the concentration of the people's power could be realized", that is, by "concentrating all forces to deal with the tasks, one by one" but not both at the same time. The post-Deng leadership under Jiang Zemin decided "to accomplish the great cause of the national reunification by adhering to the Dengist policy of peaceful reunification" through the "one country, two systems". Jiang Zemin and subsequently Hu Jintao adhered to Deng's noni-Maoist strategy which consists of two fronts.[68] It is in this context that in the next chapter the post-Deng venture of the "peaceful reunification" of Taiwan will be considered.

Conclusion

In addition to its global strategy of continuing to maintain the normalization of relations with the US-led West for its modernization revolution, Deng Xiaoping formulated the "good-neighborliness" policy in an attempt to help create a new Asian economic miracle. This policy was aimed at promoting regional and global peace and stability thus strengthening regional cooperation with the "five dragons" and other economies around the world. Deng formulated the "good-neighborliness" policy to enhance the peaceful and stable regional and international environment and induce the whole world to help modernize his country with the market-oriented development strategy. Domestically, with the aim of securing a way to integrate public ownership with the market economic elements for China's ailing state-owned enterprises without leading to privatization in its enterprise reform, Deng's "non-capitalist" policy was far from successful in trying to solve the SOE problems. In the next chapter, I will consider Jiang Zemin's efforts to speed up the integration of China's economic structure with that of the world, and, in Chapter 8, I will survey Jiang's transformation of Deng's not very successful privatization scheme.

Chapter Seven
The International Environment and Jiang's Strategy of Continuing to Induce the Whole World to Help Modernize China

In Chapter Six, we surveyed the June 1989 Tiananmen military crackdown of the pro-democracy protests, which affected Sino–US relations in the short run. The following section of this chapter concerns the anti-Chinese movements in the US Congress, starting in the early 1990s and the Chinese response to them. We will see if the impact of these anti-Chinese movements and other determinants affected or was detrimental to China's continued modernization endeavors. We will further consider the Dengist-inherited strategy of "inducing the whole world to help modernize China".

The United States as the Sole Superpower and Sino–US Relations: 1991–2002

At the beginning of the 1990s, the Chinese perceived that the Western media began to spread the so-called "China threat" theory, as a result of the rise of the PRC.[1] They argued that it was Professor Murai Tomohide at the Defense University in Tokyo who initiated this theory in August 1990 in his article entitled "On the Potential Threat of the PRC".[2] Subsequently the Japanese media propagated that the modernization of the Chinese navy led to "the PRC's strategy of seeking marine hegemonism in the 21st century". In 1992, Ross Munro, *Time* magazine's correspondent in Beijing and Hong Kong, espoused that the rapidly expanding power of China aimed to dominate East Asia. Further, journalists and strategists such as Harvard University's Professor Samuel Huntington and Lester Brown of the US-based World Watch Institute published the respective theories of "China military threat" and "China economic threat". Professor Huntington put forward a book in 1993 entitled "The Conflict of Civilizations". In this book, he claims that the end of the Cold War saw the replacement of the ideological conflict by "a clash of civilizations" of which Confucianism is "the most dangerous to the West's interests and values".[3] Further, the Chinese believed that the US military presence in the Asia-Pacific region was designed to "contain an increasing powerful China".[4] According to the Chinese, this was partly because Western military analysts perceived that China's claims to the Spratlys Islands in the South China Sea backed by naval patrols heralded a more assertive approach in Asia.[5]

It was in this context that in the early 1990s China began to call for establishing a new international order "devoid of hegemonism and domination by the First World countries". The Dengist foreign policy aimed at forming a united front with regional Third World nations to counteract "US and Japanese hegemonism".[6] The Chinese leadership created a different version of Mao's concept of the three worlds, with its perception of the emergence of a new world order dominated by "a rich-nations club" comprising the United States and Japan.[7] As the old world order based on the contention between the two superpowers collapsed, the Dengists perceived China as being in a world moving toward "multi-polarity".[8] With the demise of the Soviet Union, the United States became the sole superpower, while Japan, which belonged to the Second World in Mao's worldview, had now transformed into a First World nation in Deng Xiaoping's worldview. However, it should be noted that at this stage, the Sino–US contradiction remained non-antagonistic. According to the Chinese, other advanced Western industrialized nations remained in the Second World. The PRC's perception of the new international order now reflected its fears, firstly, that as a result of the collapse of the Warsaw bloc, the world was dominated by the United States and secondly, that along with Japan's high-level economic development this would likely be associated with a resurgence of Japanese militarism.

At a secret meeting held by the State Council representatives of the general office of the Committee of the Chinese People's Political

Consultative Conference (CCPCC) in mid-January 1991, the Dengists considered that the Persian Gulf War was a "struggle between global and regional hegemonism [...] (after the) old world order had been destroyed".[9] According to the Chinese, a "new world order" with the United States as the sole superpower had already taken shape. The US objective, they concluded, was "first, to teach Saddam Husssein a lesson, and then dominate the Middle East and then the world".[10] Occupying a key position together with Japan in the Asia-Pacific region, the Chinese continued, the United States took strategic space in junction areas of Central Asia and Middle East, which were once controlled by Britain. They also claimed that it also filled the strategic vacuum left over by the former Soviet Union after its disintegration but not yet held by Russia. As a consequence, they argued, this did not leave China any room to expand its influence in Asia. According to the PRC's new worldview, the major members of the "club" in the Asia-Pacific region they referred to were obviously the United States and Japan, which schemed at "containing China".

In an attempt to win over the regional Third World nations against "power politics in any form", the Chinese leadership formulated its own world order based on "respect for independence and sovereignty of every nation, regardless of size, wealth, or military power".[11] They argued that this "new world order" was "markedly different from the old order that harms developing countries". They perceived the rise of "American expansionism" particularly in the region and the tendency to contain the PRC. Clearly the Chinese based their anti-US arguments on the following: Firstly, the US decision to reduce its troop presence in Japan, South Korea and the Philippines by only 10 per cent totaling 120,000 soldiers and personnel was to improve its military quality and efficiency. This was a response to the changing Soviet force compositions and US budgetary constraints.[12] Secondly, of the three US armed services budgetary cuts in relative terms this would least affect the Navy which is a Pacific force.[13]

Scheming at forming a united front with the neighboring countries based on its proposed international order, Beijing aimed at curbing the US influence in the Asia-Pacific region. Although in reality the PRC could not count on the cooperation of all the neighboring countries in its endeavors of anti-"club of wealthy nations", it worked on the possibility that more "friends" meant fewer "enemies". The Dengists knew that while these Third World nations might not contribute toward the alliance of anti-hegemony, they might stand neutral. This new perception had witnessed the most significant shift in the PRC foreign policy since the late 1980s. This new Chinese strategy was meant to go hand in hand with their diplomacy of good-neighborliness.

With its perception of the neighboring Southeast Asian countries as important points for countering "US hegemony", this policy also aimed to help curtail US influence in the region. This scheme could be seen as follows:

1. During President Yang Shang-kun's visit to Malaysia in mid-January 1992, he pledged China's "full support" for the Malaysian proposed East Asian Economic Caucus, a concept opposed by the United States.[14]
2. The Sino–Malaysian anti-US stance was clear in their agreement that "a balanced application of human rights should take into account our values".[15]
3. Yang's pledge, which came a few days after President Bush's visit to Singapore, seemed to imply its disapproval of the US newly proposed plan of relocating its Seventh Fleet logistical command from Subic Bay to Singapore in 1993.

In addition, in the mid-1990s, ties between China and the United States came under further strain. Apart from the issues of Taiwan, human rights abuses and intellectual property right violations, the case of nuclear proliferation in 1994 regarding the *Yinhe* incident, in which the United States accused the PRC of selling M-11 missiles to Pakistan, aggravated the already worsened Sino–US relations. During that year, a number of US congressmen even opposed the Chinese bid to host the 2000 Olympics. The mid-term elections in the United States in late 1994 brought several long-term anti-China right-wing congressmen into the foreign relations committees of both the Senate and the House of Representatives. Since then, according to the Chinese, the Republican-dominated Congress had passed many anti-China resolutions applying great pressure on the Clinton administration.[16] Further, in October 1995, the Chinese accused anti-Chinese US strategists of proposing to restore the Southeast Asia Treaty Organization

(SEATO) with the Cold War policy of containing China.[17] The United States was certainly fearful of how the Sino–Russian cooperation in consolidating their commercial ties and in building "a strategic partnership for the 21st century" could undermine US strategic advantage as the world's only superpower. Its defense analysts considered that China's purchases of Russian missiles and warships during the 1996 tension off the Taiwan Straits could threaten the US military presence in Asia.[18] As the No. 1 customer for Russia's arms industry, China had access to the most advanced missile, thermonuclear and aerospace systems the Russians could sell. In January 1999, the US Congress intended to include Taiwan in its Tactical Missile Defense (TMD) system. Inherited from the Dengist predominantly anti-US regional model, the Jiangist perception of the regional hegemony of the "US-Japan club" further reflected China's fears that Japan would be associated with the US anti-missile forces of the TMD system. According to the Chinese, this system was to supply military technology to Japan and even more so to Taiwan. This plan, which was to form an actual military alliance between the United States, Japan and Taiwan against the PRC, would nullify the potential of China's own 700 or so medium-range missiles aimed across the Taiwan Straits. Moreover, in April 1999, the Sino–Russian governments joined forces to oppose the proposed missile defense system of the United States and warned that a new arms race could threaten global stability.[19] With the United States as the dominant international power, China setting on a pattern of growth and Russia attempting to compensate its decline from its former superpower status, both found common cause in trying to set up a balance to the US.

However, the anti-China strategies and movements in the United States were not effective owing to the following crucial factors:

1. The two countries have shared common views regarding the issues of preventing proliferation of weapons of mass destruction, maintaining regional stability in the Asia-Pacific region, promoting international trade, improving the ecological environment, etc.
2. The global multi-polarized tendency called for resolving international and regional problems through cooperation of the major powers vitally including the United States and China.

3. With the process of economic globalization, the acceleration of technological innovation and economic interdependence on each other enhanced the sphere of Sino–US economic cooperation. By September 1994 China had set up 5 special economic zones, 32 economic and technological development zones and 52 national-level new and high-tech development zones.

Understandably, therefore, less than two and a half years after the Tiananmen crackdown, Secretary of State James Baker visited Beijing in mid-November 1991 on the issues of the Korean Peninsula as well as trade and economic matters. President Bill Clinton's "engagement" policy was announced in September 1993 to resume high-level contact with the PRC. To reiterate, the United States needed to secure China's cooperation on a number of regional and global issues. In mid-March 1998, following the footsteps of the European Union, the US declined to propose to the Congress to go against China at the United Nations Human Rights Conference in Geneva. More importantly, with the aim of building the Sino–US "constructive strategic partnership", Clinton visited Beijing in June the same year, the first visit by an American President in nine years. In May 1999, the US-led NATO bombed the Chinese Embassy in Yugoslavia. With Clinton's apology, the Chinese government reacted in a restrained manner thus resolving the conflict by dialogue.

After President George W. Bush took office in January 2001, his tough policy toward the PRC defied his predecessor's aim of building a "strategic partnership" with it and redefined it as the "strategic competitive rival of the US". With the mid-air collision of Chinese military aircraft and US navy spy plane in April 2001, this policy gave rise to tension in bilateral relations. Further, as noted above, the Department of Defense of the United States began shifting the US military strategic focus from Europe to East Asia, with Bush's National Missile Defense system vitally including Taiwan.

However, the terrorist attacks on New York and Washington D.C. on September 11, 2001, which shocked the world, ushered in the new phase of Sino–US bilateral ties of "constructive cooperation", with China's anti-terrorist stance. Since then, Bush has considered the PRC a friend of his country. Further, the Shanghai Summit in mid-October

2001, China's admission to the World Trade Organization (WTO) as a formal member in November that year and its victory in July the same year for the 2008 Olympic bid all paved the way for the sound development of bilateral ties in the new century. Moreover, in October 2002, the Sino–US Summit took place at President Bush's private ranch known as the "White House in Texas". Bush considered the PRC as an ally of the United States in its fight against global terrorism. Both sides began the resumption of military exchanges, which were to bring about their strategic stability. US strategists realized that without China's cooperation, there would be no peace in Asia. Apart from China's anti- terrorist stance, the US needed the PRC's cooperation on the issue of security of the Korean Peninsula. Both China and the United States have shared common views on the issue of preventing proliferation of weapons of mass destruction.[20] In the following, we will consider this issue.

China's Position in the US-North Korean Nuclear Stalemate

Although an armistice accord ended the Korean War in 1953, no peace treaty was signed. This left the North and South Koreans still technically at war, with the US continuously stationing forces on the peninsula. Even with the end of the Cold War, the world's largest concentration of military forces continued to be located along the sensitive border. North Korea's military forces remained to be postured in an offensive mode, with huge tunnels detected under the demilitarized zone. Its unsafeguarded nuclear weapons program was discovered in late 1991. William Tow argues that, if left unresolved, the confrontation between the two Koreas could lead to explosion at any time to undermine whatever other progress may have been made in structuring a more stable regional security work.[21] Considerable progress toward reunification seemed to have taken place in the early 1990s with talks between the prime ministers of both sides. Further, in September 1990, Pyongyang initiated negotiations with Tokyo regarding normalization following the Moscow–Seoul normalization. It also sought to normalize its relations with Washington and expressed its willingness to accept nuclear inspection by the International Atomic Energy Agency as one of the prerequisites for rapprochement with Tokyo and Washington. More importantly, Pyongyang and Seoul joined the UN in the capacity of full members in September 1991. Thus, it seemed that the historic inter-Korean agreements on reconciliation, non-aggression, exchanges and cooperation would bode well for the future of their relations. Further, Seoul established diplomatic and trade relations with Moscow and improved its relations with Beijing.

The increasingly improved Beijing-Seoul bilateral relations induced Pyongyang to adopt an open-door policy. The success of China's economic reform inspired North Korea to introduce tentative agricultural reform in the spring of 1996, allowing the farmers to sell produce on the free market.[22] In early 1996, with the United States and China as participants for an armistice agreement to end the 1950–1953 Korean War, the four-nation talks were proposed to provide a forum for securing the lasting peace to the divided peninsula. The vice-ministers from Seoul and Pyongyang met in mid-April that year in Beijing to discuss an ambitious trade zone on the border between China, North Korea and Russia.[23]

However, further steps seemed to hinge on the resolution of Pyongyang's nuclear problem. Its old friends, Russia and China, discouraged it from pursuing the nuclear option. No country in East Asia, particularly China, wanted to see the emergence of a new nuclear power to induce instability. Political instability on the Korean peninsula could impede China's modernization drive. Under the US-broker 1994 accord, North Korea froze its nuclear program in exchange for two light-water reactors to replace the regime's graphite-moderated reactors, which produced greater amounts of weapons-grade plutonium.[24] Seoul was the major financier of the US$5 billion project.

Although there was undoubted progress toward lessening tensions between Pyongyang and Seoul since the end of the Cold War, the Korean problem remained unresolved. In mid-2005, the United States stepped up its pressure on the PRC over the six-party dialogue involving the two Koreas, China, Japan, Russia and the United States concerning North Korea's nuclear program. Their talks were stalled for more than a year after a third round in Beijing in June 2004. In early July 2005, President Hu Jintao sent State Councillor Tang Jiaxuan to North Korea in an attempt to prod Pyongyang back to the negotiating table and revive the six-party talks.[25]

The Chinese always emphasized that economic development and peace had become important stabilizing factors in Sino–US bilateral ties. However, the PRC had encountered problems with the United States in the areas of the most-favored-nation (MFN) status, the World Trade Organization (WTO), and the Asia-Pacific Economic Community (APEC) issues. In the following, the APEC issue will be discussed first.

The Asia-Pacific Economic Community Issue

In view of the remarkable economic growth in the Asia-Pacific region in the 1980s, Australian Prime Minister Bob Hawk proposed the establishment of APEC in January 1989. Aiming at concerns over the proliferation of regional trading blocs like the European Economic Community and the US-Canada Free Trade Agreement from which countries in the region were excluded, Hawk's proposed organization was to commit itself to the reduction of trade barriers and to seek greater interdependence among its members with the world economy. However, after consulting the United States and the region's governments, his revised proposal inevitably included the US and Canada as major members. The US trade with the Asia-Pacific region accounted for more than one-third of its total and linking to the fast growing East Asian economies was considered as ideal in solving the country's twin budget and trade deficits.[26] Thus the idea of the APEC materialized in November 1989 with the United States playing a leading role.

The US negotiators considered that the APEC mechanism should be based on the main principles as follows:

1. giving political support to the Uruguay Round of GATT or ASEAN talks,
2. exploring options for regional trade liberalization on a non-discriminatory foundation with the rest of the world, and

3. recognizing the free market policies crucial to trade liberalization as the most acceptable route for economic development.

Hawk's original proposal included China, but the US objected on the ground that the PRC was not a market economy. However, resisting the more exclusive organizations like the East Asian Economic Caucus (EAEC), in November 1991 the Asia-Pacific economic community resorted to integrating the then less open economy of the PRC as well as the vibrant newly industrializing economies of Hong Kong and Taiwan.[27] It is important to note that China pledged to use the market forces in conducting its economic activities and sought to apply the Western legal system in its international economic dealings and trade. Further, President Jiang's state-owned enterprise reform was Western-oriented. Therefore, including the PRC as a core member to liberalize trade and investment and carry out technological cooperation, APEC inevitably changed the economic map of the region as well as the whole world. Since it joined the economic community in 1991, China had pushed forward the process of opening up to the outside world and the reform of its economic system more vigorously.

Most-Favored-Nation Status

In December 1945, on the basis of mutual benefit and through the most-favored-nation (MFN) status, the United States proposed the establishment of a multilateral trading system with its trade ideas and policies favorable to itself in the world trade system. This international multilateral system, whereby each country undertook to apply the same rate of TARIFF to *all* of its trading partners, was formally adopted in the 1980s when the Eighth Round of General Agreement on Tariff and Trade (GATT) multilateral trade negotiations – the Uruguay Round – was launched. After the Uruguay Round, the WTO – the former US-initiated GATT – was formally founded in 1995 with the "most-favored-nation treatment" as one of its basic principles recognized in the world economic system. By 1997, the United States had already offered this status to more than 160 countries.

The MFN status granted by both the United States and China to each other since 1980 had stimulated rapid development of mutual trade and economic relations. Reportedly, the volume of Sino–US trade, which was only US$2.45 billion in 1979, increased nearly five-fold to US$11.76 billion in 1990.[28] However, since 1990, the US Congress had taken international political factors into consideration regarding China's MFN status. Every year the US Congress would vote whether or not to give China the MFN treatment on the grounds of China's human rights situation, its system of government and military issues. The Chinese claimed that the continual annual review of the status was associated with "US laws of the Cold War period".[29] They argued that this created the feeling of instability among the business communities of the two countries and was detrimental to the bilateral trade and economic cooperation.[30] President Clinton de-linked the human rights issue from the annual extension of the MFN status for China in May 1994. This led to the normalization of Sino–US relationship enabling them to pursue broader economic, political, security and strategic interests and international and regional cooperation.

The World Trade Organization Issue

In July 1986, China formally applied for restoring its founding member status in GATT from which it withdrew in 1950. Joining the international economic community would make the PRC equal in global economic competition by removing the barriers which impeded the development of its trade ties with other countries.

As an important signatory of the WTO, which, as mentioned earlier, was formally established in January 1995 with 134 members to replace the GATT, the United States played a crucial role in deciding China's entry into the world community. The Chinese realized that the new membership would help speed up the integration of its national economic structure with that of the world and give new impetus to its domestic enterprise reform.[31] They also realized that the rules of WTO are based solely on Western economic principles. Since late 1999, they had sorted out related laws, rules and regulations and the National People's Congress revised seven laws for the same purpose.[32]

The Sino–US agreement signed on November 15, 1999 paved the way to Beijing's entry into the international organization. The WTO membership would commit China to the principle of MFN and national treatment for *all* members as well as its pledge to gradually liberalize trade in services.[33] According to WTO rules, US Congress must grant China permanent normal trade status (PNTR), that is, the most-favored-nation status, to guarantee Chinese goods the same low-tariff access to the US markets as products from most other countries. The PRC's accession to WTO was to promote the development of the global economy and trade and the ties would be conducive to China's further economic reform and opening up to the outside world.

China's accession to WTO would help boost US exports to it. Most of these exports were high value-added commodities such as aircraft and computers produced by industries which not only were crucial to technology transfer to the PRC but also helped pay US workers above-average wages. The signing of the bilateral agreement broke the deadlock between the two countries and normalized their relations. However, after the US-led NATO bombing of the Chinese embassy in Yugoslavia, Beijing stopped its military exchanges, arms talks and human rights dialogue with Washington. Further, according to the Chinese, the US launched anti-China and anti-communist campaigns at the end of the 1980s and the beginning of the 1990s, with the collapse of the Soviet Union.[34] It also claimed that, for two years and eight months, the US had frozen negotiations with regard to China's entry to the GATT as a major sanction against it.[35]

With the announcement of China's pro-US anti-terrorist stance, its WTO accession took place on November 11, 2001. Thereafter China began to make a formal external commitment to a whole range of trade-related reforms, according to President Bush's "Economic Report of December 2001". The PRC also made new progress in its deepening reform and opening up endeavors. Its most significant progress, however, was its public law, which bound the government to the WTO rule of laws particularly relating to foreign investment and providing a mature legal environment for foreign investors.[36]

Having committed to pushing forward economic restructuring and the reform of their economic system, China's WTO membership demonstrated its involvements in international economic competition and cooperation. The Chinese investment environment further improved. In March 2002, the Chinese committed to amending other laws.[37] Since its WTO entry, multinational corporations had entered the country continuously. Reportedly, over 400 of the world's top 500 firms had invested in the PRC.[38] In the following we will consider Sino–US economic and trade relations during the period 1990–2002.

Sino–US Economic and Trade Relations: 1990–2002

We noted that the June 1989 Tiananmen Square pro-democracy military crackdown adversely affected Sino–US relations for only less than two years. Also the United States needed China to help turn the Korean Peninsula into a nuclear-free zone. Secretary of State James Baker's China mission in mid-November 1991 vitally included the issues of trade and economic exchange, in addition to arms control.[39] Furthermore, the United States sought Chinese cooperation in the United Nations on such issues as the Middle East, the prevention of proliferation of weapons of mass destruction, maintenance of regional stability, environmental protection, drug control and so forth. In the economic sphere, the United States sought to integrate the PRC fully into the global market economic and trade system and expand the US access to the Chinese market. At the end of 1992, cooperation between China and the West in the fields of trade and science and technology was normalized. Further, at the beginning of 1993, while recognizing China's market-oriented reform as a "liberal economic policy", the new Clinton administration increased political exchanges with the PRC with the policy of "keeping contact".[40] In September that year, the Clinton government initiated the so-called policy of "engagement" in resuming high-level contacts with the Beijing leadership. As mentioned above, the United States needed China's cooperation on a number of regional and global issues. Finally, in November the meeting between Jiang Zemin and Bill Clinton in the APEC Summit in Seattle broke the Sino–US deadlock that had existed since 1989. Furthermore, as mentioned earlier, Clinton decided to delink human rights from the annual extension of MFN trade status for the PRC. This "made it possible for the two countries to normalize and stabilize their relationship, to pursue broad economic, political, security and strategic interests for both nations, and to engage in international and regional cooperation".[41] Furthermore, the anti-China strategies and movements in the United States as mentioned above were not effective. Both countries needed each other, particularly in economic and trade exchange. The PRC's modernization drive needed funds, technology, management expertise and a huge market that the United States could provide. The United States saw the market potential of China. It is in this context that in the following we will survey Sino–US economic and trade relations for the period 1990–2002.

In January 1993, visiting US Secretary of Commerce Barbara Franklin recognized that China's market-oriented economic reform boosted confidence among the foreign investors and implied that the United States would sell more high technology to the PRC.[42] In November 1997, according to Wu Yi, China's Minister of Foreign Trade and Economic Cooperation, Sino–US two-way trade achieved an annual average growth rate of 20 percent, increasing from US$2.5 billion in 1979 to US$42.84 billion in 1996, 17 times the figure of 1979 when both countries established diplomatic relations.[43] In that period, Wu Yi continued, two-way trade totaled US$260.6 billion.[44] According to Chinese customs statistics, Sino–US trade volume expanded about 7-fold to reach US-$80.5 billion from US$11.8 billion during the period 1990–2001, while statistics from the US Department of Commerce showed a 6-fold growth over the period.[45] Chinese statistics indicated that in 1996 US products accounted for 11.6 per cent of the PRC's total imports, while the US statistics showed that 5.42 per cent of its imports came from China in that year.[46] China was one of the US trading partners with which the United States scored the highest export growth.[47] By the end of 1997, Jiang visited the United States and claimed the country had become China's second largest trading partner and China the fourth largest trading partner of the United States. By the end of 1996, the US-invested projects had numbered 22,240 and China had used US$14.2 billion of US capital. Excluding Hong Kong, the United States was the second largest foreign investor after Japan.

During the period, both countries were highly active in the economic and trade exchange enabling them to share each other's huge market. The PRC mainly sold to the US labor-intensive products such as textiles, garments, shoes, toys and household electrical appliances. In 2000, Chinese exports to the United States were 21 per cent of its total exports and over 5 per cent of China's GDP.[48] The US mainly sold to China capital- and technology-intensive products such as aircrafts, machinery, chemical machinery, power generation equipment, electronics, telecommunications equipment, and agricultural products including grain and cotton. In 1997, China was the biggest buyer of US aircraft. In 2002, jobs created by the US exports to China numbered 400,000 compared with 200,000 in the early 1990s.[49] The US exports to China achieved a 17 per cent growth in 2001.

The PRC is also one of the largest creditors of the United States. In 1999, China held US$51.3 billion in US treasury bonds, 4 per cent of all US treasury bonds purchased by foreign countries.[50] It acquired more than US$200 billion worth of Treasury securities over 2004.[51]

As mutual dependency between both economies increases, the economic and trade relationship became a stabilizer for bilateral relations. However, as mentioned above, the year 2001 saw great ups and downs in Sino–US relations. Thanks to the joint efforts of both Presidents Bush and Jiang, the relations gradually improved during the second half of the year. At their meeting in Shanghai in October, the two presidents agreed to build a constructive partnership of cooperation. This not only provided a direction for future development of bilateral relations, but also created favorable conditions for the development of economic and trade ties.

To conclude, in the long run, China's rapid economic growth and its WTO entry will provide an even broader space for future development of its economic and trade cooperation with the US which will introduce more capital, technology and management know-how conducive to its further development. China is already home to a growing number of US-owned factories, many of them exporting back to the United States, and an even greater number of factories that are suppliers to US companies.[52] In 1995, the US Department of Commerce ranked the PRC first among the top ten rising markets. More business opportunities particularly in information technology, communications and financial services will be provided to US businesses after further improvement of China's commercial environment and further opening up of the market.

Sino–European Community Economic and Trade Relations: 1990–2002

As noted in the last chapter, in 1987, the European Community was China's third largest trade partner after Hong Kong and Japan. In the 1990s, cooperation between China and the Community was even closer particularly in the scientific and technological fields. The huge market potential in the PRC attracted a great amount of euro capital for direct investment and further improved its structure of foreign investment. As discussed above, the European Union was always a strong backer of the PRC's entry into the General Agreements on Tariffs and Trade and supported its entry into the World Trade Organization.

The period 1985–1994 witnessed the Sino–EC trade volume increase 14-fold reaching about US$41 billion. In 1995, the PRC became the European Union's fourth largest global supplier and was the EU's seventh largest market.[53] During the period 1979–96, the EU investment in China totaled US$2.5 billion, though this was still less than half of that of the United States and Japan.[54] By 1996, Europe had not only been a major supplier to China of investment, goods and machinery, but also China's largest supplier of advanced technology with a total value of US$26.5 billion. This accounted for 49 per cent of China's total technology imports.[55] In September 1998, the Sino–French governments signed a series of scientific, economic and trade cooperation agreements in Beijing. This laid a strong foundation for developing their bilateral relations in the 21st century.[56] In 1998, China became the EU's fourth largest trade partner following the United States,

Japan and Switzerland, while Western Europe became China's third largest trade partner with a two-way trade volume of US$51 billion.[57] This ranking remained unchanged in the year 2002, with the aggregate trade volume exceeding US$69 billion.[58] In the light of the smooth Sino–EU trade development, in March 1998, Premier Zhu Rongji expressed appreciation to the EU for eliminating China from the list of "non market economy" nations.[59] According to the December 2002 issue of *Business Week* magazine, the PRC's GDP was about 80 per cent of that of the EU and will exceed that of Europe by 2007.

The "Good-Neighborly" Performance: 1991–2002

For the last 25 years, as overseas capital poured into China, a large number of foreign-invested enterprises, mainly in labor-intensive industrial sectors, were set up in the country's coastal areas. The five "little dragons" were and still are the major investors in mainland China. As noted in the last chapter, the Chinese government aimed to be part of the development miracle of these NIEs, with its "good-neighborliness" policy in creating a viable peaceful and stable Asia-Pacific international environment. China's major program of export-oriented industrialization based on its open-door policy was associated with its import-substitution strategy for manufactured exports. The rapid growth of FDI in the export-oriented, labor-intensive manufacturing was a marked feature of growth in China and Asia's five "little dragons" over the last two and a half decades.

During the period 1979–2002, the PRC's development-oriented policy was consistent, with its "good-neighborliness" strategy. As discussed above, the growth in intra-regional trade with China now at the center was associated with a dramatic increase in intra-Asia direct investment with most of the investment flowing to China. Big investors of the five Asian "dragons" helped bind their economies more closely with China. In August 2000, Vice-President Hu Jintao confirmed that "China cannot achieve development without Asia, and Asia cannot realize prosperity without China".[60]

Japan

In the last chapter, we noted that in June 1991, Japan's investment in the PRC was worth US$2.6 billion, next only to Hong Kong, Macao, and Taiwan. Sino–Japanese trade reached US$20.2 billion in 1991, and in 1996 their trade volume exceeded US$60 billion.[61] Japanese companies speeded up their shift of overseas production with the aim of reducing production costs and exploring overseas markets. With its low labor costs and huge market potential, China was attractive for Japanese companies. In 1998, the two countries agreed to build a partnership of cooperation in the fields of technology, environmental protection and agriculture. During the period, Japan was China's largest trading partner. The volume of trade between the two countries was US$85.7 billion in 2000 and was expected to exceed US$100 billion in 2001.[62] Japanese investment and technological cooperation played an important role in the PRC's modernization drive. To maintain the sustained, steady and fast growth of its economy, China needed Japanese capital, technology and market, while Japan needed China's huge market and human resources to move out of the shadow of economic depression.

Taiwan

In 1991, the mainland became Taiwan's fifth largest trade market, while Taiwan was the sixth largest trading partner of the mainland. In the first ten months of 1994, indirect trade between the two sides reached US$12.3 billion.[63] Imports from Taiwan of machinery and electronics, chemical fiber and other raw materials for use by Taiwanese enterprises were at US$10.7 billion during the same period.[64] In 1994, the mainland was Taiwan's second largest export market.[65] With contracted investment of US$22.6 billion and actual investment at US$8.2 billion, due to the increase of labor-intensive high- and new-technology enterprises, Taiwan's investment now occupied the second place among overseas investment in China's mainland.[66]

As the Taiwanese government continued to emphasize the importance of establishing itself as an Asia-Pacific regional operations center for multinational and international businesses, economists believe that such a goal could not be realized without direct links with the PRC. Despite attempts at first to prevent investment in the mainland, and then, when prevention proved impossible, to restrict it, and when this proved impossible to control it, some US$10 billion to US$20 billion was estimated to have been invested on the mainland by Taiwanese firms in 1995.

During the period 1985–1996, about 30,000 Taiwan companies invested as much as US$23 billion in the mainland.[67] Trade with the mainland accounted for 16 per cent of Taiwan's export market or 23 per cent exports to Hong Kong, the bulk of which ultimately went to China.[68] That made the China market as large as the Taiwan market in the United States. In 1996, the drop in China's export growth caused a mini-recession in Taiwan, according to the head of Taiwan's Council for Economic Planning and Development, Chiang Ping-kun.[69] Much of this money went into relocating labor-intensive industry from Taiwan to the mainland in pursuit of cheaper labor costs. Some firms saw the mainland as the location that could turn them from major Taiwan players into regional or even global giants. In mid-December 2000, the Taiwanese cabinet approved the plan known as the "mini-three links" to open up direct commercial, shipping and communications links between its offshore islands and the mainland. Wang Yung-ching, a leading Taiwanese industrialist, said the government should have opened the "three big links" in 2001 to boost up Taiwan's economy, instead of by 2003 as planned.

In mid-2003, reportedly, Taiwanese companies based in the mainland pushed China ahead of Mexico and Japan as the top supplier of hi-tech goods to the United States, surging by more than a third to US$35 billion in 2002.[70] Since 2000, Taiwanese investors had poured about US$100 billion into the mainland.[71] Almost all Taiwanese high-technology companies set up assembly lines in China in the period 2000–2003.[72]

South Korea

In the last chapter, we noted that, in 1992, South Korea was the seventh largest partner of the PRC, while the PRC became South Korea's fourth largest trading partner. Sino–South Korean diplomatic relations were established in August 1992. As a result, the value of their two-way trade was US$15 billion for 1995, rising from US$11.66 billion in 1994; and South Korean investment in China surpassed US$6 billion.[73] Vice-ministers from Pyongyang and Seoul met in Beijing in mid-April 1996 for talks on an ambitious trade zone on the border between China, North Korea and Russia.[74] All this demonstrated that China valued South Korea's model and achievements in economic development.

Hong Kong

As noted above, inherited from the colonial British in July 1997, the economic policy of the Hong Kong Special Administration Region continuously adopted a free-enterprise, market-oriented system with minimal government intervention in the private sector. Prior to 1979, the PRC and Hong Kong had been not only each other's biggest trading partners in the areas of trade, domestic exports, re-exports and services, but also each other's biggest investors. During the period, China remained the largest source of, as well as the largest market for, Hong Kong's re-exports, i.e., 90 per cent. Now, enhanced by the expansion of outward processing industries in the Pearl River Delta, re-exports continued to rise in both directions. Quoting Yun-Wing Sung's estimate, A.Y. So writes that, in 2001, 56 per cent of the PRC's total exports were consumed, re-exported or transshipped by Hong Kong.[75]

The new development after 1979 put Guangdong province on a sound economic foundation in the 1990s. For instance, in 1990, 75 per cent of Hong Kong's exports were to China and 86 per cent of imports from China and a total of 82 per cent of Hong Kong-China trade was actually trade with the Guangdong province.[76] Hong Kong was China's third largest trading partner in 2000 just behind Japan and the US, accounting for 11 per cent of the mainland's total trade value.[77]

During the period 1979–2000, there was also a great increase in investment flows between the two places. Hong Kong continued to be the largest source of external direct investments in the mainland with the cumulative value of US$171 billion in December 2000, which was about half of China's total inward direct investment.[78] During the period 1978–2003, China attracted US$460 billion of foreign capital, 46 per cent of which originated from Hong Kong.[79] Further, Hong Kong was a major funding center for China, in addition to being a direct source of funds. Hong Kong became a major service center for the mainland providing a wide range of professional and business support services, for instance, banking and finance, insurance, accounting, transport, and sales promotion. Since 1979, Hong Kong enterprises had been playing a crucial role in developing infrastructure and property, initially in South China but spreading further inland in the 1990s.[80] In 2002, Hong Kong-based investors controlled over five million Chinese factory workers in South China.

To say the least, during the period 1991–2002, Hong Kong was a facilitator and middleman for mainland trade and investment, an important source for China's technology transfer, training the mainlanders' capitalist skills and financing China's modernization drive.

Singapore

In the mid-1980s, China considered that Singapore, as one of the "four little Asian dragons", was important for its modernization program with its remarkable economic experiences. In the first half of the 1990s, Deng expressed his confidence that China could learn a lot from Singapore regarding economic development, administrative efficiency and social administration.[81]

According to Singapore's Lee Kuan Yew, in 1995, more than 3,000 MNCs operated in and out of Singapore, with an established infrastructure for venturing into the region.[82] Many MNCs set up projects in the island republic's industrial parks in partnership with companies there.[83] These MNC regional headquarters in the island republic continued to oversee their operations, marketing companies and liaison offices in China and elsewhere. In the early 1990s, the

Singapore government began to encourage its entrepreneurs to pioneer in the rising Chinese market. Their investment in China diversified, extending from the spheres of real estate and processing industry to the sectors of legal and management consultancy, insurance, finance, telecommunications and tourism, from coastal areas to inland areas and from small- and middle-sized enterprises to large companies.[84]

According to the Ministry of Trade and Industry of Singapore, Singapore's economic decline at the turn of the century was mainly due to the failure of its three economic engines, i.e., the US economy particularly in 2001, the global electronic industry and the integrated Southeast Asian economy. Under these circumstances, the Singapore government paid much attention to Singapore–China economic and trade relations. The PRC's rapid economic development provided a huge market for world economies including Singapore. Singapore increasingly exported integrated circuits and microelectronics modules which China demanded. The growth of the island republic's exports to China, to some extent, offset the decrease of its export to the United States caused by the American economic downturn. At the same time, with more and more Chinese manufacturing enterprises using Singapore as an export transshipment port, Singapore's imports from China substantially increased.

During the period 1993–2000, Singapore's exports to China increased rapidly from US$1.9 billion to US$16.2 billion; and China's exports to Singapore also grew from US$2.4 billion to US$10.6 billion.[85] In the first 11 months of 2001, Sino–Singapore trade was US$20.4 billion, with China being Singapore's fifth largest trading partner and Singapore being China's seventh largest trading partner.[86]

Singapore inspired China to develop the Singapore-styled residential housing in many Chinese cities. The Sanlin Residential Area in Shanghai is a typical example. During the period 1991–2002, the Suzhou Industrial Park, which was a large-scale Singapore-Chinese cooperative project, already absorbed over US$8 billion foreign capital for industrial projects and housed more than 210 overseas-funded enterprises of which 40 percent were European and American businesses and 30 per cent were of East and Southeast Asian origins including Nokia, Samsung and Hitachi. Other large-scale cooperative projects materialized in 2002 included Wuxi Industrial Park and Dalian Container Terminal. By June 2001, Singapore's cumulative investment in China increased to US$36 billion making Singapore the fifth largest investor in China.[87]

In sum, the leading role of post-war Japan in the economic development of East Asia was crucial. Inspired by this resource-poor developed economy, the NIEs adopted a strategy to overcome their weakness in natural resources and take advantage of their human capital. Japanese capital, technology, materials and spare parts played a key role in developing the export-processing industries of the four NIEs. Also Japan began to tighten its economic links with the PRC in the 1980s and early 1990s. With Japan's efforts to cooperate with the four "economic dragons" and increase its investment in them, the NIEs continued to rely on Japanese capital and technology to create the Asia-Pacific economic miracle. Similarly, China became the center of a large-scale transfer of technology and trade channels in the region. Japan, South Korea, Hong Kong, Taiwan and Singapore shifted their manufacturing sectors and their trade surplus from the United States to the rising Chinese economy. The later investment of Japan and the Newly Industrialized Economies in the post-Mao China helped create yet another new economic miracle.

China and the ASEAN Members

As noted above, in 1991 China became a consultation partner of the ASEAN group. More importantly, a year later, China announced its decision to shelve its overlapping claim over the Spratlys in favor of joint cooperation to develop the marine territories.[88] The territorial claims in the South China Sea put China at odds with Vietnam, Malaysia, Indonesia and the Philippines. In 1993, the PRC proposed setting up the Sino–ASEAN Science and Technology Training Center in Beijing and the Sino–ASEAN Technology Development Service Center in one of the ASEAN cities.[89] In 1994, China became a member of the ASEAN Regional Forum (ARF). In the mid-1990s, inviting China to join the Southeast Asian Partnership Dialogue and the ASEAN+3 Meeting concerning Southeast Asian and East Asian affairs, Singapore,

Malaysia and Thailand aimed at promoting their trade and economic relations with the PRC. In July 1996, the PRC was admitted to the ASEAN post-ministerial conferences as a full dialogue partner. In March 1997, China and the Philippines held a conference of the ARF in Beijing to promote cooperation on Sino–ASEAN security.[90] In July 1999, the PRC signed a joint statement on a plan of action in the economic, scientific, technological, and security fields in the ASEAN Summit with Thailand, Malaysia and Vietnam to flesh out the Sino ASEAN partnership of good-neighborliness and mutual trust.[91] In November 2001, Premier Zhu Rongji and ASEAN leaders jointly signed an agreement to create a Sino–ASEAN free trade zone within ten years.[92] In November 2002, China and ASEAN agreed on a political declaration calling for restraint and cooperation in the South China Sea.[93]

As discussed in the last chapter, Sino–ASEAN trade and economic cooperation developed quickly, mutual investment expanded and financial cooperation strengthened. In the period 1995–2002, their trade volume grew at an average annual rate of 19.1 per cent and in 2002, the volume was a record high of US$54.8 billion.[94] All this demonstrated that Sino–ASEAN political confidence in strengthening good-neighborliness and great progress in economic cooperation.

Since 1995, Sino–ASEAN bilateral trade had grown at an annual average of 15 per cent. Their trade volume was US$54.77 billion in 2002, an increase of 32 per cent over 2001, the second highest growth rate worldwide.[95] In 2003, the ASEAN group was China's fifth largest trade partner, and the PRC was the sixth largest trade partner of the group. Sino–ASEAN members pushed forward economic cooperation as well as cooperation in science, technology, tourism, resources exploration, agriculture, energy, information and personnel training. The agreement reached among the six old ASEAN members (that is, Brunei, Indonesia, Malaysia, Singapore, Thailand, and the Philippines) formed an initial free trade zone in 2005. In October 2003, the Sino–ASEAN free trade zone, which was to be established in 2015, was declared to "serve as a blueprint for fostering partnership between ASEAN and China for peace and prosperity", according to Indonesian President Soekarnoputri Megawati. Malaysian Prime Minister Mahathir bin Mohamad said that the strategy of "looking eastward" – learning from Japan and South Korea – should have included China.[96]

To conclude, the PRC's successful "good neighborliness" policy was formulated to promote trade and investment "on a long-term basis", which was aimed at tapping capital and technology for its economic reform and modernization program. Companies in the future Sino–ASEAN free trade zone were expected to have 1.7 billion consumers and a potential market of a combined GDP of US$15.2 trillion.[97]

The Post-Deng "Good-Neighborliness" Policy and Sino–Russian Relations

In mid-December 1992, the visiting Russian President Boris Yeltsin and Chinese President Yang Shangkun issued a "joint statement on mutual relations between the PRC and the Russian Federation" in Beijing. In September 1994, President Jiang Zemin who succeeded Yang signed with President Yeltsin the second joint statement and the "joint statement on mutually not using nuclear weapons against or "aiming strategic nuclear weapons at each other".[98]

Toward the end of April 1996, Boris Yeltsin revisited China for the creation of an Asia-Pacific regional security association which was aimed at Russia-China commercial ties and building a "Strategic Partnership for the 21st Century". According to Yeltsin, cooperation with China was "specially helpful to Russia's economic reform, the economic development of its Far East region".[99] China's economic reform inspired Russia; and Yeltsin proposed to consolidate the commercial ties. Yeltsin's visit highlighted the signing of the first such treaty in Asia by the presidents of China, Russia and three former Soviet Union republics of Tajikistan, Kyrgyzstan and Kazakhstan. The treaty to demilitarize their common border was hailed as a significant boost to peace and stability in the Asia-Pacific region. The accord marked the apex of the ties of the Sino–Soviet alliance, which had collapsed in the 1960s. This had been the most important treaty to reduce border tensions in Asia and make economic cooperation possible since the Cold War. The treaty was unlikely to change the balance of power in Asia or the world, with the ending of the Cold War and the United States remaining the sole superpower. During the Cold War period, the agreements would have been viewed as the two communist giants colluding against the United States. Yet the treaty was of great symbolic significance in that it formally marked the end of an era in which Russian strategic thinking had posed as a massive military threat to Asia.

During Yeltsin's visit, both countries signed 14 agreements ranging from trade deals to nuclear energy cooperation. Perhaps the biggest deal reached was the joint development of a pipeline to bring gas from the Siberian fields to the Yellow Sea. In mid-July 2001, visiting Jiang Zemin and Russian President Vladimir Putin signed a good-neighborly treaty of friendship and cooperation, with the aim of maintaining the global strategic balance and stability.[100] Alhough Russia's trade with Japan was only marginal and the value of two-way Russian–Chinese trade amounted to less than 2 per cent of China's total in 1995, Russia was now to attempt transform its centuries-old policy of military expansion into one of peaceful commercial exchange.

China's "Good Neighborliness" Policy and South Asia

In early December 1996, Chinese President Jiang Zemin, in a speech delivered to the Pakistani Senate, proposed the five principles for developing "long-term, stable and friendly ties" with the South Asian nations.[101] He stressed that both China and South Asia needed an international environment of peace and stability to develop their national economies. Apart from consolidating ties with the South Asian neighbors, Jiang visited India and Nepal in December that year, reiterating China's persistent Dengist policy of enhancing friendly relations with its neighbors.[102]

China and India resumed official talks in the early 1980s, followed by the late Indian Prime Minister Rajiv Gandhi's visit to Beijing in

1988. The nuclear-armed Asian giants, who fought a conventional war in 1962, had claimed portions of each other's territory since then. The issue of the 4,500-kilometer frontier was viewed as central to problems between them. However, both governments emphasized their common interests in promoting economic cooperation rather than border disputes, and signed an agreement in 1993 to ease tension along their frontier during Indian leader Narasimha Rao's visit to China. In August 1995, both agreed to pull back their troops from four border posts in India's northeastern state of Arunachal Pradesh, parts of which were claimed by the PRC. As a result of talks between India's Prime Minister Deve Gowda and President Jiang Zemin, the first Chinese president to visit India in late November 1996, both countries agreed to cut troops on their disputed border.[103] China also promised not to supply nuclear weapons or technology to India's rival Pakistan.[104]

In June 2003, Indian Prime Minister Atal Behari Vajpayee visited Beijing to promote trade, investment and technological cooperation.[105] Direct trade between both countries was restored in 1977 after it had been suspended for 15 years. During the period 1988–1997, Sino–Indian bilateral trade increased more than six-fold from US$246 million to US$1.83 billion.[106] Their total trade volume rose to US$3 billion in 2000.[107] Despite these increases, Sino–Indian trade was still quite marginal compared with China's world trade of about US$500 billion a year or its trade with the United States of about US$75 billion a year. However, this indicated China's determination to promote its friendly neighborhood policy to enhance the development of advanced technology.

The complementary nature of the relationship between China and India was certainly not confined to commodity exchange. India's software, which was not well known in the 1980s, had been well developed since the 1990s, and became famous in the international market. During the period 1991–2002, India had remarkable advantages in software development, while the PRC was quite strong in its production of hardware.

From "Good-Neighborliness" to Inducing the Whole World to Help Modernize China: Sino–African Economic and Trade Relations

Economic and trade cooperation is a major part of Sino–African friendly relations. During the first eight months of 2000, their trade volume was US$6.72 billion of which the PRC's exports to Africa accounted for US$3.23 billion and the rest US$3.49 billion came from its imports from Africa.[108] Since 1995, the PRC has established 11 multilateral trade and investment promotion centers in Africa. Contracting of engineering projects and labor service constituted an important part of economic cooperation between the PRC and the African continent. By 1999, Chinese enterprises had signed about 9,800 such agreements involving a contracted investment of US$14 billion.[109] In 1997, the Bank of China set up its first agency for business operations in Africa.[110] By early 2000, China had launched 46 aid projects in 21 African countries through joint ventures. By September 2000, Chinese enterprises had invested US$660 million in 485 African projects.[111] African countries had economic advantages complementary to China. For example, China learnt petroleum refining and fruit tree cultivation techniques from Africa in the past and introducd their skills in environmental protection, extracting oil from coal and diamond cutting.[112] In November 2001, joining the WTO, China entered into a new phase of reform and opening up to the outside world. During the period 1991–2002, the country took Africa as one of the major regions to practise its "market diversification" strategy. At the end of 2002, bilateral trade volume was US$12 billion and contracted projects undertaken by Chinese companies in Africa were worth over US$20 billion.[113] Based on strategic considerations for the 21st century, the Chinese government attached strategic importance to its relations with African countries. Its economic and trade cooperation with Africa was a major part of China's overall diplomatic strategy.

To conclude, during the Jiangist period, while making great efforts in promoting global peace and stability conducive to its continued modernization drive, the PRC pushed forward the process of opening up to the outside world more vigorously. Successful bilateral trade and economic ties with the US-led West not only provided a direction for future development of bilateral relations, but also created favorable conditions for the development of even closer economic and trade ties. Likewise, promoting peace and stability in the Asia-Pacific region with the aim of tapping capital and technology for its modernization program, the PRC's "good-neighborliness" policy was equally successful in that the five "economic dragons" and the ASEAN group shifted their trade surplus to the US to the rising China. Their investment in the post-Deng China helped create another new economic miracle. China's success in inducing the whole world to help modernize the country was shown in its trade and investment performance bringing about more growth of foreign trade. In November 1997, in the New York based China Chamber of Commerce, the visiting Chinese President Jiang Zemin said that with peace and stability in the international environment, "China's development relies on the world, while the world's prosperity relies on China".[114] The country's huge construction and infrastructure program, for instance, continued its domestic growth spurring imports. Its foreign exchange reserves in 2000 was US$155 billion, the second largest in the world. Since its entry to the WTO in November 2001, the PRC had speeded up the process of opening up to the outside world. Foreign investment drove the process of internationalization of the Chinese economy. In 2002, more than 26,000 investment contracts were signed with foreign companies with a record inflow of funds of US$52.7 billion. It continued to seek imports of capital and high technology particularly from the US-led West. It is not so much the capital *per se* that it needed, but rather the technology that was associated with foreign direct investments from the Western world. Since 1979, the PRC had acquired most of the technology imports from the advanced Western countries particularly the US, West Germany, Britain, France and the five Asian economic "dragons".

The Dengist Strategy of "One Country, Two Systems" and the Taiwan Question

At the beginning of the 1990s, as discussed above, with the Western "China threat" theory initiated as a result of the rise of the PRC, the Chinese leadership brought out Mao's concept of the three worlds in association with its perception of the emergence of a new world order dominated by a "rich-nations club" mainly of the United States and Japan. They claimed that both "club members" schemed at "containing" their country, though their contradiction with the "club members" remained non-antagonistic. The United States pursued a major change in its strategic thinking by shifting its focus of future major military operations from Europe to Asia and the Pacific as China gets more powerful and Russia poses less of a threat. In 1999, the US Congress planned to include Japan and Taiwan into the anti-missile forces of its Tactical Missile Defense System (TMD). As a response to the PRC's anti-secession law initiative, in mid-February 2005, the US–Japan joint agreement declared that the security in the Taiwan Straits was a "common strategic objective".[115] The vital issue on the US strategic thinking was whether the PRC's long-term interests – including its opportunities to profit from foreign investment and trade – hinged on being a "responsible" member of the international community. The US-led West wanted China to forego the use of force to pursue reunification with Taiwan

As discussed above, the ping-pong diplomacy staged in 1971 led to President Nixon's China visit and the decisive changes of China's relations with the superpowers. The rapprochement with the US which brought 20 years of confrontation to an end, promoted normalization of the bilateral relations and opened the pave to the determination of the position of Taiwan as expressed in the Shanghai Communique between the PRC and the United States in February 1972 as follows:

> The Chinese government firmly opposes any activities which aim at the creation of 'one China, one Taiwan', 'one China, two governments', 'two Chinas' and independent Taiwan, or advocate that 'the status of Taiwan remains to be determined'.

With its security hinged on the support from the United States, this agreement made Taiwan very insecure. According to the coercive PRC, Taiwan argued, "one China" meant that Taiwan accept the PRC as the Central Government and the rule of one party-state of the CCP. The Sino–US friendly relations continued and the fully fledged diplomatic relations were established in 1979 under the conditions that the United States severed the diplomatic ties with Taipei, terminated the 1954 mutual defense treaty and withdrew US military personnel from Taiwan, while the PRC accepted the continued US–Taiwan unofficial relationship in commercial, cultural and other areas and agreed to carry out the cross-straits "peaceful resolution of the Taiwan question" as demanded by the United States.[116] The latter two conditions were included in the Taiwan Relations Act determined by the US Congress in April 1979. The August 1982 Communique on US arms sale to Taiwan was signed.

Although the Dengist-Jiangst priority was the scheme of the four modernizations, the Taiwan question was and still is the PRC's major concern. However, if the Taiwanese government opted for independence, war would be unavoidable certainly involving the United States. China wants to settle its dispute with Taiwan peacefully on the condition that the island gives up any idea of independence. If Taiwan actively seeks independence, Thomas Christensen and others argue, China would act even if it means damaging profitable trade and investment relations with Taiwan, and it would do so regardless of the US military involvement.[117]

In the early 1980s, Deng Xiaoping formulated the policy of "one country, two systems" for the resumption of sovereignty over Hong Kong and Macau with the promised high degree of autonomy in terms of the social, economic and political systems different from those of the mainland. This concept was meant to set an example for the future "peaceful reunification" with Taiwan. The Sino–British joint declaration on Hong Kong was signed in mid-1984. In 1987, the Straits Exchange Foundation (SEF) of the Republic of China and the Association for Relations across the Taiwan Straits (ARATS) of the PRC were established to resolve questions arising from bilateral exchanges on the economic, personal and cultural matters when Taipei allowed its people to visit their mainland relatives.

However, this study argues that Deng's "one country, two systems" formula aimed at "peaceful reunification" with Taiwan is not in harmony with his "good neighborhood" policy.

Lee Teng-hui, elected in 1988, demanded that the PRC renounce its use of force against Taiwan as a prerequisite for the cross-straits normalization of relations. He made clear Taiwan's stand that both sides represented "two separate political entities". With Sino–US relations deteriorated as a result of the June 1989 Tiananmen Square pro-democracy military crackdown, a series of sanctions of the US House of Representatives against Beijing resulted. As noted above, led by the Summit of Seven, the leading Western industrialized nations, the West denounced China's "violent suppression in violation of human rights". All this jeopardized Deng's "one country, two systems" formula.

With his "coercive hand" particularly during the period 1990–1992, Jiang Zemin pressurized the Lee government that the PRC "could not indefinitely tolerate the postponement of negotiation". Although the first Koo Chen-fu (辜振甫)–Wang Daohan (汪道涵) meeting held (in Singapore) in 1993 was based on the "1992 Consensus of one China", with Taiwan's sense of deep insecurities, Lee had already begun to look for more international space for its international existence in the world community.

In July 1994, the Republican-dominated US Congress passed an amendment to the Taiwan Relations Act against the Clinton administration's position of disallowing Lee Ting-hui to visit the US in a "private" capacity. In addition, as noted above, in late 1994, the mid-term elections in the United States brought a number of anti-China right-wing congressmen into the foreign relations committees of both the Senate and House of Representatives.

Adhering to Deng's reunification formula of "one country, two systems", in January 1995, Jiang announced his "eight-point" proposal emphasizing his opposition to Lee's "expansion of Taiwan's international living space".[118] Jiang considered Lee's "private visit" as politically-oriented seeking collaboration with the anti-China foreign forces particularly the United States. He also argued that the eventual return of Hong Kong and Macau to China in 1997 and 1999 respectively would create the opportune time for putting the Taiwan question squarely on the policy agenda.[119] However, Lee argued that both his sovereignty entity claim and international space were to create favorable bargaining chips for the negotiation on the reunification.

Despite being under Beijing's coercion, Lee made his "six-point" statement in April 1995 after returning from the Middle East as an answer to Jiang's "eight-point" proposal with particular emphasis of "treating the reality with objectivity" on the point of "one China". This meant that Taiwan should not accept the PRC as the Central Government and the rule of one-party state of the CCP.[120] Understandably the Republic of China (ROC) was quite skeptical of the future of both Hong Kong and Macau.

In May 1995, the US Department of State approved Lee's visit to Cornell University, his Alma Mater, in June that year. In mid-June the ARATS declared that the second Koo-Wang meeting was postponed indefinitely in protest at Lee's US visit. In addition, the PRC staged six war games in the Taiwan Straits during the period July 1995–March 1996. The military exercises carried the message that Beijing was determined to use force as an option to achieve the reunification, apart from making it clear its opposition of foreign intervention in its reunification endeavors and of Lee's pro-independence tendency. In March 1996, the PRC stepped up its campaign of intimidation in an apparent effort to influence the results of Taiwan's first direct presidential election. The United States responded with the dispatch of aircraft carriers to monitor the PRC's missile tests and large-scale military maneuvers in the Straits. This was to emphasize its close ties with Taipei, despite official US recognition of the government in Beijing as the only government of China. Just three days before Taiwan's democratic presidential elections, the Clinton administration announced its anti-aircraft missiles deal with Taiwan.[121]

The cross-straits dialogue restarted with Koo Chen-fu's visit to the mainland in October 1998. However, in January 1999 the US Congress intended to include Taiwan into its TMD system. The PRC's perception of the Asia-Pacific hegemony of the "US–Japan club" linked up Taiwan with the US anti-missile forces of the TMD system thus nullifying its 700 or so medium-range missiles aimed across the Taiwan Straits. In July that year, with more confidence, Lee openly objected to the coercive one-China principle and espoused his "two-states" theory. As a result, his independence rhetoric touched off a new crisis not only putting on hold the viable cross-straits dialogue, but also making the PRC leadership more affirmative in preparing for war in the event of Taiwanese declaration of independence. Reiterating the US Taiwan policy of the one-China principle, cross-straits dialogue and peaceful resolution, the Clinton administration urged Taipei to stop using US support to provoke Beijing and putting off dialogue with the mainland indefinitely.[122]

The year 1999 was Lee's last year in office. Although the PRC felt more urgent to resolve the Taiwan problem with the successful return of Hong Kong and Macau to the mainland, it was also more concerned about the rapid changes in the Taiwan population's negative attitude toward the reunification with the mainland, while the Taiwanese leadership used the "creative ambiguity" policy to expand its international space and seek more international recognition.[123] The US House of Representatives passed its Taiwan Security Enhancement Act in February 2000 amid Beijing's warning that any attempt by Taipei to assert independence would mean war. While the cry for independence was rising, the pro-independence Democratic Progressive Party won the presidential election in March that year breaking the KMT's 55-year grip on power. In April Washington agreed to sell Taiwan long-range radar that can detect missile launches from the mainland. In 2001, the US provided 4 Kidd-class destroyers, 12 anti-submarine P-3 Orion aircraft and 8 diesel submarines as part of the biggest arms deal since 1992 for improving Taiwan's naval and air defences against the PRC.[124] In mid-August that year, rehearsing war games as part of its long-term strategy aimed at restraining the pro-independence sentiment on Taiwan, the PRC intimidation message prompted a US Navy response by conducting a "passing exercise" involving two mighty carriers, *Constellation* and *Carl Vinson*, with their 150 aircraft and supporting ships. In June 2005, aiming at defusing the threat from Beijing, the US Defense Department was to sell Taiwan the Early Warning Surveillance Radar.[125] Meanwhile, sticking to his election-campaign strategy of emphasizing his defiance toward Beijing, the pro-independence Chen Shui-bian rejected the "one country, two systems" formula. He argued that the result of this principle was to lean toward the "one China" direction and to let the "two systems" disappear.[126]

At the beginning of March 2005, with complete control as Chairman of the PRC's Central Military Commission, Hu Jintao announced that the National People's Congress was to enact an anti-secession law which authorized the use of force against Taiwan if the island declared independence.

The Sino–Taiwan confrontation, however limited in scope, would destabilize the military balance and constrict commerce and shipping, which is the region's economic lifeblood. Furthermore, Hong Kong and Macau would be put at risk if China took military action against Taiwan. Jiang was well aware of the damage to the Hong Kong economy and the smooth transition in 1997 as well as the confidence on the part of overseas investors along the Chinese coast. Confrontation would be detrimental to China's "good neighborliness" policy, which has been vital to its modernization program.

In view of the above, the PRC's "one country, two systems" policy was not compatible with its four modernizations scheme. Together, they formed two fronts, that is, the four modernizations plan and the task of the reunification with Taiwan, which Mao avoided.

Mao's national strategy was supposed to be successful only with one front at a time. A united populace was needed for "annihilating" the primary enemy, 'bit by bit, portion by portion". Therefore, starting from 1950, Mao's primary national task was to deal with the primary enemy as his top priority. During the period 1950–1958, his primary enemy was the United States, while during the period 1969–1976, his primary enemy was the Soviet Union. However, the period 1958–1969, China's primary enemy was the United States with the Soviet Union as the "No. 1 accomplice of the US", and the formation of the two superpower fronts was "disadvantageous to the PRC". Mao's economic policy formulated through his communized scheme during the entire period 1950–1976 was intimately related with the primary enemy. Therefore, understandably, with the Soviet Union as the newly perceived primary enemy, Mao had to shelve the Taiwan question for "a hundred years" as he told Kissinger in 1971 when the status of the primary enemy began to transform.

However, without the primary enemy, the PRC's two national fronts evolved out of the post-Mao strategy. With the two fronts, the leadership could not fully concentrate its attention on its four modernizations program. Sino–US relations are quite fluid, owing to the Taiwan issue. If not handled well, the thorny issue could jeopardize its modernizations program. Although the PRC's "good neighborliness" policy has been and still is basically sound for its reunification aim by first seeking to forge closer economic ties with Taiwan, its "one country, two systems" formula is contradictory to this policy.

In recent years, Taiwan's economic slump and an exodus of the manufacturing activities to the mainland increased pressure from the business community to make moves toward unity with China. In April 2005, several originally pro-DPP business tycoons such as Stan Shih of the Acer group, Taiwan's largest computer company, and Shih Wenlong, founder of Chi Mei Electronics-Liquid Crystal Display consortium, resigned as presidential advisers.[127] They claimed that Taiwan could not develop its economy without the mainland. Taiwanese computer makers are the biggest in the world, but more than two-thirds of their output comes from their factories on the mainland where labor and production costs are much lower. Over the past few decades, the Taiwanese business community has invested about US$100 billion in the mainland.[128] Two other Taiwanese tycoons – Chang Yung-fa of Evergreen Marine and Wang Yung-ching of the Formosa Plastics Group – had long been fierce critics of the government for focusing on pro-independence only at the expense of the economy.[129] The business community believes that Taiwan is in an ideal position to enhance the mainland's growth. In May 2005, Vice-Chairman of the KMT, Chiang Pin-kung, argued that Taiwan's economy had been sluggish for four or five years because "the government had overlooked the rise of the mainland" and that "cross-straits tensions had driven away investors".[130]

Weixing Hu writes that in 1999 Beijing was well aware of the public opinion in Taiwan, which was nowhere near contemplating any form of reunification with the mainland.[131] A survey carried out in the island in 1996 suggested that the majority of the Taiwanese population preferred to maintain the *status quo* supporting neither independence nor reunification and not to accept Communist rule.[132] The DPP's defeat in legislative elections in 2004 showed that Chen Shui-bian's attempt to move Taiwan much closer to independence by making big constitutional changes was fruitless. Thus, in mid-May 2005, James

Soong Chu-yu's (宋楚瑜) deal of "two sides, one China" with President Hu Jintao should be understood in this light. The deal provided the DPP an opportunity to reconcile with the mainland offering a great range of concrete economic incentives likely to bode well with the Taiwanese people especially the influential business community. If public support for ties with the mainland grows and Chen opts to resist it, it would likely deal a heavy blow to the DPP in the 2008 presidential election. In the presidential election in March 2000, Chen won 39.6 per cent of the vote marginally, while the KMT support was split between Party rebel Soong with 36.8 per cent and official candidate Lien Chan (连战) with 23 per cent.[133]

The "One Country, Two Systems" Formula and the Case of Hong Kong

We noted above that Lee Teng-hui was quite skeptical about the future of both Hong Kong and Macau and that Chen Shui-bian rejected the "one country, two systems" formula. That Beijing aspired to the leadership of Hong Kong Chief Executive Tung Chee-hwa (董建华) for plausible application of the formula to the case of Taiwan did not help. As it turned out, Tung's weak leadership failed to have Beijing's aspirations fulfilled.

Firstly, in March 1998, only less than a year after Hong Kong was handed back to China, the territory's rule of law suffered a damaging blow as a result of the decision of the Department of Justice not to prosecute media tycoon Sally Aw Sian, a friend of Tung. While prosecuting two and a former senior executives of the newspaper *Hong Kong Standard* for fraudulently inflating daily circulation figures, the Department refused to explain why the well-connected co-conspirator Aw was not charged. The government's decision, which caused a scandal damaging the confidence in Hong Kong's legal system, led to Justice Secretary Elsie Leung facing a no-confidence motion in the Legislative Council.

Secondly, in July 2000, a leading pollster, Dr Robert Chung Ting-yiu, director of the Public Opinion Programme of the Journalism and Media Studies Centre at the University of Hong Kong, claimed that Chief Executive Tung put pressure on him a year earlier through a "third party", the Hong Kong University Vice-Chancellor Professor Patrick Cheng Yiu-chung, that his public-opinion surveys showing the slumping trend of Tung's popularity and the government's credibility should stop. Chung's claims sparked a public inquiry on the interference of academic freedom and freedom of speech and led to the resignation of Professor Cheng. In mid-July, as the row over pressure on academics widened, a legal adviser to the Hong Kong University staff claimed that "several of them had been asked by their superiors to write positively about Chief Executive Tung in newspaper columns and other commentaries".[134]

Thirdly, the scandal regarding Financial Secretary Leung Kam-chung's purchase of a car ahead of an increase in vehicle taxes in the budget of 2003 further demonstrated Tung Chee-hwa's weak leadership. In March when Leung first offered his resignation as a result of the public outcry against him, Tung chose not to accept it and stood by his troubled financial secretary. Tung dealt the accountability system a devastating blow.

Fourthly, Tung Chee-hwa was again under fire as a result of an official inquiry into the SAR administration's handling of the 2003 outbreak of the Severe Acute Respiratory Syndrome (Sars) failing to blame any individual. Instead of establishing an independent probe into the government's handling of the Sars outbreak, he appointed Health Chief Dr Yeoh Eng-kiong, who was most closely associated with the government's handling of the crisis, to head the panel. An independent investigation by international experts found that Yeoh and the former Health Director Dr Margaret Chan did not pay enough attention when the disease first appeared in southern Guangdong province. Yeoh had even played down the danger of the epidemic as the disease began to spread in Hong Kong in March subsequently killing 299 and infecting 1,755 people. The outbreak spread to Europe and North America. The failure of Tung's government to respond to the crisis in its early stages was in sharp contrast to Hu Jintao's decisiveness in handling the Sars outbreak in Beijing. Hu sacked the Health

Minister Zhang Wenkang (张文康) and Beijing Mayor Meng Xue-nong (孟学农) for fraudulently falsifying the infected numbers of cases in Beijing.

Fifth, the SAR Government was again engulfed in crisis, as 500,000 people took to the streets on July 1, 2003, the sixth anniversary of Hong Kong's return to China, against Tung's governance and the national security legislation.

The proposed legislation required under Article 23 of the Basic Law – Hong Kong's mini-constitution – to outlaw treason, subversion, secession, disclosure of state secrets and political bodies with overseas affiliation, but the legislation, which contained controversial provisions that would empower the Secretary for Security Regina Ip Lau Suk Yee to outlaw local organizations affiliated to mainland organizations whose operations had been banned on national security grounds, prompted the rally against Tung's government.[135] The proposed bill's provisions on unauthorized disclosure of state secrets had already caused a lot of anxiety among journalists and civil servants. Anyone who was a passive receiver of confidential information obtained through illegal means could face prosecution, even if they did not participate in the illegal act.[136] Thus, freedom of the press and the public's right to know would be put at risk. The massive protest called for more time and more consultation as Tung was determined to push ahead on July 9 with the enactment of the highly unpopular and poorly conceived legislation which would affect overseas confidence in Hong Kong's implementation of the "one country, two systems" formula. Further, unemployment, salary cuts, the destruction of people's wealth through falling property prices, the slow response to the Sars outbreak and the government's tarnished accountability system all contributed to the demonstration. Tung's popularity had already fallen from almost 70 per cent when he assumed the SAR leadership to a low of less than 40 per cent, with his government characterized by being weak, indecisiveness and out of touch. Further, on July 7, Executive Councillor James Tien Pei-chun, a key Tung ally, announced his resignation from the cabinet after his calls to delay the national security bill were rejected. The Liberal's departure crippled the government's authority and further undermined public confidence in the Tung team. All this put the mainland government in an embarrassing position deepening doubts about whether he could govern effectively.[137] Local members of the National People's Congress and others started to discuss whether he should resign or be sacked.[138] Further, following the second rally of about 50,000 people in the city on July 9 demanding the embattled Chief Executive to step down, for the third time in two weeks, more than 20,000 people took to streets on July 13 demanding the speedy introduction of full democracy for Hong Kong.

The resignation of Secretary for Security Ip, who had become inextricably associated with the intransigency on the national security bill and the deferral of the bill with the promise of due consultation did not retrieve the situation. A "brutal public dressing down" by Hu Jintao in Macau in December 2004 signalled the beginning of the end of Tung's turbulent eight years as the Hong Kong SAR Chief.[139] The removal of Tung Chee-hwa no doubt was a popular move with his failure to win the people's support. His departure might be seen as an admission of failure by the central government in its implementation of the "one country, two systems" formula.

Conclusion

The US realism in dealing with the PRC was that it recognized its huge stake in engaging the PRC constructively on economic, security and strategic issues. For instance, with both sharing common views on the global issues of preventing proliferation of weapons of mass destruction and the maintenance of peace and stability in the Asia-Pacific region, the impact of the anti-Chinese movements in the US Congress in the early 1990s was marginal. The United States-related anti-Chinese factors were not detrimental to China's continued modernization endeavors. While China made vigorous efforts in promoting regional as well as global peace and stability conducive to its continued modernization drive, its success in opening up to the outside world was shown in its trade and investment performance. The country continues its imports of capital and hi-tech from the US-led West, the Asia-Pacific "economic dragons" and the world at large. Their investment in the post-Deng China helped create another new economic miracle. However, Taiwan remains a thorny issue in the Sino–US bilateral relations. Deng's "one country, two systems" formula, which aimed at "peaceful reunification" with Taiwan, contradicts his "good neighborhood" policy which is vital to China's modernization endeavors. Both formula and policy created two fronts which Mao would avoid. Even Beijing's reliance on the leadership of the Hong Kong SAR Chief Executive Tung Chee-hwa to inspire plausible application of the formula to Taiwan did not help. Tung's weak leadership failed to have Beijing's aspirations fulfilled. If not handled properly, the "one country, two systems" formula can jeopardize China's modernization efforts.

Chapter Eight
Jiang Zemin's Approach to Privatization

Characteristic of the present global economy is its pattern of globalization. In this chapter, we will consider Jiang Zemin's approach to the issue of privatization, his privatization model in relation to economic globalization and its role in shaping the global economic system.

Jiang Zemin's Approach to Privatization

This section concerns Chairman Jiang's approach to the privatization of the national economy. This was established to further "improve the livelihood of the people", alongside continuing modernization efforts, by further opening up the country to the outside world to tap capital inflow and science and advanced technology. The international environment remained favorable to the PRC's continued modernization program, although anti-Chinese initiatives did crop up in the US Congress in the early 1990s. Adopting the market-oriented economic principles and further privatizing the national economy importantly including the industrial and agricultural sectors, Jiang aimed ultimately for entry to the World Trade Organization (WTO). In this section, I will also consider other targets of the ninth FYP (1996–2000). First, let us consider the question of the state-owned enterprises (SOEs) as addressed in the eighth and ninth FYPs.

The Emerging Private Sector

The reforms and relaxation policies initiated in December 1978 witnessed the experimental nature of the private sector, which was limited to "individual businesses" called *getihu* (个体户). In the first five years before 1983, the private sector was generally successful among the vast peasantry. As mentioned above, each of the small privately owned enterprises (*siying qiye*) (私营企业) typically from the trade and service sectors was allowed to employ the maximum of eight workers. However, the period 1984–1992 witnessed the rise of enterprises permitted to employ more than eight people. Gradually the scope of the private sector expanded. From 1993, with the new market structure established and property rights reforms in place, the private economy became more powerful. In September 1997, the Fifteenth National Congress of the CCP treated the private sector as an important component of the national economy. It was addressed in the Constitution in March 2000.

China's startling economic success in the past two decades was achieved primarily because of the growing private sector, the most dynamic component of its national economy. Absorbing a large number of laid-off workers from declining state-owned enterprises, the private sector became the chief source of new employment. Since 1980, according to the International Finance Corporation, a member of the World Bank Group, the output value of, and employment in, China's private economy grew by 71 per cent and 41 per cent each year on average.[1] The IFC also reported that by the end of 1997, the number of people employed by private businesses was about 67.9 million.[2] In June 1999, private companies totaled 1.3 million with total registered capital valued at Rmb 817.7 billion (US$98.94 billion).[3] In 2000, the private sector accounted for 33 per cent of the nation's GDP, compared with the state sector's 37 per cent, which was less than half of the privatization of the SOEs completed, according to the Chinese.[4]

The Party's transformation from representing "advanced elements of the proletariat" to "advanced productive forces" and "advanced culture", led to a new Party, well represented among not only managers and professionals, but also private entrepreneurs. This situation stood in contrast with Mao's time, when Party members were primarily workers and peasants. In Shenzhen, in March 2002, for example, 35.7 per cent of managerial personnel, 27.2 per cent of professionals and 22.2 per cent of private entrepreneurs were found to be Party members.[5] In contrast, only 10.4 per cent of workers in the service industry were Party members.[6] The survey revealed a similar pattern in other parts of China.[7] At the beginning of 2002, reportedly more than 200 million workers were employed in private enterprises.[8]

Acute SOE Problems and the Eighth Five-Year Plan of 1991–1995

The Eighth and Ninth FYPs were designed to support the PRC's continuing modernization scheme. As mentioned above, problems concerning the SOEs appeared in the early modernization drive.

In December 1990, the Seventh Plenary Session of the Thirteenth Central committee of the CCP adopted the proposals to draft the Eighth FYP (1991–1995) for national economic and social development and the Ten Years Program (1991–2000). The plenary session listed the key points of agriculture, industry and infrastructure, and educational, scientific and technological modernization in economic construction of the previous five-year plans as well as the ten years program and the Eighth FYP. Both Plan and Program were firmly based on the traditional guiding principles such as pushing forward reform and further opening up the country to the outside world. Apart from raising the people's living standards, their strategic objectives were to establish an economic structure and operating mechanism (1) that promoted the development of a socialist planned commodity economy based on the public ownership, and (2) to combine planning with market regulations. The public ownership proved to be ineffective, however.

In response to the following major economic problems particularly those the SOEs confronted during the Eighth FYP, the Chinese endeavored to change the economic structure, which marked a major turning point for reform:

- Serious inflation led to an overheated economy and price hikes. Consumer prices rose on an average 12 per cent per year, with the 1994 rate reaching 24.1 per cent.
- Limited financial inputs to agriculture forced state-owned units to reduce the proportion of investment in this sector to total investment in fixed assets. The lack of long-term planning on the part of both enterprises and individuals on input to agriculture prevented improvements in agricultural production conditions. Price increases in agricultural capital goods had raised agricultural production costs which, in turn led to rising prices for farm and sideline products.
- More importantly, slow reform of state-owned enterprises incurred heavy losses. The growth rate of state-owned enterprises during the 8th FYP period was slower than that of non-state enterprises. In 1994, 45.9 per cent of state-owned enterprises recorded losses.
- An underdeveloped financial market and lagging financial reforms were due to the lack of independence of the central bank, as a result of excessive government interference and control. Further losses in the state-owned enterprises led to acute problems in the banking system.

It was in this context that the Ninth FYP and long-term objectives concerning the SOE question were approved at the Fourth Session of the Eighth NPC in March 1996. In the following section, I will consider the Ninth FYP.

Jiang's SOE Reform and the Ninth Five-Year Plan of 1996–2000

In September 1995, in the Fifth Plenary Session of the 14th CCP Central Committee, General Secretary Jiang addressed the SOE problems. In tune with the establishment of a modern enterprise system, the government aimed at speeding up reform as follows:

(1) Giving greater play to the SOE's dominant role in the national economy and
(2) Quickening the market-oriented reform of the national economy.

As noted above, the state sector's share of industrial output declined from 76 per cent in 1980 to 50 per cent in 1991. By 1995, the figure significantly decreased to about 30 per cent reflecting the expansion of the non-state-owned sector, including township and village enterprises and various forms of individual enterprises and foreign ventures. Despite this, the state sector remained the largest employer, with more than 100 million workers. The overall performance of the state sector had been disappointing over the years, incurring huge losses that necessitated large loans from the banking system, thus hindering China's banking reform. According to the State Planning Commission Director, Chen Jinhua, 75 per cent of China's industrial SOEs suffered losses in 1996.[9] Thus, without significant transformation of the ailing SOEs, any further deepening of China's economic reform would not be effective.

China's enterprise reform in the early stage was aimed at securing a way to integrate public ownership with the market economy for its SOEs without leading to the privatization of these enterprises. The reform was to faithfully stick to the Marxist theory to avoid the exploitation of the majority of the people by the minority. In his report at the 15th National Congress of the CCP in September 1997, Jiang claimed that the state-owned sector was still dominant and competitive, even if "it accounts for a smaller proportion of the economy".[10] It was only with the rule of law that privatization of the state economy could be enhanced, even though the latest constitutional amendments raised the status of private firms.[11] This meant that, in the process of reforming the state sector, privatization had not become a dominant factor. Professor Wei Xinghua of the People's University argued: "If the state-owned sector failed, private and foreign economies would become the main components of the economy; and China's socialist economic system would not survive".[12] In 1999, China had one million private enterprises.[13] The building of a workable modern enterprise system by the end of the century in most of the key large- and medium-sized state-owned enterprises was envisaged, however. This meant that the SOEs remained subject to further transformation.

In the continued restructuring of the state sector, emphasis was placed on promoting efficient management, reaping profitability and reforming the price system. Thus, in January 1998, China's public ownership structures developed in the following diversified forms:

- Solely state-funded companies.
- Collective economy. This was a form of public ownership in which the means of social production and the fruits of production were held collectively by the masses.
- Joint-stock system. This system featured the principle of voluntary participation, autonomous management and the assumption of sole responsibility for profits, losses and risks.
- Joint-stock partnership system. This was a new collective system with a new form of public ownership in which employees became shareholders and equal rights and interests among employees were ensured.
- Social-fund ownership economy. This kind of social security fund ownership by major investors in such funds as old age pension, medical insurance and housing funds was a new form of social property organization. Its assets belonged neither to the state nor to enterprise collectives or individuals, but to the members of society concerned.
- Entrusted management.
- Property management responsibility system.

All of these diversified forms were designed to adhere to President Jiang's idea of "retaining a dominant position for public ownership with diverse forms of ownership development side by side", according to Meng Xianggang, Deputy Secretary-General of the State Economic and Trade Commission.[14] Considered as "an important component of China's socialist market economy", the non-public sector was structured to provide more opportunities for foreign investment. Foreign investment was now to take the following forms:

- Foreign investment in technical upgrading and the structural readjustment of SOEs,
- Foreign investment in the strategic reorganization of the state economy through exclusive funding, joint ventures, or partnership with the SOEs,

– Foreign investment in the reform of large- and medium-sized SOEs,
– Foreign investment in the reform of small- and medium-sized SOEs,
– Foreign investment in the construction of non-fixed assets projects.

It was anticipated that China would gradually evolve into a society with "a fairly developed market-oriented economy" where "the socialist public ownership would be dominated by different types of ownership developed side by side" as Jiang Zemin envisaged.[15] In essence, to speed up the process of privatization of the SOEs, the central government would give up its control and allow foreign and private investors to take the controlling stakes in the SOEs. More importantly, the majority of Jiang's "people" would inevitably become the capitalists.

Jiang's "Three Represents" and the Private Economy

As discussed above, in the Plenary Session of the Fourth Session of the Eighth NPC in March 1996, Jiang Zemin addressed the acute problems of the SOEs. This reform responded to declines in the industrial output of the state sector, from 50 per cent in 1991 to about 30 per cent in 1995. This decline reflected the expansion of the non-state-owned sector which included various forms of individual enterprises and foreign ventures. Subsequently, further reform in the SOE sector was seen vital. It was in this context that Jiang's development ideology of the "Three Represents" – addressing private entrepreneurs, capitalists and professionals – was espoused to "develop productive forces" for the purpose of "rejuvenating the nation". This was described as "the third theory of Marxism with Chinese characteristics".[16] In the following section, I will discuss how this latest Jiangist theory materialized to form "part of Mao Zedong Thought".

Mao Zedong's "concrete analysis of the concrete conditions" resulted in his original theory that the Chinese peasants must be won over if the Chinese revolution was to succeed, because the peasantry made up the majority of the Chinese population. Therefore Mao realized "the strongest force in the world" through his policies of uniting, that is, organizing "the whole population" in the Chinese peasantry. This was the essence of Mao Zedong's Thought, "the great theory of Marxism with Chinese characteristics". Calling this "the first great theory of Marxism with Chinese characteristics", President Jiang Zemin called Deng Xiaoping's Theory as "removing China's two mountains of economic and technological backwardness" "the second great theory of Marxism with Chinese characteristics". The motive seemed clear in the light of the new solutions proposed to the chronic problems faced by the troubled SOEs.

The Constitution of the CCP revised at the 11th Party Congress convened in November 2002, elevated the third generation CCP leader President Jiang to the same level of the CCP founder Mao and the second generation CCP leader Deng. It designated all three men chief representatives of the Communists during their respective periods. The ideology of the "Three Represents", together with Marxism-Leninism, Mao Zedong's Thought and Deng Xiaoping's Theory, according to the Jiangists, was to "become a theoretical foundation for the CCP's governance and a program of the CCP in the 21st century".[17] While vitally including Deng's emphasis on "the development trend of China's advanced productive forces and Mao's original espousal of the fundamental interests of the overwhelming majority of the Chinese people", Jiang's "Three Represents" was adopted to implement his view of the "orientation of China's advanced culture" for SOE reform.[18] Jiangist thought was carried out in "keeping pace with the times" to follow the international trend of private economy and, more importantly, economic globalization. The newly revised Constitution thus aimed to make Jiang's "Three Represents" a guiding ideology for the CCP to bring the "new forces" to the cause of "rejuvenating the nation". Needless to say, the "new forces" in the ranks of the Party were private entrepreneurs or capitalists or professionals, who were previously defined as exploiters of the workers, according to Marxist theory. Now, accepted as playing a vital role in the same Party, these private forces, "builders of socialism with Chinese characteristics" were described by Jiang as follows:

> Emerging in the process of social changes, entrepreneurs and technical personnel employed by non-public scientific and technological enterprises, managerial and technical staff employed by overseas-funded enterprises, the self-employed, private entrepreneurs, and employees in intermediaries, free-lance professionals and members of other social strata are all builders of socialism with Chinese characteristics.[19]

Jiang's reference to these private entrepreneurs as members of "advanced culture" was meant to justify their membership in the Party.[20] He also emphasized that "in stimulating economic growth creating more jobs and activating the market, [...] all legitimate income, whether from work or not, should be protected".[21] As he elaborated, even "income not from one's labour such as 'money earned from money', which was previously regarded as exploitation by the CCP, is now protected as long as it is lawful".[22]

It is important to note that Jiang's stance on protecting the capitalists began with Mao's 1971 law, stipulated in his Fourth FYP, that the private entrepreneurs would be allowed to employ "a limited number of workers":

> Non-agricultural individual laborers were allowed to engage in individual labor provided involving no exploitation of others within the limits permitted by law.

The essence of Jiang Zemin's "theory of the Three Representatives" was that the Party had to open its doors to private business people and professionals. It needed the support of the private sector to sustain its economic growth and thus to keep it in power.

Privatization of the State-owned Enterprises

We discussed above the plight of the SOEs. The early transformation of the SOE system witnessed the emergence of deep-rooted problems that conflicted with the demands of the PRC's market environment. These were rigidity in operations management, lack of technical innovation, heavy debt, social burdens, an overbundance of workers and difficulties in production and business operations. Therefore a new guideline for reform and development of the debt-ridden SOEs was adopted during the Fourth Plenary Session of the 15th Central Committee of the CCP.[23] Special efforts were made to separate administrative and enterprise functions and to make enterprise operation more market-oriented.[24] Furthermore, to enhance competitiveness, the SOEs were aimed to speed up technical renovation and to promote structural optimization and industrial upgrading to improve quality, enhance efficiency and enlarge export volume.[25]

As a result, during the SOE reform period of September 1997 through November 2000, the number of unprofitable large- and medium-sized SOEs reportedly decreased to 4,391 accounting for 66.5 per cent of the 1997 figure of 6,599.[26] During the same period, China's state sector laid off 25.5 million workers of which 17 million had found new jobs and 3 million retired and 5.5 million remained jobless.[27] As the above figures illustrate, the transformation from a planned to a market economy was enormous.

In another step toward speeding up the process of privatization of the SOEs, the central government allowed foreign and private investors to take controlling stakes of SOEs in its initial public offerings. This meant that the central government effectively gave up its policy of state control of the listed SOEs. It realized that so long as the state retained control of the listed SOEs, obstacles to restructuring the chronically ailing sector would occur, because of intimate links to the public ownership system.

In mid-March 2002, State Development and Planning Minister Zeng Peiyan reminded NPC delegates that many SOEs were plagued with inefficiency which led to acute unemployment pressure.[28] China reportedly planned to shut down 2,900 SOEs by 2005, entailing 5.7

million job losses.[29] Since the mid-1990s, the State Council had singled out several "sunset industries" including coal, steel, and textiles and companies in these sectors were ordered to shut down within 10 years. Meanwhile, the government planned to close down companies producing military supplies.[30] During the period 1996–2001, the problems of only half of the SOEs had been completed, however.[31] By March 2003, the problematic SOEs had absorbed 80 per cent of the country's total resources but contributed only 40 per cent of the industrial output.[32] In March 2005, the central government continued to speed up the restructuring, bringing the remaining 179 SOEs to about 80, with about 20 of the original 196 SOEs merged into larger conglomerates.[33]

In mid-2002, China's invitation to foreign capital was another important step toward diffusing the state's shareholding, which accounted for an average of 39 per cent of its publicly listed companies.[34] However, under the central government's new industrial restructuring, the state retained control of companies producing materials for military and of industries that provided important public utilities and services, including SOEs in petrochemicals, automobiles, the provision of information, and machinery and high technology.[35] In March 2003, the Assets Supervision and Administration Commission was established to manage these SOEs, with the aim of producing 30 to 50 business enterprises and conglomerates on par with the highest international standards within 8 years.[36] They retained the features of a planned economy but incurred problems of overstaffing, low efficiency and heavy debt.

Jiang's Market-Oriented Enterprise System and Economic Globalization

Transnational operations and businesses are an inevitable outcome of economic globalization characterized by private enterprise development. At the 21st Century Forum in Beijing in June 2000, President Jiang Zemin emphasized that "for countries to be successful, they should explore international resources and markets".[37] Since 1979, the Chinese leadership had adopted market-oriented factors as fundamental principles to reform its national economy. In addition, China had continued in full swing to further its market-oriented structural reform guided by the goals of privatization and opening the country up to the outside world.[38] The 15th Party Congress marked the transition from planned to market economy, while the 16th Congress heralded the new market economy at turn of the 21st century. The post-Mao policies of adopting market-oriented economic principles and privatizing the national economy was aimed at China's ultimate entry to the World Trade Organization, which had been established in January 1995. China's policy to this end over the past two decades was to create favorable conditions for the country to participate in economic globalization.

In 1992, UN Secretary General Butros Butros Ghali declared that the first truly globalization era had arrived. Since that date, increased globalization enabling the integration of various economies throughout the world in the areas of production, distribution and consumption became a common trend, with transnational corporations rapidly developing into a dominant force in the world economy. By the end of 1998, reportedly there had been about 60,000 transnational corporations. These accounted for 40 per cent of the world GDP, 60 per cent of all international trade, 60 to 70 per cent of international technological trade and 90 per cent of the total FDI.[39]

Economic globalization, which aims to enhance the interdependence on market and production of different countries, encourages the transnational flow of labor, capital, commodities, service, technology and information. Jiang Zemin emphasized that the market-oriented economic system promoted the efficient and optimized allocation of various productive elements and resources.[40] Economic globalization created a worldwide market in which all countries could compete according to the rules of the market economic system. Admitted to the WTO in December 2001, the Chinese government pledged to adopt stronger measures to open its market in the areas of commodities and service trades and, more importantly, to expedite market-oriented reform. Its WTO membership thus encouraged the reform process and enhanced China's modern market-oriented enterprise system. This system aimed to improve its legal system as it related to the market economy in the realm of international policy and procedures, for instance, with respect to the proper treatments in market access, tax collection and credit, sufficient transparency in administration, law enforcement. Furthermore, to encourage overseas investment to enter the Chinese market, the PRC adopted measures to improve its approval system and management. In short, China's entry into the WTO reflected its active participation in economic globalization as well as in international competition and cooperation.[41]

At the 21st-Century Forum, Premier Zhu Rongji argued that "China cannot develop without help from the world, just as the world cannot develop without China".[42]

> (China's) WTO entry can help (itself) to gain a more stable international economic and trade environment and enjoy the convenience of trade and investment liberalization. As the largest developing country in the world, China has a population of more than 1.2 billion. With its GDP ranking seventh and foreign trade ninth in the world, it is now an indispensable part of the global economy [...]. Without China's membership, the WTO is incomplete.[43]

By September 1999, among the world's top 500 transnational corporations, more than 100 had invested in China.[44] These included involvement in such businesses as automobile manufacturing, telecommunications, petroleum, banking, insurance, space and aviation, electronics, computers, medicine and biology and industry and agriculture.[45] The great impact of China's new WTO membership was the increased confidence of the global business community in China's continued economic growth. In the year 2002, China attracted a record US$52.7 billion in FDI and US$620 billion in foreign trade.[46]

Jiang's Private Economy and the Effects of WTO Membership

Thanks to the peaceful and stable international environment, at the end of 1999 and the beginning of 2000, China was in a position to sign the agreements on its accession to the WTO with the United States and the European Union respectively. China's WTO membership also promised to open its markets to foreign companies. Entrepreneurs in China, now an official WTO member, were in a position to compete on an equal footing in both national and international markets. As a result of the Chinese government's relaxation of policies, the previously restricted sectors to overseas investment and domestic private capital were now accessible to them. The agreement with the WTO also meant the progressive elimination of quotas in export markets such as textiles and shoes. Further, the development of its newer private industries has helped the sectors with modern factory techniques and large-scale production units, which competitors in even lower-cost manufacturing countries could not match. China's next stage of development will see enormous potential for improved distribution of and logistics related to a wide range of domestic private industries, from agriculture to banking, insurance retailing and marketing, in which they have to face foreign competition. Needless to say, the opening up of these Chinese sectors will lead to improvement in the efficiency of these services.

The Chinese leadership has encouraged small- and medium-sized and private businesses, because they create jobs. In addition, they have changed the finance, tax and accounting systems to support the creation of new jobs.[47] However, the impact of globalization on China's continual reform and on the privatization of state-owned enterprises will subsequently increase the numbers of displaced workers, who will have to fend for themselves in the absence of adequate social security.[48]

New policies were formulated that business mergers, acquisitions and failures would be regulated strictly by the market.[49] The Financial and Securities Institute of Renmin University of China predicted that with further opening up of its economy, the post-WTO PRC would see a large number of enterprises engaged in mergers and acquisitions during the period 2001–2010.[50] Large-scale mergers and acquisitions can help enlarge the scale of Chinese enterprises and upgrade the industry optimizing the allocation of resources and improving the overall quality of the Chinese economy.[51]

The further strengthening of legal protections will be critical in eradicating graft in the Chinese market, thereby preventing official corruption while allowing private businesses to flourish. Post-WTO China will likely continue to evolve into a modern market economic structure based on the legal system, with more efficient allocation of capital, less government intervention and improved corporate governance. Nicholas Lardy of the Brookings Institution, the Washington-based economic research organization, considered that China's current reform program will eventually "lead to a more efficient system of resource allocation and utilization".[52]

In sum, Jiang's idea of "retaining a dominant position for public ownership with diverse forms of ownership development side by side" was considered "a fairly developed market-oriented economy", for which the central government allowed foreign and private investors to take control of the SOEs. In addition, in speeding up the process of privatization of the SOEs, Jiang's "people" became dominated by the capitalists and professionals. Post-WTO China continued to evolve into a modern market economic structure based upon the legal system, with more efficient allocation of capital, less government intervention and approved corporate governance.

Other Objectives of the Ninth Five-Year Plan of 1996–2000

The 9th FYP period was to fulfill the quadrupling the 1980 GNP thereby enabling the population to lead a fairly comfortable life. The main objective in the proposal for the year 2010 was to double the 2000 GNP thereby enabling the people of the nation to lead an even more comfortable life. However, in 1995, the Chinese were confident that, due to extensive efforts carried out during the three five-year plans since the 1980s, the original target of quadrupling the 1980 GNP by 2000 would be fulfilled ahead of schedule in 1995. Indeed this original target was fulfilled in 1996.

To speed up economic and social development in the 9th FYP, the following were among the major principles adopted during the previous five-year plans since the 1980s.

(1) To ensure a strong agricultural base to suit the growing needs for farm products as a result of the country's increasing population,
(2) To strengthen primary industries, adjust and upgrade secondary industry and boost tertiary industry,
(3) To use science and education to revitalize the country and at the same time to integrate the economy with science, technology and education,
(4) To persist in efforts to open the country to the outside world,
(5) To adhere to the coordinated development of the regional economies and to gradually narrow the gap in the development of different localities.

The Jiangist Rural Economic Reform

Agriculture, which supports more than half of the country's population, accounts for less than 16 per cent of the GDP. As has been well known, to guarantee national food security and stabilize grain prices, the central government directed farmers to sell part of their grain harvests to state agencies at a guaranteed price, which was usually higher than the market rate. The government then paid the agencies the price difference. This arrangement led to excess stocks and rampant corruption, however. Farmers also seldom got the price they deserved for their produce thus worsening rural poverty. With the introduction of a new direct-subsidy scheme, the central government aimed to improve the lot of rural families by directly subsidizing them cash rather than forcing them to go through procurement agencies. However, the plan, aimed at grain farmers, only benefited a few and failed to address the root problems of excessive agricultural taxes.

In March 2003, Premier Wen Jiabao reintroduced his predecessor Zhu Rongji's taxes-for-fees reform, which was aimed at standardizing the rural tax system and abolishing a wide range of fees imposed on farmers by local officials.[53] Zhu's reform had resulted in an average 30 per cent reduction on average of farmers' financial burden, though the complex reform of the fees system could take as long as a decade to complete.[54]

Tapping China's "Reserve Strength" in its Central and Western Regions

Uneven development in differing regions was a basic condition in the reforming PRC. Although economic reforms brought about overall growth in the economy, there were regional variations. Reforms generally achieved better results in the SEZs designated for foreign investment. Having de-emphasized Maoist egalitarianism, Deng Xiaoping's strategy was to make some regions well off first, which, in turn, would help develop inland China. During the 9th FYP period, emphasis was placed on the development of the central and western parts of the country. This was to slow down the widening of regional disparities and narrow the gap.

In February 2000, the Chinese government announced its decision to shift the focus of economic development from the eastern coastal provinces to the western regions. The area covers 5.4 million square kilometers, that is, about 56 per cent of China's total land mass and is home to 23 per cent of its population. They are comprised of the six provinces of Shaanxi, Gansu, Qinghai, Schuan, Yunnan and Guizhou, the three autonomous regions of Ningxia, Xingjiang and Tibet, and the Chongqing Municipality, which is under the direct administration of the Central Government. This development scheme was "to tap the reserve strength" in these regions, which, the Chinese claim, possess rich natural resources, plentiful labor power, low investment costs and tremendous market potential.[55] They estimated that in the 21st century, about 60 per cent of the raw materials and 50 per cent of the energy needed by the industries in the eastern coastal provinces would be from these central and western regions.[56]

While the eastern coastal areas developed fast during the period 1979–2000, the central and western regions clearly lagged behind. While the former contributed 65 per cent of the national GDP in the late 1990s, the latter achieved only 15 per cent.[57]

In November 1999, Premier Zhu Rongji recalled that in the 1980s, Deng Xiaoping advanced the strategy of "two major concerns" in China's modernization drive.[58] It was first to develop the eastern coastal areas beginning in 1979, and then the central and western areas by the turn of the century. This was Mao Zedong's original development strategy, formulated in his celebrated "Ten Major Relationships" in April 1956. The second major relationship Mao emphasized was the relationship between industry in the coastal regions and industry in the "interior". Mao's argument was that "(m)aking good use of the old industries in the coastal regions and developing their capacities will put us in a stronger position to promote and support industry in the interior".[59] This was because

> In the past our industry was concentrated in the coastal regions [...]. About 70 per cent of all our industry [...] is to be found in the coastal regions and only 30 per cent in the interior. This irrational situation is a product of history [...]. (B)ut, to even out the distribution of industry as it develops, we must strive to promote industry in the interior.[60]

According to Mao, to realize this "reserve strength", "the basic policy" would optimally "mobilize all positive factors, internal and external".[61] Mao's positive factors, internal and external, were "internally, the workers and the peasants as the basic forces and, externally all the forces that can be united with must be united". In short, according to Mao, "we should mobilize all forces, whether direct or indirect, and strive to make China a powerful socialist country".[62]

Inspired by Mao's industry-oriented development plan, the Dengist modernization strategy was announced in December 1978. This was first to focus on the development of the eastern coastal regions. In 2000, about 20 years after the PRC had introduced the opening of the country and reform, the government decided to begin the economic development of the central and western regions. According to Premier Zhu Rongji's government work report of the 2000 NPC session, the government aimed to meet the following major objectives with the market economy mechanism:

- implementing pro-active financial policies,
- speeding up the construction of the infrastructures,
- strengthening the protection of the ecological environment,
- developing science, technology, and education, and
- absorbing investment from the eastern regions, which had been moderately developed in the year 2000.[63]

Economic Performance and the Resultant Abuse of Power, Inflation and Corruption

In the light of the relatively peaceful and stable international environment conducive to his scheme of opening up the country to the outside world, in 1971 Mao initiated his relaxed policies to improve the livelihood of the people in the real term. As a result, China's successful structural transformation of its economy in the post-Mao 1980s and early 1990s impressed the world. In the period 1984–1985, foreign trade and local industry increased 68 and 59.6 per cent respectively, including the substantial growth of domestic services.[64] Improvements in the standard of living were noted in both rural and urban areas. China's annual GDP growth rate averaged 9.8 per cent during the period 1979–1992, reminiscent of Japan's high growth period.[65]

However, with the previously sacrosanct tenet of selflessly serving and uniting with the collective giving way to the Western capitalist concepts of liberalism and material incentives, new problems began to appear in the early 1980s. The negative aspects associated with the PRC's economic reforms, particularly corruption, were felt nationwide. In the mid-1980s, as market forces gathered momentum, abuse of power and corruption rose dramatically alongside a worsening inflation crisis. Economic reforms had created opportunities for government officials to "use power for personal gain". Illegally charging excessive fees, collecting commissions and seeking unjustifiable benefits were common in the police force, educational institutes, at news agencies and in the public health sectors.[66] Corruption increased among the government officials, many of whom were the top officials of organizations and agencies of the government and the Party. The result was the erosion of popular confidence leading to the mass demonstrations in Beijing and many other cities in May and June of 1989.

Bernstein argues that the reforms strengthened rather than weakened the old networks of administrative and personal relationships.[67] Local authorities and the enterprises, he continues, used the power given to them by the central government "in ways not corresponding to central goals" but to personal gains.[68] Corruption has reportedly been prevalent in most all the economic and administrative sectors of the Party and government, since the beginning of the Dengist period.[69] Bernstein even further argues that local officials colluding with enterprise managers "focused on growth rather than on efficiency resulting in highly inflationary local investment rates".[70] The expansion of local economic power therefore contributed to the massive inflation experienced in China.

Among the peasantry, farmers' incomes rose rapidly because of the rise of productivity in agriculture. By the mid-1980s, the peasants could also make additional money in non-agricultural enterprises. While the prices of major agricultural goods were officially set at 1979–1981 level, those of the industrial commodities rose dramatically. The resultant inflation spiral led to a chain reaction in other sectors nation-wide. According to official records, a massive inflationary trend in the country in 1985–1988 meant that prices increased by 8.8 per cent in 1985, 6 per cent in 1986, 7.3 to 7.9 per cent in 1987 and 20 per cent in 1988.[71] Inflation was rampant in 1988. With panic buying and withdrawals of low-interest savings in many major cities, it reached 30 per cent and unofficial estimates were even higher.[72] Inflation affected the intellectuals and professionals on fixed salaries much more than the peasants and entrepreneurs. Despite the leadership's fight against rampant inflation through price reform in 1988, it continued to be an acute problem well into the first half of the 1990s.

However, the World Bank reported a major victory in its continued battle against inflation in late 1995. This victory, due to the central government's macro-economic policies of administrative intervention, economic legislation and improved law enforcement, combined with a two-year old credit squeeze that began in 1993 and in centives to boost agricultural output particularly of grain, was hard won.[73]

China's rapid growth has resulted in dramatic transformation of its countryside, with fertile farmland turned into industrial estates. It has been common in this process for local officials to abuse their power inforcing farmers to give up their land for "public purpose". Often failing to pay compensation or share the fruits of development with the farmers, officials have later sold this land for huge profits. Abuse of power and corruption in fact has become so rampant that violent and bloody confrontations have often flared up. For instance, thousands of villages of Qiaoxiang near Dongguan city in Guangdong province, reportedly took to the streets in January 2002, demanding that authorities report on alleged graft on the part of officials in relation to land-lease profits.[74] In another instance in Changping country, villagers accused officials of reaping more than 100 million yuan over the period 1992–2002 in dubious land deals.[75]

In October 1987, Zhao Ziyang's proposal to the 13th Party Congress concerning a new economic mechanism that would ensure that "the state regulates the market and the market guides the enterprises" worsened the abuse of power and corruption in the urban areas. Cheng argues that this was due to the absence of an effective market, which in turn gave rise to speculation, *guanxi* (networked ties), privileges and corruption.[76] The populace at large considered abuse of power from top down for private benefits more harmful than inflation. It was common knowledge that family members of high-ranking officials assumed positions within the administrative scope of their parents or spouses. Further, Party leaders used their influence to give their children opportunities to study abroad, while their children were also able to establish lucrative businesses in large cities or Hong Kong.[77]

In 1990, the Party stepped up its anti-corruption drive. Reportedly, as a result of the drive, about one-third of a million offenders were arrested in its first 18 months of operation.[78] In addition, in 1992, the Supreme People's Procuratorate instituted a system that encouragd the general public to come forward with information concerning corruption or abuse of power.[79] Over 80 per cent of the 1.03 million cases reported involving embezzlement or bribery were investigated.[80] According to the CCP Central Commission for Discipline Inspection, among those punished in 1999, 17 were ministerial-level officials, and more than 4,400 were responsible for bureaus, prefectures, departments and division offices.[81] In addition, China closed 110 illegal pharmaceutical markets and 7,594 pharmaceutical plants in 1999 and investigated 8,745 related cases of malpractice.[82] Further, about 20,000 illegal companies run by the PLA, the People's Armed Police, the police and legal departments were shut down.[83] Despite all this, according to Wei Jianxing, Secretary of the CCP Central commission for Discipline Inspection, rampant corruption was still to be curbed effectively. The situation remained serious.[84]

The CCP continued to carry out its anti-corruption drive targeting the top echelons of the Party which lead to the executions of a number of senior officials at central and provincial level.[85] Official figures showed that 175,364 cadres were investigated for corruption in the year 2001.[86] Vowing to investigate and prosecute corrupt cadres, Premier Zhu Rongji renewed his scathing attack on corruption and extravagance on the part of officials in his Fourth Report to the NPC in March 2002.[87] In addition to the law of the existing Central Commission for Discipline Inspection, a new law enacted in March 2002 required governments at or above county level to establish separate accounts to deal with financial management at the grassroots level in order to reduce embezzlement and other fraud.[88]

Ke Lin warned in September 1997 that corruption on the part of officials had become a rapidly developing cancer in Chinese society in spite of the CCP's claimed efforts to fight this fraud.[89] It might become the CCP's Achilles' heel if it grew complacent. In his report at the 15th NPC in mid-September 1997, General Secretary Jiang admitted that corruption, extravagance and waste were still proliferating.[90] Speaking at the closing ceremony of the NPC in April 1996, Qiao Shi vowed to punish corrupt officials.[91] In the presence of widespread corruption particularly at higher levels, it is difficult to tap people's power in the course of advancing the four modernizations.

In keeping the public sector alive, China will probably become a fairly developed market-oriented economy, with socialist public ownership gradually supplanted by different types of ownership. In a step toward speeding up the process of privatization of the SOEs, the central government designated its control to the foreign and private investors. In speeding up this process, Jiang's "people" were now dominated by capitalists, entrepreneurs and professionals. The Jiang Zemin Thought was adopted "to keep pace with the times" with respect to international trends of private economy and, more importantly, economic globalization. The Chinese economy became not only a more capitalist model, but also aimed for integration into the globalized economic system through WTO membership. Economic globalization had created a worldwide market, which provided the mechanisms for all countries to compete in the same market using the rules of the market economic system. China's entry into the WTO in December 2001 thus reflected its active participation in economic globalization and in international competition and cooperation. the PRC's WTO membership helped to promote its reform process and to enhance its modern market-oriented enterprise system based on the rules of law with more efficient allocation of capital, less government intervention and improved corporate governance. Because of the increasingly improved investment environment and foreign direct investment, China witnessed a sustained and sharp increase in recent years particularly from North America, Western Europe and the Asia-Pacific economic "dragons". China also continued to import hi-tech from the US-led Western world. All of this was enhanced by Jiang's vigorous efforts to promote regional and global peace and stability as would be conducive to the country's continued modernization drive.

As in the case of the previous five-year plans, the Ninth FYP was formulated to aim with the goal of continuing the modernization revolution, with particular attention to developing the central and western regions and to combating the negative consequences of the economic reforms such as rural poverty, unemployment and corruption.

Chapter Nine
China in the New Century

The main emphasis of the PRC's economic reform and open-door policy has been to promote economic development, a trend which presently continues with even greater force. Deng Xiaoping aimed at "quadrupling economic production by the end of the 20th century and achieving a better living standard of the population overall". He devised a three-step strategy for the country's modernization drive with the following objectives:

1. Doubling the per-capita GNP of 1980 (about US$250) and solving the problems of food and clothing for the people in ten years, starting from the beginning of the 1980s;
2. Redoubling the per-capita GNP to reach US$800–US$1,000 in ten years from the early 1990s to 2000, basically eliminating poverty and enabling the people to live a fairly comfortable life; and
3. Reaching the per-capita GNP level of moderately developed countries by the mid-21st century and basically accomplishing modernization.[1]

During his thirteen-year leadership, Jiang Zemin successfully transformed Deng's development strategy from the PRC's planned-cum-market economy to one based on market forces. By the end of 2002, China had accomplished the first two steps of Deng's three-step strategy. During the past two decades, the PRC has maintained an average real GNP growth of 9.5 per cent, demonstrating the continued expansion of the economy, more rapidly than that in the Newly Industrialized Economies, though less so than in Taiwan during its start-up period. The Guangdong province has done even better. During the period 1979–1996, China's real GNP rose five times from US$150 billion to US$750 billion.[2] The State Council reported that it had 250 million people living in dire poverty in 1978, but the number was reduced to 42 million in 1999.[3] The strengthening of the economy has thus brought about significant improvements in its standard of living.

Housing as a Verifiable Factor of Improvement in the People's Livelihood

As noted above, due to extensive efforts carried out during the three five-year plans since the 1980s, the original target of quadrupling the 1980 GNP by 2000 was fulfilled in 1996. The main target of the proposal for the year 2010 was to double the 2000 GNP, thereby enabling the people to lead an even more comfortable life. China's economy in terms of liberalization, internationalization and privatization will eventually converge progressively with those of the neighboring NIEs.

The PRC's economic reform and opening-up to the outside world have continued relentlessly. The strengthening of the economy, which has resulted in significant improvement in the people's livelihood overall, can be verified particularly in the rural as well as urban housing.

Before 1978, low investment in housing and the spiraling growth of the population made housing shortage one of its severest social problems.[4] Since 1979, local governments and enterprises have invested heavily in urban housing construction, while rural housing development has boomed.[5] However, the proportion of investment from individuals in both rural and urban areas has always been small.[6]

Prior to 1978, about 100 million square meters of new houses were built for the peasants each year. However, during the period 1981–1985, this figure increased dramatically to some 3.2 billion square meters.[7] The quality of these newly built houses greatly improved with better-structured elements to replace adobe walls, thatched roofs and paper-pasted windows.[8] In 1991, however, more than 85 per cent of the new houses were built of bricks, tiles, and prefabricated cement materials.[9] In 1980, only 3 per cent of the new houses were two- or more-storeyed buildings; but the figure shot up to 37.4 per cent in 1989.[10]

During the Sixth FYP of 1981–1985, the newly built urban houses accounted for 48 per cent of the total building area for the period 1950–1985, while those in the rural areas amounted to 47 per cent of the total houses for the same period.[11] The *Beijing Review* quoted the data released by the United Nations that China led the world during the period 1979–1993 in terms of both the volume of housing completed and growth in per-capita floor space.[12]

Despite all this, the standard of housing remained low in the late 1980s, with a quarter of China's population suffering from insufficient housing. The problem, however, was given top priority in the 1990s, as approved by the Fourth Session of the Seven National People's Congress in the Ten Year Program, and the Eighth FYP of 1991–1995 for the national economic and social development.[13]

Although the government provided urban housing as a welfare service until the late 1980s, a new privatization policy to sell half of the country's 2.4 billion square meters of public housing on the market was formulated in 1980 to improve the people's livelihood.[14] The central government's goal of this housing reform strategy was to convert the heavily subsidized housing industry into a self-financing venture.[15] The PRC's investment in its value-added construction was Rmb 550 billion (US$67 billion) in the 1990s. This contributed about 1.4 billion square meters of buildings under construction, with about 600 million square meters completed each year.[16] Much of the urban residential portion of this construction was to replace old and dangerous housing, though it also involved more than 200 large, new housing estates each year.[17] Further reform in the year 2000 involved housing subsidies, housing loans, selling of government-owned apartments, supplying apartments for families with different levels of income and improving the housing market mechanism.[18] More importantly, this policy of urban housing privatization was to slow down the spending spree on consumer durables, while encouraging the people to buy their own homes.[19]

In the countryside, all houses were and still are privately built and owned. However, in the cities, almost all housing was built and maintained with state funds and then rented out at a very low cost of about 3 per cent of the tenant's monthly income.[20] During the period 1981–1987, the country spent about 25 per cent of its total fixed asset investment on housing construction.[21] In 1991, the per-capita building floor space in the rural areas was about 20 square meters and the living space an average of 17.8 square meters. The farmers had better living conditions than the urban residents.[22] Generally, they profited from the diversified economy and the household contract responsibility system with remuneration linked to output, introduced in 1979. Thus, as farmers' income increased, the construction of rural housing boomed. The *Beijing Review* reported that farmers spent a total of about RMB 64 billion on building houses in 1988, and that an average of 700 million square meters of new houses were built each year after 1979.[23] By 1991, half of the rural households had moved into new houses.[24]

Although the per-capita living space in the peasantry expanded greatly, the heating, drinking water and hygiene facilities lagged behind the urban centers. In 1991, 90 per cent of the rural villages still lacked running water, and 30 per cent were without electricity.[25]

By the end of 1992, China had established a total of 11,985 towns. The country planned to transform 20 per cent of them into modern towns featuring improved housing conditions, convenient transport facilities, complete infrastructure and so on.[26] The emerging modern towns were aimed at promoting overall social-economic development among the peasantry.[27]

In 1995, a five-year national drive called the "Green China" project was proposed to provide a clean and healthy environment for the cities.[28] Through the project, the urban sewage disposal rate was to be raised from 17 per cent in 1995 to 25 per cent by the year 2000.[29] At the same time, a five-year program from 1996 to 2000 was initiated to treat urban domestic refuse and improve the technology for cleaning up public areas in the cities.[30]

In the next thirty years, China will face a rapid growth in demand for housing both in quality and quantity. The Ministry of Construction (MC) has estimated that 1.2–1.5 billion square meters of housing will be built yearly over the next three decades.[31] The huge demand comes from better living standard of the people, increased per-capita floor space, the growing population and increasing urbanization.

The MC's plan is that China would continue to strive in the first decade of the twenty-first century to improve the quality of housing projects.[32] Efforts would be made to ensure energy-saving and high-tech applications in housing construction and to establish a standardized system for the use of building materials.[33]

An Emerging Economic Giant

The PRC introduced its latest economic reform concerning its emerging private sector as that sector seemed to be the major driving force for the economy, and the government realized that it was difficult to sustain growth with state expenditure.[34] Jiang proposed to gradually deregulate interest rates to help the private sector to develop and state-owned commercial banks to reform. This was to allow interest rates to be decided by market forces.[35] According to Jiang, strengthening regulations and preventing financial risks would provide better banking services for economic and social development.[36] All this ultimately was to nudge the economy towards a more capitalist model.

According to the *Business Week* magazine, by December 2002, the PRC's GDP had almost reached 80 per cent of that of the European Union, and would move "ahead of Europe by 2007".[37] This had helped fuel China's economic growth of 7.5 per cent following an 8 per cent increase in GDP in 2002 predicted by the World Bank.[38]

China's success in getting the whole world to help modernize the country can also be seen in several measures of trade and investment performance. Compared with only 9.7 per cent in 1978, China's trade was 27.6 per cent of its GNP value in 1988, with exports increasing by 25 per cent and imports by 23 per cent. Since the beginning of the 1990s, China has further opened up to the outside world bringing about higher growth of foreign trade. It was forecasted that to imported goods would be worth US$287 billion in 2003 as against US$324 billion of exports, thus producing a trade surplus of US$37 billion.[39] Its huge construction and infrastructure programs, for instance, have spurred its domestic growth of imports. The country became the world's biggest steel importer, taking over from the United States, with imports totaling 25 million metric tons in the first nine months of 2002.[40]

China's foreign exchange reserves in the last quarter of 1999 stood at US$154.675 billion, the second largest in the world.[41] In February 2006, the PRC overtook Japan as the world's largest holder of foreign currencies, with reserves of US$853.7 billion.[42]

With its greatly improved investment environment and its WTO membership, China's foreign direct investment has witnessed a sustained and sharp increase in recent years particularly from North America, Western Europe, and the five economic "dragons".[43] In addition to the industrial sector, foreign investors have accelerated their activities in the banking, insurance, service and commerce fields. Richard Wagoner, CEO of industry leader General Motors, has said, "no globalization program of a business is realizable without a resolute China strategy".[44] In the last decade, China attracted US$411 billion in direct foreign investment.[45] By the end of the second quarter of 2002, it had already received paid-in investment of US$412.15 billion.[46] Since 1992, foreign capital inflow has risen on an unprecedented scale in its history. During the period 1997–2002, it ranked first in using foreign direct investment among developing countries and second in the world.[47] Foreign investment has driven the process of internationalization of the Chinese economy. In 2002, reportedly more than 26,000 investment contracts were signed with foreign companies with a record inflow of funds amounting to US$52.7 billion, an increase of 12.5 per cent over 2001.[48] This is in contrast to Japan's situation and problems faced by other regional economies since the East Asian crisis of 1997. Reportedly in 2002, the PRC was the global chief executives' preferred country for direct investment, which surpassed the United States for the first time.[49] In 2004, Chinese official data indicated that the nation's FDI was US$60.6 billion.[50] The reported rationale was that for companies facing an economic downturn and stiff international competition, the combination of a local market of 1.4 billion people, low operating costs, lower labour costs and advancing technology had proved irresistible.[51] The Vice-Chairman of the State Trade and Economic Commission reported that China would be opening up the economy even further, and improve its investment-related legislation and the investment environment, as well as putting more effort into priority industries especially into the infrastructure and high-tech industry.[52]

China will continue to seek direct investments from the US-led West. It is not so much the capital *per se* that it needs, but the technology that is associated with foreign direct investments from the Western world. Since 1979, the PRC has acquired most of the technology imports from the advanced Western countries, particularly the United States, West Germany, Britain, France and Japan. It has also sent more students abroad to enhance the process of technology transfer. During the period 1978–1998, about 320,000 Chinese students and research scholars were in 103 countries studing or researching in almost all subjects.[53] The PRC's institutes of higher learning have also invited foreign experts to give lectures and conduct cooperative research and joint training of postgraduates. For instance, in 1997, Chinese universities invited about 3,700 foreign experts and lecturers.[54]

In November 1995, the country mapped out a development plan for science and technology for the period 1996–2000. There was another plan for the period 1996–2010 in which research in agriculture was to be given top priority.[55] High-tech projects were to be boosted for large- and medium-sized enterprises.[56] According to the Asian Development Bank, China is "the workshop of the world" for computers and cars.[57] The PRC's largest outputs in 2002 were electronic goods and products from the motor industry, having taken over from Japan as the world's second biggest producer of electronic hardware.[58]

International business giants, such as Microsoft, Intel, Lucent, and HP have established more than 120 R&D (research and development) institutions in the PRC.[59] Thus, the US *Fortune* magazine has listed the PRC as a rising global technological center.[60] Furthermore, establishing regional headquarters or operational centers in China responsible for coordinating and supervising their markets in the region have been another trend among the multinationals. A 2002 survey by *Fortune* magazine showed that about 92 per cent of the world's leading enterprises planned to establish regional headquarters in China in the near future.[61] Singapore's Lee Kuan Yew has also predicted that in the next three decades, China will still need huge amounts of Western capital, technology, and know-how.[62]

At the beginning of the new century, it seems that Chinese consumers are driving the Asian region and stimulating the whole global economy, according to the *Time* Magazine.[63] It concluded in December 2002 that China was in the process of filling the role in Asia once played by Japan whose loans, investment, and consumer spending had helped lift Asia out of poverty.[64]

Conclusion

With the stable and peaceful international political environment, the PRC's economic reform based on Western market economic principles and its opening of the economy to the outside world have promoted economic development and continues in full swing. The strengthening of the economy has brought about significant improvements in the people's housing in both urban and rural areas and in their livelihood overall – the prime mover for furthering China's modernization revolution.

Chapter Ten
Concluding Remarks

This work contends that each of Mao's twin national development models was designed based on a unique set of international conditions.

Firstly, Mao's post-World War II perception of the world led to his conception of a strategy for the new PRC's national development. With the post-war United States as China's primary enemy and the Soviet Union as its *de facto* enemy in his worldview, Mao's collectivization scheme, which was aimed at "wiping out capitalism", became central to the country's defense-oriented development scheme of communization. Therefore, power politics was a vital determinant of his approach to China's development program. This meant that, in response to the pressures of the US and Soviet superpowers, singly or in unison, during the period 1950–1970, his communization project, based upon the anti-Japanese Yenan experience as a prototype, was intimately related to the hostile international environment.

Having completed his cooperativization scheme in 1957, Mao accelerated his communization endeavors. His commune, in which he developed organizational and leadership techniques for linking military efforts and rural economic and social activities in a basic program of mobilization to penetrate to every village and every family, involved every individual. Therefore, Mao's economic-social-defense strategy was a political solution designed to face China's external enemies. Although his GLF was an economic disaster, Mao's mobilization of the masses against imperialism with one mind was impressive.

Therefore this study argues that characteristic of the period 1950–1970 was Mao's aim to inspire a quarter of mankind to generate the will power to "wipe out capitalism". This was the crucial prerequisite to his communization goal, a tool for "removing the mountain of imperialism". The mass line strategy he devised for this great task, which required the moral incentive of "serving the people", was to "unite all who can be united". His aim of creating a selfless communist man was based on the same argument of "uniting all who can be united" in confronting the imperialist primary enemy or "the superpower enemies in collusion". Moreover, the unparalleled emphasis on mass movements and class struggle for the purpose of maintaining the people's ideological integrity was to combat a revival of capitalism and bureaucracy, both of which could not unite the masses for his anti-imperialist task. Thus, Mao's collectivization goal was ultimately aimed at materializing his defense-oriented communization system.

However, the Liuist onslaughts on Mao's collectivization drive were detrimental to his mass line strategy in the face of the hostile international climate. The origins of his Cultural Revolution can be traced to the Liuist onslaughts. Liu Shaoqi's "rightist" and "revisionist" approaches, which were purely economically oriented, neglected the then crucial power politics. Mao felt that Liu had ignored the cold hard fact that in Mao's worldview the Soviet Union had emerged as China's *de facto* enemy after 1950 and became "the accomplice of the US primary enemy" during the period 1958–1969.

However, the year 1971 saw the beginning of the transformation of Mao's worldview in which the United States was replaced by the Soviet Union as the primary enemy, and became a non-antagonistic secondary enemy. With the new international environment conducive to his scheme of opening the country to the outside world, Mao began to adopt his relaxed economic policy "to improve the livelihood of the people". This national primary task was Mao's second model of development in action. As a consequence, Mao needed to discard the element of moral incentive and introduce that of material incentive in China's economic development. A budding Western-styled economic approach was adopted in the period 1971–1976. consequently, Mao's consistent strains of class struggle and aspirations for a more egalitarian society, which both aimed at "uniting with all possible" against the United States in collusion with the Soviet Union, were no longer relevant. Likewise, his tenet of "serving the people" and his aim of making a communist man, which contradicted his new policy, eventually had to be abolished. He began to activate his four modernizations scheme to acquire United States-led Western capital and modern technology together with capitalist economic principles. His modernization initiatives, as spelled out in the Fourth FYP of 1971–1975, were primarily related to the favorable international environment.

Agriculture was related to the growth of light and heavy industry, and the precondition for the gigantic modernization task was to improve the livelihood of over 80 per cent of the Chinese peasantry. With his strategy of "walking on two legs", Mao organized the whole population to carry out his modernization revolution.

Mao's approach inspired the post-Mao leadership to continue to organize a quarter of mankind to carry out the modernization revolution in phases for "ten thousand generations". During Deng Xiaoping's time, the international situation was primarily different from that of the Maoist period 1950–1970. With a peaceful and stable international environment, post-Mao economic development in the real sense was possible by relying on the application of vital US-led Western economic principles enhanced by Sino–Western trade. Deng's economic reform and opening up the country to the outside world as well as his "good neighborhood" policy were aimed at the acquisition of advanced science and technology plus the vital Western capital and Western-styled business and administrative management. Thus, the four modernizations scheme inherited from Mao called for the dismantling of the outdated commune system, and the abolition of the Maoist element of class struggle. Mao Zedong's "continuous revolution", which was aimed at preventing the comeback of Liuist "revisionism", also had to go.

Apart from its global strategy to continue maintaining normalized relations with the US-led West, Deng's "good-neighborliness" policy was aimed at promoting regional peace and stability to create a new Asian economic miracle. This policy was eventually extended to include the South American and African continents and elsewhere. During Jiang's time, he made vigorous efforts in promoting global peace and stability conducive to China's continued modernization drive. In mid-1996, the Jiangist foreign policy included Russia as a "Strategic Partner for the 21st Century". As a result, the PRC emerged as a key player in the global economy, making the Dengist tenet of inducing the whole world to help modernize China possible. China's global economic strategy, however, would not have been successful without its market-oriented approach.

However, associated with Deng's "one country, two systems" policy which aimed at "peaceful reunification" with Taiwan and contradicts his "good neighborliness" policy vital to China's continued modernization revolution, Taiwan remains a thorny problem in Sino–US bilateral relations. Both formula and policy created two fronts which Mao would have avoided.

Deng's staunch Maoist "non-capitalist" strategy aimed at developing effective "productive forces". However, integrating public ownership with market economic principles but without encouraging privatization in enterprise reform, this staunch "non-capitalist" stance to prevent the growth of capitalism was not bold enough to reform the state-owned enterprises (SOEs), which had experienced heavy losses. Understandably therefore, Jiang Zemin subsequently allowed China's socialist public sector to gradually be dominated by different types of ownership. As a further step towards speeding up the process of privatization of the SOEs, the Jiangist government transferred its control over SOEs to foreign and private investors. As a result, Jiang's "people" were now dominated by the capitalists, private entrepreneurs, and professionals. The Jiang Zemin Thought was adopted "to keep pace with the times", that is, the popular international trend of the private economy and, more importantly, economic globalization. The economy took on not only a more capitalist model, but also helped integrate it into the globalized economic system with its World Trade Organization (WTO) membership. China's entry into the WTO in December 2001 reflected its active participation in economic globalization as well as international competition and cooperation. The post-WTO China has continued to progress toward a modern market economic structure based on the rules of law, with more efficient allocation of capital, less government intervention and approved corporate governance.

By rationalizing Mao's strategy of long-term modernization, the post-Mao Chinese leadership has truly brought about significant improvements in the people's livelihood. By the year 2000, the Chinese population had grown to around 1.3 billion, but the per-capita GNP had already quadrupled the figures for 1980; poverty was basically eliminated; and a quarter of mankind were enjoying relatively comfortable living standards.

In its influential 1996 annual publication *Asian Development Outlook*, the Asian Development Bank forecasted that with China's outstanding performance, the region was to grow 7.1 per cent in 1996 and 7.3 per cent in 1997, while the world economy would expand by 3.2 per cent and 3.5 per cent for the two years. During the period 1980–2002, according to the HSBC's 2003 *Premier* magazine, the world had grown accustomed to the PRC's role as a major exporting power, a magnet for foreign investment, and one of the fastest developing economies on the planet. It went on to emphasize that "China's transformation is leading the advanced sectors in the economy forward in a way which [...] will make the country even more of a powerhouse and enable it to rival Japan as the most significant economic force in Asia". With the continued development of modern industry, services, and the infrastructure, the biggest domestic market on earth, its huge power as an exporter and further reform in key sectors, the PRC has now emerged as a key player in the global economy. It seems that China's success story will change the "flying geese" theory, provided that its growth can be maintained. However, its strategy of inducing the whole world to help modernize the country would not have been successful without its market-oriented development policy.

In sum, this book has taken a holistic approach that, dictated by the hostile international climate at the time, Mao's economic development during the 1950–1970 period was not very successful in contrast with the impressive post-Mao modernization revolution initiated by Mao himself in 1971 when the international environment became relatively more peaceful and stable.

Notes

Chapter One
Introduction

1 Mao, *Selected Works of Mao Tsetung, Vol.III* (hereafter *SWIII*), [Beijing: Foreign Languages Press (hereafter FLP), 1967], p.254, p.268.
2 Chen, Jin (陈晋), ed., *Explaining Mao Zedong's Reading Notes, Vol.I*, (Shenzhen: Guangdong People's Press, 1996), p.588.
3 Mao, *SWV*, (Beijing: FLP, 1977), p.479.
4 Lam, Lai Sing, *Mao Tse-tung's Purposive Contention with the Superpowers* (hereafter *Book I*), (Lewiston/Queenston/Lampeter: Mellen University Press, 1995), p.86, p.97.
5 Chen, Jin, op.cit., p.588.
6 Mao's notes as a result of his reading the section on socialism, that is, "The time alloted for achieving socialism" in the *Textbook of Political Economics*, see *Mao Zedong Si Xiang Wan Sui* (hereafter *Wan Sui*), (Beijing: 1967), p.194.
7 *People's Daily* (hereafter *PD*), (Beijing: April 20, 1962), p.1.
8 Zhou, Enlai, *Selected Works of Zhou Enlai*, (Beijing: FLP, 1989), p.427.
9 Ibid., p.504.
10 Ibid., p.458; see also *PD*, (Beijing: December 31, 1964), p.1.
11 *New China News Agency* (hereafter *NCNA*), (Beijing: January 20, 1975).
12 Zhou, Enlai, op.cit., p.504; *PD*, (Beijing: January 21, 1975), p.1.
13 Zhou, Enlai, "Marching Towards the Splendid Goal of the Four Modernizations", op.cit., p.373.
14 *Peking Review* (hereafter *PR*), (Beijing: January 24, 1975), p.23.
15 Deng, Xiaoping, *DXP Wensuan 1975–82*, [(Hong Kong: People's Press and Joint Publishers (hereafter PP and JP), 1983], p.261.
16 Mao, *SWV*, (Beijing: FLP, 1977), p.419.
17 Deng, *Selected Works of Deng Xiaoping 1975–82* (hereafter *SW of DXP 1975–82*), (Beijing: FLP, 1983), p.280.
18 Mao, *SWV*, (Beijing: FLP, 1977), pp.287–9.
19 *The Party Documents*, 4th issue, (1993); see also Chen, Jin, op.cit., *Vol.I*, p.617.
20 Bernstein, Thomas P., "China: Change in a Marxist-Leninist State", in *Driven by Growth: Political Change in the Asia-Pacific Region*, ed., Morley, James W., (Armonk: M.E. Sharpe, Inc., 1993), p.41.
21 Chiou, C.L., *Maoism in Action: the Cultural Revolution*, (Brisbane: University of Queensland Press, 1974), p.67.

22 Ibid.
23 Mao, *Poems of Chairman Mao*, (Beijing: People's Literature Press, 1967), p.42.
24 Lam, Lai Sing, *Book I*, pp.83–4.
25 Ibid.
26 Mao, "Letter of August 23 1917 to Li Shaoxi", in Li Rui (李锐), "The Thought Direction of the Young Mao Zedong", in *Li Shi Yan Jiu Monthly*, (Beijing: January 1979), p.36.
27 Li Rui, ibid., 100; see also Mao, *Mao Tse-tung's Works*, (毛泽东集) (hereafter *Works*), *Vol.I*, ed., The Research Section of Chinese Communism, (Hong Kong: I Shan Press, 1976), p.53, pp.57–69.
28 The first four issues of the *Xiang Jiang Review*, (July 1919); see also Li Rui, *Comrade Mao Zedong's Early Revolutionary Activities*, (Beijing: Chinese Youth Press,1957), p.100, p.103.
29 Hammond, Ed, "Marxism and the Mass Line", in *Modern China*, *Vol.4, no.1*, (Beverly Hill: SAGE Publications, January 1978), p.16.
30 Mao, *Wan Sui*, (1967), p.128.
31 Mao, *SWIV*, (Beijing: FLP, 1954), p.111.
32 Hammond, Ed, op.cit., p.12.
33 Selden, Mark, "The Yenan Legacy: The Mass Line", in Barnett, A. Doak, ed., *Chinese Communist Politics in Action*, (Seattle: University of Washington Press, 1969), p.151.
34 Li, Ying (李颖), and Cheng, Meidong (程美东), ed., *Experiencing History With Mao Zedong* (与毛泽东一起感受历史), *Vol.II*, (Wuhan: Hubei People's Press, 2005), p.58.
35 Lam, Lai Sing, *The Role of Ch'i in Mao Tse-tung's Leadership Style* (hereafter *Book III*), (San Francisco: Mellen University Press, 1993), pp.104–5.
36 *PD*, (Beijing: New Year Day Editorial of January 1, 1968).
37 Lam, Lai Sing, *Book III*, p.205.
38 Mao, *Xiang Jiang Review*, in "A Periodical Introduction of the May 4th Period", Editing Section of the Works of Marx-Engels-Lenin-Stalin, ed., *Vol.I*, (Beijing: PP, 1958), p.145.
39 Mao, *SWII*, (Beijing: FLP, 1967), p.186.
40 Ibid. Nevertheless, it should be noted that in the anti-Japanese war as a whole the defensive and the counter-offensive were stages in which regular warfare was primary and guerilla warfare supplementary.
41 Lam, Lai Sing, *Book III*, p.148.
42 Ibid.
43 Ibid.
44 Ibid.
45 Ban Gu (班固), *Han Shu* (汉书) "Basic Biography", (Hong Kong: Chung Hua Press), p.1970.
46 Mao, *SWII*, (Beijing: FLP, 1967), p.26, p.247, pp.422–3.

47 This strategy was first brought out by Li Ding Ming (李鼎铭), Vice Chairman of the Border Areas, and was approved by the Central Committee of the CCP. See Mao, *SWIII*, (Beijing: PP, 1969), p.905.

48 Mao, *SWII*, (Beijing: FLP, 1967), p.232.

49 Lam, Lai Sing, *Book III*, p.155.

50 Ibid.

51 Mao, *SWIV*, (Beijing: FLP, 1961), p.150.

52 Ibid., pp.159–61.

53 This was with the exception of the period 1950–3 in which the new PRC's development policy was largely Soviet-dictated.

54 *PD*, editorial, (Beijing: February 9, 1979).

55 Deng's words in his conversation with officials in Shanghai during his "Southern Inspection Tour". This was recorded in the Macau TV series *The Hundred Years of Deng Xiaoping* (百年小平), 10.15–11.00 p.m., October 8, 2004. Mao, *SWV*, (Beijing: FLP, 1977), pp.473–4; see also Deng, *SW of DXP 1975–82*, (Beijing: FLP, 1983), p.58, p.141.

56 Deng, *SW of DXP 1975–82*, (Beijing: FLP, 1983), p.217.

57 In September 1953, Mao stated that "The transformation of capitalism into socialism is to be accomplished through state capitalism". See Mao, "The Only Road for the Transformation of Capitalist Industry and Commerce", *SWV*, (Beijing: FLP, 1977), p.112.

Chapter Two
Mao's Post-War Worldview
and the Defense-Oriented Collectivization Scheme

1 Mao, *SWIV*, (Beijing: FLP, 1967), p.99; also see Lam, Lai Sing, *Book I*, p.90.

2 Mao, *SWIV*, (Beijing: PP, 1969), pp.1089–90; also Lam, Lai Sing, ibid.

3 Ibid.

4 Mao, *Mao Zedong Si Xiang Wan Sui* (hereafter *Wan Sui*), (Beijing: 1969), p.239, p.256. Also Lam, Lai Sing, ibid., p.91

5 Mao, *SWIV*, (Beijing: PP, 1969), pp.1380–81.

6 Mao, *SWIV*, (Beijing: FLP, 1969), pp.448–9.

7 *People's Daily* (hereafter *PD*), (Beijing: April 13, 1950), p.1.

8 It should be noted that the principles, which governed Mao's worldview of US imperialism and later of social imperialism, had their origins in his worldview of the Japanese imperialism, which started World War II in East Asia. See Mao, *SWI*, (Beijing: PP, 1969), pp.232–3.

9 Garver, John W., "The Opportunity Costs of Mao's Foreign Policy Choices", in *The China Journal, no. 49*, (Canberra: Contemporary China Centre, Research School of Pacific and Asian Studies, The Australian National University, January 2003), p.128, p.129.

10 Salisbury, Harrison E., *The New Emperors: Mao and Deng, A Dual Biography*, (London: HarperCollins Publishers, 1992), p.85.

11 Ibid.

12 Garver, John W., op.cit., p.129.

13 Mao, *SWIV*, (Beijing: FLP, 1967), p.172.

14 Mao, *SWIV*, (Beijing: FLP, 1967), pp.425–9.

15 Ibid.

16 Mao, *SWIV*, (Beijing: FLP, 1967), p.426, p.433.

17 Mao, *Wan Sui*, (Beijing: 1969), p.164.

18 The interview took place on July 23, 1936. "When the people's revolution has been victorious in China, the Outer Mongolian Republic will automatically become a part of the Chinese federation at its own will". See Schram, Stuart R., *The Political Thought of Mao Tse-tung*, (New York: Frederick A. Praeger, 1963), p.419. Also Lam, Lai Sing, *Book I*, p.89.

19 Snow, Edgar, *Red Star Over China*, (New York: Grove Press, 1973), pp.444–5.

20 Ibid., p.396.

21 Snow, Edgar, *The Other Side of the River*, (London: Victor Gollancz Ltd., 1963), p.49.

22 Ibid.

23 Snow, Edgar, *Red Star Over China*, op.cit., pp.49–50.

24 Ibid.

25 Mongolian President Yumjaaglyn Tsedenbal related all this. See *Far Eastern Economic Review* (hereafter *FEER*), (Hong Kong: February 7, 1975), p.37.

26 Ibid.

27 Mao, *Wan Sui*, (Beijing: 1969), p.164.

28 *FEER*, (Hong Kong: February 7, 1975), p.37.

29 Ibid.

30 Salisbury, Harrison E., op.cit., p.13.

31 Mao, *Wan Sui*, (Beijing: 1969), p.164. Also see Mao, *Mao Zedong Wenji* (hereafter *Wenji*), *Vol.7*, (Beijing: PP, 1999), p.393.

32 Ibid., p.165.

33 Salisbury, Harrison E., op.cit., p.14.

34 Ibid., p.13. Also see Mao, *Wenji, Vol.7*, (Beijing: PP, 1999), pp.120–2, p.388.

35 This was a statement from Mao's former security guard, Chang Muqi (张木奇). Source: Phoenix Cable TV, Hong Kong, hosted by Lu Yu (鲁豫) (8.00–8.45 p.m., January 5, 2004).

36 Mao, *Wan Sui*, (Beijing: 1969), p.163.

37 Ibid.

38 Li, Ying, and Cheng, Meidong, op.cit., *Vol.I*, (Wuhan: Hubei People's Press, 2005), pp.455–6.
39 Khrushchev, Nikita, *Khrushchev Remembers: The Last Testament*, tran. and ed., Strobe Talbott, (Boston: Little Brown & Co., 1974), p.244.
40 Mao, *Wan Sui*, (Beijing: 1969), p.163.
41 Salisbury, Harrison E., op.cit., pp.107–15.
42 Snow, Edgar, *The Other Side of the River,* op.cit., p.654.
43 Garver, John W., op.cit., p.129.
44 Ibid., pp.112–3.
45 Ibid., pp.113–4.
46 Garver, John W., op.cit., p.131.
47 Mao, *Wenji, Vol.6*, (Beijing: PP, 1999), p.97.
48 Mao, *SWV*, (Beijing: FLP, 1977), p.82, p.117. Also see Welfield, John B., "Australia and Japan in the Sino-US Cold War, 1949–72, Some Notes and Observations", (Canberra: ANU Seminar, April 1974), p.6. Also see Lam, Lai Sing, *Book I*, p.86.
49 Welfield, John B., ibid.
50 Mao, *Wan Sui*, (Beijing: 1969), p.239; also see Lam, Lai Sing, *Book I*, p.91.
51 Ikira Iriye, *Across the Pacific: The Sino-American Crisis,* (Chicago: Imprint Publications, Inc., 1992), p.292.
52 *New York Times*, (New York: August 5, 1953), p.1, p.10.
53 Lam, Lai Sing, *Book I*, p.92.
54 *The Times*, (London: January 13, 1954), p.2.
55 Li, Ying, and Cheng, Meidong, *Vol.II,* op.cit., p.146.
56 *The Times*, (London: January 22, 1954), p.5.
57 Ibid.
58 *The Times*, (London: January 27, 1954), p.6.
59 Li, Ying, and Cheng, Meidong, *Vol.II,* op.cit., p.146.
60 Snow, Edgar, *The Other Side of the River*, op.cit., p.641.
61 *PD.*, (Beijing: November 19, 1957), p.1.
62 *PD,* (Beijing: April 12, 1955), p.1.
63 *PD*, [Beijing: (December 26, 1957), p.1; (December 28, 1957), p.5; (December 30, 1957), p.5; (December 3, 1958), p.1]. Also see Lam, Lai Sing, *Book I*, p.87.
64 *1967 Yearbook of Chinese Communism* (hereafter *1967 Yearbook*), (Taipei: Institute for the Study of Chinese Communist Problems, 1967), p.403.
65 *1967 Yearbook*, 403. This included the establishment of treaties of friendship and mutual non-aggression with 11 of these nations. China had already established (a) trade relationships with more than 50 nations, (b) cultural relationships with more than 50 nations and (c) aid commitments of US$970 million to 22 nations.
66 Mao, *SWII*, (Beijing: FLP, 1967), p.186.
67 Mao, "Refute Right Deviations Views That Depart from the General Line", *SW V*, (Beijing: FLP, 1977), p.93.

68 Mao, *SWV*, (Beijing: FLP, 1977), p.156.
69 Ibid., p.157.
70 Ibid.
71 Ibid. p.289.
72 Li, Ying, and Cheng, Meidong, *Vol.II,* op.cit., p.58; see also Li Yinqiao (李银桥), *Beside Mao Zedong for 15 Years* (在毛泽东身边 15 年), (Hong Kong: Cosmos Books Ltd, 1992), p.231.
73 Eckstein, Alexander, Galenson, Walter, and Liu, Ta-Chung, *Economic Trends in Communist China*, (Edinburgh: Edinburgh University Press, 1985), p.5. Also see Lam, Lai Sing, *Book II*, p.136.
74 Hsu, C.Y. Immanuel, *Rise of the Chinese People's Republic*, 5th edition, (New York: Oxford University Press, 1995), p.652.
75 Mao, *Wenji*, *Vol.6*, (Beijing: PP, 1999), p.183.
76 Ibid.
77 Ibid., pp.180–1, pp.214–5.
78 Mao, *SWV*, (Beijing: FLP, 1977), p.214. Also see Lam, Lai Sing, *Book II*, p.137.
79 Ibid.
80 Lam, Lai Sing, *Book III*, p.186.
81 Mao, *Wenji*, *Vol.6*, (Beijing: PP, 1999), p.420.
82 Ibid.
83 Part of this section depends on my published work *Mao Tse-tung's Ch'i and the Chinese Political Economy With Special Reference to the Post-Mao Modernization Revolution* (hereafter *Book II*), (Lewiston: The Edwin Mellen Press Ltd., 2000), pp.138–47.
84 Mao, *SWV*, (Beijing: PP, 1977), p.231.
85 Mao, *SWV*, (Beijing: FLP, 1977), p.29.
86 Ibid.
87 Mao, *Works, Vol.9*, (Hong Kong: I Shan Press, 1976), p.75.
88 Mao, *SWV*, (Beijing: FLP, 1977), p.254.
89 Ibid.
90 Gurley, John G., *China's Economy and the Maoist Strategy*, (New York: Monthly Review Press, 1976), p.212.
91 Mao, *SWIV*, (Beijing: FLP, 1967), p.203.
92 Mao, *SWV*, (Beijing: FLP, 1977), p.105.
93 Li, Ying, and Cheng, Meidong, *Vol.I*, op.cit., p.405.
94 Chi Chao-ting, "Capitalists Cross Over in China in Transition", in Oh, S.K., *Land Reform in Communist China and Postwar Japan*, PhD dissertation in International Relations, (Philadelphia: University of Pennsylvania, 1966), p.104.
95 Private businessmen were the targets of the Five-Antis Movement, which was designed to aim against bribery, tax evasion, theft of state assets, cheating in labor and materials and stealing state economic intelligence.
96 Oh, S.K., op.cit., pp.101–7.

97 Hughes, Trevor Jones, and Luard, Evan D.T., "The Economic Development of Communist China, 1949–58", pp.88–9, in Oh, S.K., op.cit., p.107.

98 Gurley, John G., op.cit., p.213.

99 Ibid.

100 Zhou Enlai, "Report on the Proposals for the Second Five Year Plan for the Development of the National Economy to the Eighth Party Congress", September 16, 1956, in Oh, S.K., op.cit., p.107.

101 Mao, *SWIII*, (Beijing: FLP 1967), pp.160–1, see note 4.

102 Wong, John, *Land Reform in the PRC: Institutional Transformation in Agriculture*, (New York: Praeger, 1973), p.218.

103 *PD*, (Beijing: April 10, 1952), p.1.

104 Mao, *SWI*, (Beijing: P.P., 1969), pp.110–1.

105 Mao, *SWI*, (Beijing: FLP, 1967), p.144.

106 Mao, *SWIII*, (Beijing: FLP, 1956), p.56.

107 It was doctrinairism of cadres – a kind of "subjectivism" – that Mao was primarily concerned about. To Mao, it was difficult for cadres to unite with the masses if they refused to recognize the objective realistic conditions of China that the peasant masses constituted the majority of the population. The reality was the peasant masses, which constituted the majority of the population.

The remnants of sectarianism were independence – "without considering the whole". Sectarianism was not compatible with Mao's strategy of "uniting with all possible" (Ibid., pp.47–8). Mao considered that "sectarian tendency" was where one "overbears in his relations with non-Party people, looks down on them, refuses to respect them or appreciate their strong points" [*SWIII*, (Beijing: FLP, 1967, p.48)]. This occurred "within the Party and, on the whole, between the individual and the Party, between outside and local cadres, between army cadres and other cadres working in the locality, between different military units, localities and departments and between old and new cadres" (Ibid., p.47). Mao argued that this was a modern version of the stereotyped writing of "Party eight-legged essays", which had existed for centuries. It is manifested in empty long-windedness with no substance "pretentiousness with deliberate intention of intimidating people", not being up to the point, "drab language, "complicated arrangement", and "irresponsibility" reflecting self-centeredness and showing off. The eight-legged essays could cause divorce between the leadership and the masses.

108 Mao, *SWIV*, (Beijing: FLP, 1960), p.215.

109 Mao, *SWIV*, (Beijing: FLP, 1967), p.374.

110 Ibid., see also Chao, Han, *On Rectification Campaigns of the CCP*, (Beijing: Chinese Youth Press, 1957), p.27.

111 Ibid., see also *PD*, [Beijing: (September 20, 1950), p.1; (June 7, 1950), p.1]. Also see Lam, Lai Sing, *Book III*, p.207.

112 Mao, *Fight for the Basic Improvement of the National, Financial and Economic Situation*, (Beijing: PP, 1950), p.9.

113 Teiwes, Frederick C., *Politics and Purges in China*, (NewYork: M.E. Sharpe Inc, 1993), pp.105–65. Also see Lam, Lai Sing, *Book III*, p.209.

114 Mao, *SWV*, (Beijing: FLP, 1977), pp.64–9.

115 Teiwes Frederick C., "Establishment and Consolidation of the New Regime", in *Cambridge History of Chinese History, Vol.14*, Twitchett, Denis C., and Fairbank, John K., (Cambridge: Cambridge University Press, 1987), p.90.

116 Chao, Han, op.cit., pp.29–30.

117 Mao, *SWV*, (Beijing: FLP, 1977), p.139.

118 Teiwes, Frederick C., op.cit., pp.134–7.

119 *PD*, (Beijing: February 16, 1952); Mao, *SWV*, (Beijing: FLP, 1977), p.65, p.68, p.72.

120 Directive drafted by Mao for the C.C. of the CCP, January 26, 1952, see *SWV*, (Beijing: FLP, 1977), pp.65–6. The two campaigns were officially merged on December 30, 1951, when the *Directive on Production Increase and Austerity and the Struggle Against Corruption, Waste and Bureaucratism* of the Chinese People's Political Consultative Conference was issued [*PD*, (Beijing: December 31, 1951)]. Also see Lam, Lai Sing, *Book III*, p.209.

121 Ibid.

122 Teiwes, Frederick C., op.cit., pp.159–60; Mao, *SWV*, (Beijing: FLP, 1977), p.101. See also Lam, Lai Sing, ibid.

123 Mao, *SWV*, (Beijing: FLP, 1977), pp.84–6.

124 Li, Ying and Cheng, Meidong, *Vol.I*, op.cit., p.404.

125 Mao, *SWV*, (Beijing: FLP, 1977, 84); *PD*, (Beijing: April 2, 1953); see also *Current Background*, no.46, (Hong Kong: US Consulate General), p.1.

126 Mao, *SWV*, (Beijing: FLP, 1977), p.84.

127 Mao, *SWV*, (Beijing: FLP, 1977), pp.85–6.

128 Myers, Ramon, "Agricultural Development", in Hinton, Harold C., ed., *The PRC*, (Boulder: Westview Press, Inc., 1979), p.180.

129 Mao, *SWV*, (Beijing: FLP, 1977), p.139.

130 Mao, *SWV*, (Beijing: FLP, 1977), pp.132–3.

131 Mao, *Wenji, Vol.6*, (Beijing: PP, 1999), p.296.

132 Mao, *SWV*, (Beijing: FLP, 1977), p.93.

133 Mao, *SWV*, (Beijing: FLP, 1977), p.94.

134 *PD*, (Beijing: September 21, 1954), p.2.

135 Mao, *SWV*, (Beijing: FLP, 1977), p.242.

136 Mao, *SWV*, (Beijing: FLP, 1977), p.248.

137 Mao, *SWV*, (Beijing: FLP, 1977), pp.243–4.

138 *PD*, (Beijing: October 17, 1955), p.1.

139 Mao, *SWV*, (Beijing: FLP, 1977), pp.196–7.

140 Wong, John, op.cit., p.199.

141 *PD*, (Beijing: October 17, 1955), p.2.

142 Mao, *SWV*, (Beijing: FLP, 1977), p.197.

143 Ibid.

144 Ibid.
145 Ibid.
146 Ibid., p.198.
147 Ibid., pp.411–2.
148 Harrison, James P., *Long March to Power*, (London: Macmillan, 1973), p.473; see also Goldman, Merle, "The Party and the Intellectuals", in *Cambridge History of China, Vol.14*, op.cit., p.242.
149 Mao, *SWV*, (Beijing: FLP, 1977), p.411.
150 *NCNA*, (Beijing: June 1, 1957).
151 Mao, *SWV*, (Beijing: FLP, 1977), p.411; also see Teiwes, Frederick C., op.cit., p.278; *PD*, Editorial, (Beijing: June 22, 1957).
152 Deng, Xiaoping, *Report on the Rectification Campaigns,* delivered at the Third Plenum (Enlarged) of the 8th C.C. of the CCP, (Beijing: FLP, September 23, 1957), p.7.
153 Goldman, Merle, op.cit., p.257.
154 Ibid.
155 *NCNA*, (Beijing: September 10, 1957).
156 Teiwes, Frederick C., op.cit., p.288.
157 Ibid., p.321; see also MacFarquhar, Roderick, *The Origins of the Cultural Revolution (2) The GLF, 1958–60*, (London: Oxford University Press, 1974), pp.293–7.
158 *NCNA,* (Beijing: June 18, 1957); see also Harrison, James P., op.cit., p.474.
159 MacFarquhar, Roderick, op.cit., p.295.
160 Eckstein, Alexander, *China's Economic Development*, (Ann Arbor: The University of Michigan Press, 1975), p.281.
161 Ibid.
162 Mao, *Wan Sui*, (Beijing: 1969), p.416.
163 Ibid.
164 Eckstein, Alexander, *China's Economic Development,* op.cit., (1975), p.14.
165 *Peking Review*, (Beijing: 1963).
166 Ibid.
167 Eckstein, Alexander, Galenson, Walter, and Liu, Ta-Chung, op.cit., p.551.
168 Gurley, John G., op.cit., p.218.
169 Ibid.
170 Yeh, Kungchia, in Eckstein, Alexander, Galenson, Walter, and Liu, Ta-Chung, "Introduction", op.cit., Chapter 8, Table 3, p.16.
171 Chao, Kang, "Politics and Performance in Industry", in Eckstein, Alexander, Galenson, Walter, and Liu, Ta-Chung, op.cit., p.555.
172 Mao, *Wan Sui*, (Beijing: 1969), p.432.
173 Ibid.
174 Mao, *SWV*, (Beijing: FLP, 1977), p.288.
175 Ibid., p.289.
176 Gurley, John G., op.cit., p.218.

177 Mao, *Wan Sui*, (Beijing: 1969), p.356.
178 Ibid.
179 Ibid.

Chapter Three
1958–1969: The US as Primary Enemy with the USSR as "No. 1 Accomplice"– Mao Launches the Great Leap Forward, the Commune and the Cultural Revolution

1 *PR*, (Beijing: April 30, 1965), p.15.
2 Ibid.
3 Mao, *SWV*, (Beijing: FLP, 1977), p.411
4 *PD*, (Beijing: May 13, 1958), p.7
5 Mao, *Wan Sui*, (Beijing: 1969), p.432.
6 Ibid.
7 Lam, Lai Sing, *Book I*, pp.93–5.
8 Snow, Edgar, *The Other Side of the River*, (New York: Random House, 1961), p.640; see also Li, Ying, and Cheng, Meidong, op.cit., p.70, p.73.
9 Li, Ying, and Cheng, Meidong, ibid., pp.70–71.
10 Snow, Edgar, *The Other Side of the River*, op.cit., p.641.
11 Khrushchev, Sergei Nikitich, tran., Benson, Shirley, *Nikita Khrushchev and the Creation of a Superpower*, (Pennsylvania: The Pennsylvania State University, 2000), p.268.
12 Yahuda, Michael B. writes: "The signing of the partial Nuclear Test Ban Treaty in July 1963 was the turning point in Sino-Soviet relations". See "Chinese Foreign Policy After 1963: The Maoist Phases", in *China Quarterly*, no.36, (October–December 1968), p.93. However, I would argue that the turning point could even be dated further back to the outcome of the Taiwan Straits Crisis.
13 Lam, Lai Sing, *Book I.*, pp.78–9; also see Mao, *Wenji, Vol.8,* (Beijing: PP, 2001), p.358.
14 *PR*, (Beijing: November 8, 1963), p.25.
15 Mao, *Wenji, Vol.7*, (Beijing: PP, 1999), p.412.
16 Goodman, David S.G., *Deng Xiaoping and the Chinese Revolution: A Political Biography*, (London: Routledge, 1994), p.73.
17 Mao, "On the Question of the International Situation", in *Wenji, Vol.7*, p.412.
18 Lardy, Nicholas R., "The Chinese Economy Under Stress, 1958–65", in Twitchett, Denis C., and Fairbank, John K., *The Cambridge History of China*, op.cit., p.363.

19 Mao, *SWV*, (Beijing: FLP, 1977), pp.288–9.

20 Chen, Jian, "How to Pursue a Critical History of Mao's Foreign Policy", in *The China Journal*, no.49, op.cit., (Canberra: January 2003), p.137; Lieberthal, Kenneth, "The GLF and the Split in the Yenan Leadership", in *Cambridge History of China*, op.cit., p.294.

21 Mao, *Wan Sui*, (Beijing: 1969), p.69.

22 Mao, *Wan Sui*, (Beijing: 1969), p.267, p.606.

23 Hsu, C.Y. Immanuel, op.cit., p.654.

24 Mao, *Wan Sui*, (Beijing: 1969), p.225, p.240.

25 Mao, *Wenji, Vol.6*, (Beijing, PP, 1999), p.93.

26 Eckstein, Alexander, Galenson, Walter, and Liu, Ta-Chung, op.cit., p.7.

27 Teiwes, Frederick C., op.cit., p.334, p.337.

28 Meisner, Maurice J., Mao's China: *A History of the People's Republic*, (New York: The Free Press, 1977), p.230.

29 Lam, Lai Sing, *Book II*, pp.159–67.

30 *PD*, Editorial, (Beijing: September 4, 1958).

31 *Hongqi*, 10th issue, (1958), p.1; *PD*, (October 1, 1958), p.1.

32 "The New Development of the Labor-Military Forces Combined", in *Yenan Liberation Daily*, (Yenan: October 15, 1944), p.3; "The Road of the Soldiers and People Behind the Enemy – Fighting and Production Combined", in *YLD*, (Yenan: March 2, 1944), p.1; "The New Development of the Labor-Military Forces Combined in the Ch'in Sui (晋绥) Border Area Last Year", in *YLD*, (Yenan: February 1, 1945), p.3.

33 Lardy, Nicholas R., op.cit., p.365.

34 Mao, *Wenji, Vol.7,* (Beijing: PP, 1999), pp.434–5.

35 Ibid., p.440.

36 Mao, *SW V*, (Beijing: FLP, 1977), p.112.

37 Ibid.

38 Mao, *Wenji, Vol.7,* (Beijing:, PP, 1999), p.437.

39 Lardy, Nicholas R., op.cit., p.365.

40 *PD*, Editorial, (Beijing: September 3, 1958); see also Lethbridge, Henry J., *The Peasant and the Communes*, (Hong Kong: Dragonfly Books, 1963), p.74.

41 Mao's commune system was meant to be the prototype for the whole of the oppressed and exploited third world with each nation as a basic unit. The dictum of "uniting all that can be united" was meant to work for Mao's anti-capitalist and ultimately anti-imperialist schemes in which all self-sufficient and independent units represented by all third world oppressed and exploited nations were to be united with both anti-capitalist and anti-imperialist aims.

42 Schram, Stuart R., *The Political Thought of Mao Tse-tung*, (New York: Praeger, 1969), p.182.

43 Han Suyin, *China in the Year 2001*, (London: C.A. Watts, 1967), p.41.

44 "Resolution of the C.C. of the CCP on the establishment of People's Communes in the Rural Areas", in *People's Communes in China*, (Beijing: FLP, 1958), p.2; see also *PD*, (Beijing: August 29, 1958); see also Han Suyin, op.cit., p.47.
45 Han, Suyin, op.cit., p.46.
46 Mao, *Wenji*, *Vol. 8*, (Beijing: PP, 1999), p.12.
47 Ibid.
48 *NCNA*, (Beijing: August 15, 1967).
49 Ibid.
50 Ibid.
51 Teiwes, Frederick C., op.cit., p.401; *PD*, (Beijing: September 17, 1959); also see Mao, *Wenji, Vol. 8*, (Beijing: PP, 1999), p.76.
52 *NCNA*, (Beijing: August 26, 1959).
53 Li Ying, and Cheng, Meidong, *Vol. II,* op.cit., p.147.
54 Teiwes, Frederick C., op.cit., p.311, p.328.
55 Ibid., p.328.
56 Mao, *Wan Sui*, (Beijing: 1969), p.94; see also Mao's Letter to *Shi Kan* (诗刊), (Beijing: January 1959).
57 Mao, *SWV*, (Beijing: FLP, 1977), p.340.
58 *PR*, [Beijing: (August 18, 1967), p.8; (August 25, 1967), p.6; (September 1, 1967), p.12].
59 Li Jie, "Changes in China's Domestic Situation in the 1960s and Sino-US Relations", in *Re-examining the Cold War: US-China Diplomacy, 1954–73*, ed., Ross, Robert S., and Jiang Changbin, (Cambridge, Mass. and London: Harvard University Press, 2001), p.298.
60 Ibid.
61 Mao's conversation with Wu Zhi-pu (吴芝圃) on June 22, 1959; see "Documents of the Party"(党的文献), 4th edition, (Beijing: 1959).
62 "Documents of the Party", 5th edition, (Beijing: 1994).
63 Chen, Jian, op.cit., p.1441.
64 Eckstein, Alexander, *China's Economic Development,* op.cit., p.287.
65 Eckstein, Alexander, Galenson, Walter, and Liu, Ta-Chung, op.cit., p.11.
66 Eckstein, Alexander, op.cit., p.280.
67 Chao, Kang, op.cit., p.555.
68 Skinner, William, "Marketing and Social Structure in Rural China", in *Journal of Asian Studies*, [Ann Arbor: (November 1964), pp.3–43; (February 1965), pp.195–228]. See also Richman, Barry, *Industrial Society in Communist China*, (New York: Random House, 1969), pp.316–7. See also Hoffmann, Charles, *Work Inductive Practices and Policies in the People's Republic of China 1953–65*, (New York: State University of New York Press, 1968), p.108. See also Gurley, John G., op.cit., p.215.
69 Gurley, John G., Ibid.
70 Ibid.
71 Harrison, James P., op.cit., p.485.

72 Even as far back as 1954, the entire length of the Trans-Siberian Railway was noted as "military territory" and Khabarvosk on the Amur as a "great military city". See Salisbury, Harrison E., *The Coming War Between Russia and China*, (New York: W.W. Norton & Co., Inc., 1969), p.105.

73 *PR*, (Beijing: June 16, 1961), pp.17–21.

74 Li Jie, op.cit., p.295.

75 Ibid.

76 This was because the Russians had denied them the resources to develop a nuclear bomb under the "false claim that they would be prepared to defend Chinese interests".

77 *PR*, (Beijing: October 11, 1963), p.14.

78 Ibid.

79 Ibid.

80 *PR*, (Beijing: July 17, 1964), p.7.

81 Ibid.

82 *PR*, (Beijing: April 30, 1965), p.15.

83 Ibid.

84 *PR*, (Beijing: December 3, 1965), p.14.

85 Also see *Hongqi*, (Beijing: August 21, 1965).

86 Ross, Robert S., "Introduction", op.cit., p.12.

87 *Red Flag*, no.34, (Beijing: 1963, 13). Although not mentioned, the USSR was certainly considered as part of the "devil" in Mao's worldview as "the Russian revisionists (who) are the No.1 accomplice of the US imperialist scheme of subjugating the world". See *PD*, and *Red Flag*, (Beijing: February 4, 1964). Also see Lam, Lai Sing, *Book I*, p.100.

88 *1967 Yearbook*, p.403; see also Van Ness, Peter, *Revolution and Chinese Foreign Policy: Peking's Support for Wars of National Liberation*, (Berkeley: University of California Press, 1970), p.16. Also see Lam, Lai Sing, ibid., p.101.

89 After the Communists came into power in 1949, the UK and Holland, due to their desire to maintain their interests in China, recognized the PRC whereas Finland, Sweden and others did so due to influence from the Russians. Also see Lam, Lai Sing, ibid., p.101.

90 Lie Jie, op.cit., p.296.

91 Ibid.

92 *PR*, (Beijing: July 21, 1961), p.11.

93 Harrison, James P., op.cit., p.485.

94 Ibid., pp.486–7.

95 Ibid., p.488.

96 MacFarquhar's three books are as follows: (1) *The Origins of the Cultural Revolution: The Coming of Cataclysm 1961–66*, (Oxford: Oxford University Press, 1997); (2) *The Origins of the Cultural Revolution: The GLF, 1958–60*, (Oxford: OUP 1983); (3) *The Origins of the Cultural Revolution: Contradictions Among the People*, (New York: Columbia University Press, 1974).

97 MacFarquhar, Roderick, (3), op.cit., p.6.

98 Ibid.

99 Ibid.

100 Ibid.

101 MacFarquhar, Roderick, (1), op.cit., p.11.

102 Chiou, C.L., *Maoism in Action: the Cultural Revolution*, (St Lucia: Queensland University Press, 1974), pp.3–11.

103 *PR*, (Beijing: April 14, 1967), p.8.

104 Lethbridge, Henry J., op.cit., pp.101–2.

105 Ibid., p.105.

106 PR, (Beijing: April 14, 1967), p.8.

107 Chiou, C.L., op.cit., p.47.

108 Robinson, Joan, *The Cultural Revolution in China*, (UK: Pelican, 1970), p.32.

109 Ibid.

110 Even Mao himself believed that certain aspects of the GLF were so. See the section on the 1959 Rectification Campaign against "Opportunism".

Chapter Four
1969–1976: The USSR as Primary Enemy and the US as Secondary Enemy – Mao's Relaxed Development Policies

1 The editorial of the *People's Daily* on October 1, 1972 was much harsher towards Moscow than towards Washington. While "US imperialism" came in for fewer lines and fewer attacks, the "Soviet revisionist renegade clique", it elaborated, "was reaching out it hands everywhere" [...] and was "even more deceitful than the old-line imperialist nations and, therefore more dangerous".

2 Lam, Lai Sing, *Book I*, p.112.

3 *TASS News Agency*, see *The Guardian*, (London: December 1971). Also see Lam, Lai Sing, *Book I*, p.113.

4 The essence of the Brezhnev doctrine was that when socialism itself was threatened in a socialist country, military intervention by other members of the socialist community might be necessary. Also see Lam, Lai Sing, ibid.

5 Li Jie, "Changes in China's Domestic Situation in the 1960s and Sino-US relations", in Ross, S. Robert and Jiang Changbin, ed., *Re-examining the Cold War: US-China Diplomacy, 1954–73*, (Cambridge, Mass. and London: Harvard University Press, 2001), p.306.

6 Ibid., 296.

7 Nixon, Richard, *The Memoirs of Richard Nixon*, (New York: Grosset & Dunlap, 1978), p.347.

8 Ibid., p.384.

9 Kissinger, Henry, *White House Years*, (Boston: Little Brown, 1979), p.685.

10 Nixon, Richard, "Inaugeral Address", January 20, 1969, in *Public Papers of the Presidents of the United States: Richard Nixon, 1969*, (Washington, D.C.: Government Printing Office, 1971), p.3; also see Gong Li, "Chinese Decision Making and the Thawing of US-China Relations", in Ross Robert S. and Jiang, Changbin, op.cit., p.333.

11 Li Jie, op.cit., p.314.

12 Foot, Rosemary, "Reflections: The Domestic Context of America's China Policy in the 1960s", in Ross, Robert S. and Jiang Changbin, op.cit., p.286.

13 *PD*, (Beijing: December 25, 1970), p.1.

14 Gurley, John G., *China's Economy and the Maoist Strategy*, (New York: Monthly Review Press, 1976), p.224.

15 Ibid., p.223.

16 Gong Li, "Chinese Decision Making and the Thawing of US–China Relations", op.cit., p.357.

17 Kissinger, Henry, *Diplomacy*, (New York: Simon & Schuster, 1994), p.726.

18 The Sino-Soviet talks began in September 1969 and ended in May 1971. It may be assumed that efforts had been made from both sides to relief the hostility, judging from the following activities:

(a) On June 13, 1970, Zhou Enlai sent a consolatory telegraph to Kosygin on the Russian earthquake and floods;

(b) In mid-July 1970, the Sino-Soviet Border River Navigation Committee Talks began;

(c) On October 1, 1970, the Russians telegraphed the Chinese congratulating them on their National Day;

(d) On November 12, 1970, the Sino-Soviet Commodity Exchange and Payment Agreements were signed;

(e) In March 1971 the Soviet Ilukson 62 long-range planes were sold to China for Chinese foodstuff;

(f) During the period May 10–20, 1971, the Soviet delegates toured Nanjing, Shanghai and Hungzhou. See *1971 Yearbook*, section 6, 4.

19 Mao, *Wenji, Vol.8*, (Beijing: P.P., 2001), p.441.

20 Adie, W.A.C., *World or Power? China as an Alternative Model of the International System*, (Canberra: The Australian National University Seminar Paper, 1974), p.36. Also see Lam, Lai Sing, *Book I*, p.119.

21 Ibid.

22 In February 1973, China invited Bulgaria's Vice Minister of Foreign Trade, K. Kozmov, to talk on trade, and agreements on exchange of commodities and payment were signed on February 29, 1973. On February 14, 1974, Chinese trade delegates headed by Chen Chi visited Bulgaria to sign the agreements on

commodity exchange and payment. On March 3, 1973, Vice Minister for Trade Zhou Huamin arrived in Hungary to sign an agreement on trade.

China carried out similar trade relations with East Germany, Poland, Czechoslovakia, etc. See *1974 Yearbook*, section 6, p.42–4.

It was well known that Chinese relations including trade with foreign nations had political implications. Also see Lam, Lai Sing, *Book I*, p.121.

23 Mao, *Works*, *Vol.II*, op.cit., pp.269–70; also see Chen, Jin, *Vol.II*, op.cit., pp.922–3.

24 Chen, Jin, ed., *Explaining Mao Zedong's Reading Notes, Vol.II*, (Shenzhen: Guangdong People's Press, 1959), p.588.

25 Ibid.

26 Ibid., p.923.

27 Mao, *Wenji, Vol.8*, op.cit., p.71, p.86.

28 Chen, Jin, *Vol.I*, op.cit., pp.587–8.

29 *The Party's Documents*, 4th issue, (1993); also see Chen, Jin, *Vol.I*, op.cit., p.617.

30 Mao, *Wenji., Vol.8*, op.cit., p.152, p.162.

31 Ibid., p.351.

32 Deng, *SW of DXP 1975–82*, (Hong Kong: PP & JP, 1983), p.49. Also see Mao, *Wenji., Vol.8*, op.cit., p.351..

33 Mao, *SW V*, (Beijing: FLP, 1977), pp.330–1, also see Deng, ibid., p.87. Also see Lam, Lai Sing, ibid.

34 Ibid.

35 Mao, *SW III*, "On Coalition Government", (Beijing: F.L.P., 1967), p.252.

36 Mao *SW V*, "Correct Handling of Contradictions Among the People", (Beijing: FLP, 1977), p.419.

37 Ibid., p.477

38 *PD*, Editorial, (Beijing: February 9, 1979).

39 Ibid.

40 Deng, *SW of DXP 1982–92*, (Beijing: FLP, 1994), p.190, p.358.

41 Bernstein, Thomas P., "A Giant Economy", in Morley, James, W., ed., *Driven by Growth: Political Change in the Asia-Pacific Region*, (New York: M.E. Sharpe, Inc., 1993), p.45.

42 Chen, Yuen, "The Responsibility System in Mainland China: An Analysis", in Chang, King-yuh, ed., *Perspectives on Development in Mainland China*, (Boulder: Westview Press, 1985), p.155.

43 *PD*, (Beijing: January 1, 1971), p.1.

44 Ibid

45 Mao, *SW V*, (Beijing: FLP, 1977), p.148, p.149. Also see *PR*, (August 17, 1973), p.4.

46 Lam, Lai Sing, *Book II*, pp.187–93.

47 *PR*, (Beijing: June 6, 1975), p.5.

48 Ibid.

49 Ibid.

50 *PR,* (Beijing: August 17, 1973), p.4, p.5.

51 Ibid.

52 Ibid

53 Ibid.

54 *PR,* (Beijing: July 2, 1971), p.14.

55 Ibid.

56 *PD,* (Beijing: January 1, 1971), p.1.

57 Ibid.

58 Ibid.

59 Ibid.

60 *Beijing Review* (hereafter *BR),* (Beijing: October 22, 1971), p.5.

61 Ibid. p.6.

62 Ibid.

63 Ibid.

64 Gurley, John G., op.cit., p.223.

65 Ibid., p.210, p.223, p.310.

66 Liu Suinian and Wu Qungan, ed., *China's Socialist Economy*, (Beijing: Beijing Review Press, 1986), p.384.

67 Ibid.

68 For instance, in 2003 foreign invested enterprises accounted for 52.2 percent of China's exports in increasing from 20.4 percent in 1992 [*SCMP*, (Hong Kong: February 13, 2003), p.20]. This represented a tenfold increase in their export shipments from US$17.4 billion in 1992 to US$169.9 billion in 2002 (Ibid.) The rest of China's exports were about a twofold increase in the same period (Ibid.). Characteristic of these foreign invested enterprises was that with ownership and control, they worked on the market principles. According to the statistics released by the Ministry of Foreign Trade and Economic Cooperation in mid-February 2003, the fastest growth of exports in 2002 was in the Jiangsu province where foreign-invested companies accounted for more than 60 percent of exports [*SCMP*, (Hong Kong: February 12, 2003), p.1]. (Of those exports of US$38.48 billion in 2002, foreign-invested companies accounted for US$24.26 billion).

69 Gurley, John G., op.cit., p.223.

70 *PR*, (April 9, 1974), p.10.

71 Ibid.

72 Ibid.

73 *PR*, (Beijing: January 5, 1973).

74 Ibid.

75 US Foreign Broadcast Information Service: *PRC Daily Report*, FBIS-CHI-75-13, (January 20, 1975), *Vol.1*, No.13, D10–D11.

76 Gurley, John G., op.cit., p.311.

Chapter Five
Mao's Legacy: Deng Xiaoping's Economic Reform and Open-Door Policy

1 *PR*, (Beijing: January 2, 1976), p.10.
2 Deng, *SW of DXP 1982–92*, (Beijing: FLP, 1994), p.p.35–6. Also see Lam, Lai Sing, *Book II*, p.210.
3 PR, (Beijing: June 9, 1978), p.6.
4 *BR*, (Beijing: October 6–12, 1997), p.14.
5 Deng, *SW of DXP 1975–82*, (Beijing: FLP, 1983), p.282, p.283. Also see Lam, Lai Sing, *Book II*, p.205.
6 Mao, *SWV*, (Beijing: FLP, 1977), p.419. Also see Lam, Lai Sing, *Book II*, p.206.
7 Deng, *SW of DXP 1975–82*, (Beijing: FLP, 1983), p.280.
8 Mao, *SWV*, (Beijing: FLP, 1977), p.p.287–289. Also see Lam, Lai Sing, ibid.
9 Mao, *SW V*, (Beijing: FLP, 1977), pp.473–4; see also Deng, *SW of DXP 1975–82*, (Beijing: FLP, 1983), p.58, p.141. Also see Lam, Lai Sing, *Book II*, p.207.
10 Deng, *SW of DXP 1975–82*, (Beijing: FLP, 1983), p.263.
11 Bernstein, Thomas P., op.cit., p.47. Also see Lam, Lai Sing, ibid.
12 Deng, *DXP Wensuan 1982–92*, (Hong Kong: PP and JP, 1993), p.190, p.358.
13 *BR*, (Beijing: February 23, 1979), p.5; *PD*, (Beijing: February 9, 1979), p.1.
14 Deng, *Deng Xiaoping Wensuan 1975–82*, (Hong Kong: PP and JP, 1983), p.199.
15 *BR*, (Beijing: April 27, 1979), p.11.
16 Lam, Lai Sing, "A Short Note on ASEAN-Great Power Interaction", in *Contemporary Southeast Asia*, (Singapore: Institute of Southeast Asian Studies, March 1994), p.454. Also see Lam, Lai Sing, *Book II*, p.218.
17 Kau, Michael Y.M., and Marsh, Susan H., *China in the Era of Deng Xiaoping: A Decade of Reform*, (New York: M.E. Sharpe, Inc., 1993), p.xviii.
18 Deng, *SW of DXP 1975–82*, (Beijing: FLP, 1983), p.180.
19 Lam, Lai Sing, op.cit.
20 A massive military concentration in the Soviet Far East and Outer Mongolia was established from 1969.
21 *Straits Times*, (Singapore: July 29, 1984), p.1.
22 Lam, Lai Sing, *Book I*, pp.97–112.
23 Ibid., 226; see also Deng, *DXP Wensuan 1982–92*, (Beijing: PP, 1993), p.50, p.57, p.82, p.94, p.116, p.350.
24 Deng, *SW of DXP 1982–92*, (Beijing: FLP, 1994), p.122; see also *DXP Wensuan 1982–92*, (Beijing: PP and JP, 1993), p.244, pp.286–7, p.331, p.332, p.348; *SW of DXP 1975–82*, (Beijing: FLP, 1983), p.205, p.215.

25 Deng, *SW of DXP 1982–92*, (Beijing: FLP, 1994), p.133.
26 Yeh, Kungchia, "Foreign Trade, Capital Inflow and Technology Transfer Under the Open Policy", in Kau, Michael Y.M., and Marsh, Susan H., op.cit., pp.141–4.
27 Ibid.
28 *The Nation*, (Sydney: December 1, 1982), p.6. Also see Lam, Lai Sing, ibid.
29 Lam, Lai Sing, "From Mikhail Gorbachev's Policy to China's Regional Role", in *The Journal of East Asian Affairs*, (Seoul: The Research Institute of International Affairs, August 1993), p.587. Also see Lam, Lai Sing, ibid.
30 Mao, *Notes Book*, in Li Jui, *Comrade Mao Tse-tung's Early Revolutionary Activities*, (Beijing: The Chinese Youth Press, 1957), p.38.
31 Mao, *Works, Vol.I*, ed., p.41, p.44; *SWIII*, (Beijing: PP, 1969), p.1002; *SWV*, (Beijing: FLP, 1977), p.469.
32 Deng, *Deng Xiaoping Wensuan 1975–82*, (Hong Kong: PP and JP, 1983), p.199.
33 Deng, *SW of DXP 1982–92*, (Beijing: FLP, 1994), pp.123–4.
34 Ibid. Also see Lam, Lai Sing, *Book II*, 201.
35 The first four issues of the *Hsiang Chiang Review*, (July 1919); see Li Jui, op.cit., p.36, p.100, p.103; Mao, "Letter of August 23, 1917 to Li Shao-hsi".
36 Ibid.
37 Deng, *SW of DXP 1982–92*, (Beijing: PP, 1993), pp.274–5.
38 Ibid.; Mao, *Wenji, Vol.7*, p.1.
39 Deng, ibid., p.274; Also see Mao, ibid., p.269, p.351.
40 Ibid., p.107. Also see Lam, Lai Sing, *Book II*, p.204.
41 Deng, *DXP Wensuan 1975–82,* (Hong Kong: PP and JP, 1983), pp.37–38. Also see Lam, Lai Sing, ibid.
42 Deng, ibid., p.46. Also see Lam, Lai Sing, ibid.
43 Deng, *SW of DXP 1982–92*, (Beijing: FLP, 1994), p.74.
44 Ibid.
45 Ibid.
46 Deng, *SW of DXP 1982–92*, (Beijing: FLP, 1994), p.79, p.101.
47 Ibid., p.142.
48 Ibid.
49 Ibid., p.207.
50 Ibid.
51 Ibid., p.73.
52 Ibid., p.344.
53 Deng, *SW of DXP 1982–92*, (Beijing: FLP, 1994), p.190.
54 Ibid., pp.274–5, p.344.
55 Deng, *SW of DXP 1982–92*, (Beijing: FLP, 1994), p.115.
56 Chiou, C.L., op.cit, p.48.
57 Deng's words in his conversation with officials in Shanghai during his "Southern Inspection Tour". This was shown in the Macau TV series *The Hundred Years of Deng Xiaoping* (百年小平), 10.15 p.m.–11.00 p.m., October 8, 2004.
58 Deng, *SW of DXP 1982–92*, (Beijing: FLP, 1994), p.72.

59 Ibid., p.86. Also see Lam, Lai Sing, *Book II*, p.216.
60 *SCMP*, (Hong Kong: June 22, 2002), p.14.
61 Beinstein, Thomas P., op.cit., p.49.
62 Deng, *SW of DXP 1982–92*, (Beijing: FLP, 1994), p.152.
63 Li, Luye, in Kau, Michael Y.M., and Marsh, Susan H., op.cit., p.444.
64 Deng, *SW of DXP 1982–92*, (Beijing: FLP, 1994), p.9.
65 Cheng, Joseph Y.S., ed., *China: Modernization in the 1980s*, (Hong Kong: The Chinese University Press, 1989), p.xii.
66 Ibid.
67 Ibid.
68 Ibid.
69 Kau, Michael Y.M., and Marsh, Susan H., op.cit., p.342.
70 Deng, *SW of DXP 1975–82*, (Beijing: FLP, 1983), p.215, p.217, p.342.
71 Ibid., p.217.
72 Deng, *SW of DXP 1982–92*, (Beijing: FLP, 1994), p.152.
73 Ibid.
74 Pradeep Taneja, etc., in *China Since 1978*, second edition, (Melbourne: Longman, 1998), p.71.
75 *NCNA*, (Beijing: July 27, 1997); see also ibid.
76 *FEER*, vol. 135, no. 12 (Hong Kong: March 1987), p.62; see also Cheng Joseph Y.S., op.cit., p.xvi.
77 Ibid.
78 Deng, *SW of DXP 1982–92*, (Beijing: FLP, 1994), p.72.
79 Deng, *SW of DXP 1975–82*, (Beijing: FLP, 1983), p.53
80 Ibid., p.54.
81 Bonavia, David, *Deng*, (Hong Kong: Longman, 1989), p.156; Deng, *SW of DXP 1975–82*, (Beijing: FLP, 1983), p.64.
82 Deng, *SW of DXP 1982–92*, (Beijing: FLP, 1994), p.270.
83 Goodman, David S.G., op.cit.
84 *BR*, (Beijing: February 1–7, 1999), p.17.
85 Ibid
86 Ibid., p.18.
During the period 2001–2, China sent more than 17,000 undergraduates to British universities [*SCMP*, (Hong Kong: June 21, 2003), p.E2].
87 *BR*, (Beijing: February 1–7, 1999), p.18. For instance, in 1997, Chinese universities under the Ministry of Education invited 3,658 foreign experts and lecturers.
88 Ibid.
89 Ibid.
90 *BR*, (Beijing: May 23, 1983), p.II.
91 *BR*, (Beijing: October 12, 1981), p.3.
92 *BR*, (Beijing: May 23, 1983), p.II.
93 Deng, *SW of DXP 1982–92*, (Beijing: FLP, 1994), p.20.
94 *BR*, (Beijing: September 13, 1982), pp.15–6.

Chapter Six
The Transformation of the Bipolarity: From "Good-Neighborliness" to "Inducing the Whole World to Help Modernize China"

1 In December 1989, the Soviet Union signed the arms-control treaty of reduction of the intermediate-range nuclear weapons with the US in Washington, in quest of the European security. In October 1990, they reached an agreement in New York in principle on the reduction of the conventional forces in Europe. In July 1991, they also reached an arms-control accord of slashing their arsenals of long-range nuclear weapons by about a third.

2 Estimates by the International Institute of Strategic Studies put total Soviet troop strength at 5.2 million of which about 2.2 million were deployed in Europe. See *Asian Wall Street Journal*, (Hong Kong: December 8, 1988), p.1.

3 Huang, T.W. and Li, Z.Y., "The Changing Security Scene in East Asia – An Analysis of the US Perspective", in *ASEAN-China, Hong Kong Forum 1990*, (Hong Kong: Royal Park Hotel, Shatin, August 7–9, 1990).

4 Ibid.

5 *Wen Wei Po*, (Hong Kong: May 19, 1991), p.1.

6 *BR*, (Beijing: April 23, 1984), p.16.

7 *BR*, (Beijing: July 8, 1985), p.20.

8 *BR*, (Beijing: June 20–6, 1988), p.14.

9 *BR*, (Beijing: April 23, 1984), p.17.

10 *BR*, (Beijing: July 8, 1985), p.20.

11 Ibid

12 Ibid.

13 *BR*, (Beijing: April 23, 1984), p.16.

14 *BR*, (Beijing: July 25–31, 1988), p.21.

15 Ibid.

16 *BR*, (Beijing: October 17, 1983), p.9.

17 *BR*, (Beijing: July 25–31, 1988), p.22.

18 Ibid., p.22.

19 Ibid.

20 *BR*, (Beijing: March 11–7, 1991), p.11.

21 *BR*, (Beijing: November 30–December 6, 1992), p.10.

22 Ibid.

23 Ikuo Kabashima, "Japan: There May Be a Choice", in Morley, James W., ed., op.cit., p.255.

24 Shinichi Ichimura and Morley, James W., "Introduction: The Varieties of Asia-Pacific Experience", ed., Morley, James W., op.cit., p.7.

25 Ibid.
26 Ibid.
27 *BR,* no. 38, (Beijing), p.10.
28 Ibid.
29 Ibid.
30 *BR,* (Beijing: April 6–12, 1992), p.5.
31 *BR,* no. 38, (Beijing), p.10.
32 *BR,* (Beijing: December 23–29, 1991), pp.9–10.
33 Ibid.
34 *BR,* (Beijing: January 28–February 3, 1991), p.22.
35 *BR,* (Beijing: April 27–May 3, 1992), p.26.
36 Ibid.
37 Il Sakong, *Korea in the World Economy*, (Washington D.C.: Institute of International Economics, 1993), p.21.
38 Ibid.
39 Woo-Hee Park, "The Role of Science and Technology in Korean Economic Development", in *Conference on Problems and Prospects of the Asian Pacific Region*, (Hong Kong: Centre of Asian Studies, University of Hong Kong, August 5–7, 1987), p.9.
40 Ibid., p.14.
41 Kim Jeong-Hyun and Ro Kwang-Hae, "New World Order and Korea", in *The Journal of East Asian Affairs*, vol. 6, no. 2, (Seoul: 1992), p.239; see also Chung Jae- Ho, "South Korea and China Economic Relations: The Current Situation and Its Implications", in *Asian Survey*, vol. 38, no. 10, (Berkeley: University of California Press, 1988), pp.1031–48; *Asahi Shimbun*, (August 30, 1989).
42 Hong Kong enterprises normally provide machinery, facilities, raw materials and parts to the factories for processing and manufacturing in the Pearl River Delta, where labor, water, electricity and other base facilities are provided. The finished products are exported by Hong Kong enterprises, which also pay for all the processing and assembly cost.
43 Toyojiro Maruya, ed., "Economic Relations Between Hong Kong and Guangdong Province", in *Guangdong "Open Door" Economic Development Strategy*, (Tokyo: Institute of Developing Economies, 1992), p.138.
44 Toyojiro Maruya, *A Decade of "Open-Door" Economic Development, 1979–89*, (Tokyo: Institute of Developing Economies, 1991), p.153.
45 Toyojiro Maruya, op.cit., (1992), p.27.
46 Ibid.
47 Ibid.
48 This is a new industrial township of 70 square kilometers with a comprehensive industrial, residential and recreational development, which was to house 600,000 people. Japanese businessmen also pay a role in the project. In early 1994, an agreement was signed in Beijing.

49 Goh, Chok Tong, Singapore Prime Minister, "Positioning Singapore for the 21st Century", in *Speeches*, a bimonthly selection of ministerial speeches, (Singapore: Ministry of Information and the Arts, May–June, 1995), p.4.
50 Ibid., 3.
51 Ibid.
52 *BR,* (Beijing: February 7, 2002), p.7.
53 Ibid.
54 *The Nation*, (Sydney: December 1, 1982), p.6.
55 Lam, Lai Sing, "From Mikhail Gorbachev's Policy to China's Regional Role", in *The Journal of East Asian Affairs*, vol. vii, no. 2, (Seoul: August 1993), pp.593–6
56 *BR,* (Beijing: November 15, 1999), p.13.
57 Ibid.
58 *BR,* (Beijing: October 28, 1985), p.15.
59 Ibid.
60 Ibid.
61 Ibid.
62 Ibid., p.17.
63 Ibid.
64 Ibid.
65 Deng, *SW of DXP 1982–92* (Beijing: FLP, 1994), pp.58–9.
66 Deng, *SW of DXP 1982–92*, (Beijing: FLP, 1994), p.41.
67 Deng, *DXP Wensuan 1982–92*, (Beijing: PP, 1993), p.59.
68 Jiang, Zemin, *Jiang Zemin Wenxuan* (hereafter *SW of JZM*), *Vol.III*, (Beijing: PP, 2006), pp.169–72.

Chapter Seven The International Environment and Jiang's Strategy of Continuing to Induce the Whole World to Help Modernize China

1 *BR*, (Beijing: July 14–20, 1997), p.7.
2 Ibid.
3 Ibid., see also Huntington, Samuel P., *The Clash of Civilizations and Remaking of World Order,* (New York: Simon & Schuster, 1996), p.106, p.108, pp.169–74, pp.312–4. Also see Jiang, Zemin, *SW of JZM, Vol.III*, op.cit., p.520.
4 *BR*, (Beijing: March 1–7, 1993), p.10.
5 *SCMP*, (Hong Kong: November 17, 1995), p.8.

6 *SCMP*, (Hong Kong: January 18, 1991), p.11.
7 *SCMP*, (Hong Kong: December 15, 1990), 11.
8 *BR*, (Beijing: January 7, 1991), p.9.
9 *SCMP*, (Hong Kong: January 18, 1991), p.11.
10 *FEER*, (Hong Kong: January 31, 1991), p.6.
11 "Qian Qichen on Our Changing World", in *Ta Kung Po*, (Hong Kong: December 15, 1990), p.1. Qian's thesis was based on Deng Xiaoping's new international political and economic order he proposed in 1988 in accordance with the "Five Principles of Peaceful Co-existence".
12 US Defense Secretary Dick Cheney's announcement was made in Tokyo in February 1990.
13 Polomka, Peter, "Strategic Stability and the South China Sea: Beyond Geopolitics", in *The International Academic Conference on Territorial Claims in the South China Sea*, (Hong Kong: Centre of Asian Studies, University of Hong Kong, December 4–6, 1990), p.7.
14 *SCMP*, (Hong Kong: January 13, 1992), p.8.
15 *SCMP*, (Hong Kong: January 12, 1992), p.5.
16 *BR*, (Beijing: October 21–7, 1996), p.8.
17 *BR*, (Beijing: October 16–22, 1995), p.4. SEATO formed in 1954 was aimed at containing communism and China but disbanded in 1977.
18 Reportedly toward the end of 1996, the Chinese purchased two Sovremenny class destroyers equipped with SS-N-22 anti-ship cruise missiles, which the US feared most due to their deadly supersonic speed. See *SCMP*, (Hong Kong: January 16, 1997), p.19.
19 *SCMP*, (Hong Kong: April 18, 1999), Sunday Focus section, p.3.
20 Jiang, Zemin, *SW of JZM*, *Vol.III*, op.cit., p.527.
21 Tow, William, "Reshaping Asian-Pacific Security", in *The Journal of East Asian Affairs*, vol.viii, no.1, (Seoul: 1994), pp.90–1.
22 *SCMP*, (Hong Kong: September 19, 1996), p.B7.
23 *SCMP*, (Hong Kong: April 18, 1996), p.15.
24 *SCMP*, (Hong Kong: November 12, 1996), p.13.
25 *SCMP*, (Hong Kong: July 9, 2005), p.A11.
26 Walsh, J. Richard, "A Pillar of the Community: The Role of APEC in US Policy", in *The Journal of East Asian Affairs*, vol.vii, no.2, op.cit., (Seoul: 1993), pp.545– 6.
27 Ibid., p.559.
28 *BR*, (Beijing: May 20–6, 1991), p.6.
29 *BR*, (Beijing: October 27–November 2, 1997), p.15.
30 Ibid.
31 Ibid, p.16.
32 *BR*, (Beijing: March 21, 2002), p.20.
33 Both the US and China agreed on terms and conditions of access to China's market including specific commitments on industrial goods, agricultural products

and services. According to the agreement, the PRC was to reduce average import duties to 17 percent from 22.1 percent after its WTO entry and export subsidies were to be phased out and tariffs on farm goods, automobiles and auto parts reduced. See *BR*, (Beijing: November 22, 1999), p.4.

34 *BR*, (Beijing: November 29, 1999), p.8.
35 Ibid.
36 *China Today*, (Beijing: November 2001), pp.6–8.
37 *BR*, (Beijing: March 21, 2002), p.20.
38 *BR*, (Beijing: March 21, 2002), p.21.
39 *BR*, (Beijing: November 25–December 1, 1991), p.4.
40 *BR*, (Beijing: November 15–21, 1993), p.11.
41 *BR*, (Beijing: November 14–20, 1994), p.7.
42 *BR*, (Beijing: December 28, 1992–January 3, 1993), p.5.
43 *BR*, (Beijing: October 27–November 2, 1997), p.14.
44 Ibid.
45 *BR*, (Beijing: February 28, 2002), p.7.
46 *BR*, (Beijing: April 7–13, 1997), p.20.
47 Ibid.
48 *BR*, (Beijing: February 28, 2002), p.8.
49 Ibid.
50 Ibid., p.7.
51 *SCMP*, (Hong Kong: June, 25, 2005), p.A5.
52 Ibid.
53 *BR*, (Beijing: February 2–15, 1999), p.10.
54 "Opinion on Relations between the EU and China", Economic and Social Committee of the European Communities, (Brussels: March, 19–20, 1997), p.4.
55 *BR*, (Beijing: January 2–5, 1999), p.10.
56 *BR*, (Beijing: February 22–28, 1999), p.8.
57 *BR*, (Beijing: April 12–18, 1999), p.6.
58 *BR*, (Beijing: January 24, 2002), p.23.
59 *BR*, (Beijing: March 9–15, 1998), p.7.
60 *BR*, (Beijing: August 14, 2000), p.4.
61 *BR*, (Beijing: July 26, 1999), p.10.
62 *BR*, (Beijing: March 21, 2002), p.10.
63 *BR*, (Beijing: March 13–19, 1995), p.16.
64 Ibid.
65 Ibid.
66 Ibid.
67 *SCMP*, (Hong Kong: October 1, 1996), p.9.
68 Ibid.
69 *Newsweek*, (New York: October 1, 1996).
70 *SCMP*, (Hong Kong: June 21, 2003), p.1.
71 Ibid.

72 Ibid.
73 *SCMP*, [Hong Kong: (November 11, 1995), p.8; (November 14, 1995), p.8].
74 *SCMP*, (Hong Kong: April 18, 1996), p.15.
75 *China Perspective*, no.35, (Hong Kong: May–June 2001), p.41.
76 Toyojiro Maruya, op.cit., (1992), p.132.
77 *Hong Kong 2000*, (Hong Kong: Hong Kong SAR Government Information Services Department, 2001), p.49.
78 Ibid.
79 *SCMP*, (Hong Kong: June 30, 2003), p.42.
80 Speak, Steven, "A Capital Location: Hong Kong's Emergence and Future as a Financial Center", in *Geography*, vol.82, (1997), pp.261–3, see also Lo, A.Y., in *China Perspective*, op.cit., p.41.
81 *BR*, (Beijing: February 7, 2002), p.7.
82 Lee Kuan Yew, Senior Minister, Singapore, "Growth Opportunities in East Asia", in *Speeches 95*, (Singapore: September–October 1995, Ministry of Information and the Arts), p.37.
83 Ibid.
84 *BR*, (Beijing: February 7, 2002), p.7.
85 Ibid.
86 Ibid., p.8.
87 Ibid.
88 *The Star*, (Singapore: July 24, 1992), p.4.
89 *Straits Times*, (Singapore, July 24, 1993), p.26.
90 *BR*, (Beijing: February 28–March 1, 1998), p.6.
91 *BR*, (Beijing: August 16, 1999), p.10.
92 *SCMP*, (Hong Kong: November 3, 2002), p.11.
93 *SCMP*, (Hong Kong: November 2, 2002), p.10.
94 *BR*, (Beijing: May 1, 2003), p.18.
95 *BR*, (Beijing: July 3, 2003), p.42.
96 *BR*, (Beijing: November 21, 2002), p.11.
97 Ibid., p.10.
98 *BR*, (Beijing: November 15, 1999), p.13.
99 *Xinhua*, (Beijing: April 23, 1996).
100 *BR*, (Beijing: August 2, 2001), pp.8–11.
101 *BR*, (Beijing: December 23–29, 1996), p.10.
102 Ibid.
103 *SCMP*, (Hong Kong: November 30, 1996), p.9.
104 Ibid.
105 *SCMP*, (Hong Kong: June 22, 2003), p.6.
106 *BR*, (Beijing: February 14, 2002), p.8.
107 Ibid.
108 *BR*, (Beijing: May 9, 2002), p.8.
109 Ibid.

110 *BR*, (Beijing: December 4, 2003), p.41.
111 *BR*, (Beijing: May 9, 2002), p.8.
112 Ibid.
113 *BR*, (Beijing: December 4, 2003), p.41.
114 Jiang, Zemin, *SW of JZM, Vol.I*, op.cit., p.481.
115 *SCMP*, (February 19, 2005), p.A6.
116 These two conditions were included in the Taiwan Relations Act determined by the US Congress in April 1979. See Lee, Nan-Shong Peter, "Jiang Zemin Versus Lee Teng-hui", in *China Review 1997*, note 7, pp. 109, 130, ed., Brosseau, M., etc., (Hong Kong: The Chinese University Press, 1997).
117 *Foreign Affairs*, (New York: Council on Foreign Relations, July 1996).
118 Jiang's "Eight-Points" proposal can be summarized as follows:
(a) We adhere to the principle of 'one China' for peaceful reunification.
(b) We oppose Taiwan's activities of "expanding its living space internationally", aimed at creating "two Chinas" or "one China, one Taiwan".
(c) We insist that there is only one China.
(d) We strive for the peaceful reunification.
(e) We hold that political differences should not affect economic cooperation between the two sides.
(f) We hold that all ethnic Chinese groups constitute the basis for the peaceful reunification.
(g) We fully respect the Taiwanese life style.
(h) Taiwanese leaders are welcome to visit the mainland.
119 *China Review 1997*, ibid., p.112
120 Lee's "Six-Points" proposal can be summarized as follows:
(a) Consensus of "one China" should be based on treating the reality with objectivity.
(b) To enhance cultural exchanges.
(c) Bilateral trade is mutually beneficial.
(d) Leaders of both sides to meet on international occasions.
(e) The ROC denounces the use of force as a way to achieve unification.
(f) The ROC is concerned with the future of both Hong Kong and Macau.
121 The Taiwan Relations Act passed in 1979 on recognition of China obliges the US to sell Taiwan enough hardware to allow it to defend itself against attack.
122 Hu, Weixing, "Two-State Theory Versus One-China Principle: Cross-Strait Relations in 1999", in *China Review 2000*, ed., Lau Chung-ming and Shen Jianfa, (Hong Kong: The Chinese University Press, 2000), p.142.
123 Ibid.
124 *FEER*, (Hong Kong: May 3, 2001), p.12.
125 *SCMP*, (Hong Kong: June 25, 2005), p.A5.
126 *FEER*, (Hong Kong: July 31, 2003), p.16.
127 *SCMP*, (Hong Kong: April 2, 2005), p.A7.
128 Ibid.

129 Ibid.
130 Ibid.
131 Hu, Weixing, in *China Review 2000*, op.cit., p.151.
132 Lee, Nan-shong, Peter, "Strained Mainland-Taiwan Relationship", in *China Review 1997*, op.cit., p.123.
133 *FEER*, (Hong Kong: March 30, 2000), p.16.
134 *HK iMail*, (Hong Kong: July 20, 2000), p.A3.
135 *SCMP*, (Hong Kong: July 4, 2003), p.A14.
136 Ibid.
137 *SCMP*, (Hong Kong: July 7, 2003), p.1.
138 *SCMP*, (Hong Kong: July 8, 2003), p.A14.
139 *Macaubusiness*, ed., Kareem Jalal, vol.1, no.12, (Macau: De Ficao-Projectors Multimedia, April 2005), p.58.

Chapter Eight
Jiang Zemin's Approach to Privatization

1 *BR*, (Beijing: December 18, 2000), p.20.
2 Ibid.
3 Ibid.
4 Ibid.
5 *SCMP*, (Hong Kong: March 17, 2002), p.11.
6 Ibid.
7 Ibid.
8 *BR*, (Beijing: February 27, 2002), p.24.
9 Wong, John, "Some Thoughts on China's Post-Deng Economy", in Wang, Gungwu and Wong John, ed., *China's Political Economy*, (Singapore: Singapore University Press & World Scientific Press, 1998); see also *Asia Times*, (Bangkok: January 17, 1997).
10 *BR*, (Beijing: October 6–12, 1997), p.19.
11 The new law will "grant individual proprietorship the same status as other forms of ownership", according to a deputy director of the NPC's finance and economic committee office, Li Luyang, *SCMP*, (Hong Kong: April 5, 1999), p.2.
12 *SCMP*, (Hong Kong: March 14, 1999), p.6.
13 *China Daily*, (Beijing: February 12, 1999), p.1.
14 *BR*, (Beijing: March 22–28, 1999), p.24.
15 *BR*, (Beijing: October 6–12, 1997), p.16, p.18.
16 Jiang, Zemin, *SW of JZM, Vol.III*, op.cit., p.2.

17 *BR*, (Beijing: November 28, 2002), p.21.
18 Jiang, Zemin, *SW of JZM, Vol.I*, op.cit., pp.440–54.
19 Ibid., p.p.22–3.
20 *SCMP*, (Hong Kong: March 17, 2002), p.11.
21 *BR*, (Beijing: November 28, 2002), pp.22–3.
22 Ibid.
23 *BR*, (Beijing: October 11, 1999), p.5.
24 Ibid., p.25.
25 *BR*, (Beijing: February 8, 2001), pp.20–1.
26 Ibid., p.19.
27 *SCMP*, (Hong Kong: March 9, 2002), p.3.
28 *SCMP*, (Hong Kong: March 6, 2002), p.8.
29 *SCMP*, (Hong Kong: February 17, 2002), p.4.
30 *Wen Wei Po*, (Hong Kong: February 16, 2002), p.3. Since 1996, China had spent more than 280 billion yuan (about US$36 billion) to finance the bankruptcies of 5,335 SOEs sacking 4.3 million workers.
31 Ibid.
32 *SCMP*, (Hong Kong: March 14, 2005), p.A7.
33 Ibid.
34 *Hong Kong Standard*, (Hong Kong: July 10, 2002), p.20.
35 *Hong Kong Standard*, (Hong Kong: July 10, 2002), p.3.
36 Ibid.
37 *BR*, (Beijing: June 26, 2000), p.4.
38 Jiang, Zemin, *SW of JZM, Vol.III*, op.cit., pp.10, 204, 313–8.
39 *BR*, (Beijing: February 15, 2001), p.8.
40 Jiang, Zemin, *SW of JZM, Vol.III*, op.cit., p.520.
41 Jiang, Zemin, *SW of JZM, Vol.II*, pp.195–204.
42 *BR*, (Beijing: June 26, 2000), p.4.
43 *BR*, (Beijing: November 20, 2000), p.23.
44 *BR*, (Beijing: September 20, 1999), p.17.
45 Ibid.
46 *SCMP*, (Hong Kong: December 21, 2002), p.7.
47 Overholt, William, in *SCMP*, (Hong Kong: November 16, 2002), p.10.
48 *SCMP*, (Hong Kong: November 16, 2002), p.11.
49 Overholt, William, op.cit.
50 *BR*, (Beijing: October 25, 2001), p.20.
51 Ibid., p.21.
52 *HSBC Premier*, (Hong Kong: Hong Kong & Shanghai Banking Corporation), p.12.
53 *SCMP*, (Hong Kong: March 20, 2003), p.A6.
54 Ibid. However, at the beginning of 2006, the central government under Chairman Hu Jintao abolished the agricultural tax while increasing funding for rural areas.

55 *BR*, (Beijing: February 7, 2000), p.11.
56 Ibid.
57 Ibid.
58 Ibid.
59 Mao, *SW, Vol.V*, (Beijing: FLP, 1977), p.287.
60 Ibid.
61 Ibid.
62 Ibid., p.285.
63 *BR,* (Beijing: April 10, 2000), p.15.
64 Wong, Christine, P.W., "Interpreting Rural Industrial Growth in the Post-Mao Period", in *Modern China*, (Beverly Hills: 1988), p.14, pp.13–30; see also Bernstein, Thomas P., op.cit., p.51.
65 Chan, Thomas, Man Hong, "Changes in China's Growth Pattern Since the Reform", in Cheng, Joseph Y.S., *China in the Post-Deng Era,* (Hong Kong: The Chinese University Press, 1998), p.273.
66 Ke Lin, op.cit., p.48.
67 Bernstein, op.cit., p.51.
68 Ibid.
69 Ke Lin, "On China's Corruption Problem", in *China Strategic Review*, September-October 1997, (Washington: The China Strategic Institute), p.47.
70 Ibid.
71 Beinstein, op.cit., p.52.
72 *China Daily*, (Beijing: December 15, 1988); *Guangming Ribao*, (Beijing: December 20, 1988).
73 *SCMP*, (Hong Kong: December 31, 1995), p.1.
74 *SCMP*, (Hong Kong: January 13, 2002), p.4.
75 Ibid.
76 Cheng, Joseph, Y.S., op.cit., (1989), p.655.
77 Berstein, Thomas P., op.cit., p.55; *FEER*, (Hong Kong: September 18, 1986); *Ming Pao Monthly*, (Hong Kong: July 1986).
78 Baum, Richard, *Bury Mao: Chinese Politics in the Age of Deng Xiaoping*, (Princeton, N.J.: Princeton University Press, 1994), p.317.
79 *BR*, (Beijing: February 28, 2000), p.21.
80 Ibid.
81 *BR*, (Beijing: January 24, 2000), p.4.
82 Ibid.
83 Ibid.
84 Ibid.
85 *SCMP*, (Hong Kong: January 27, 2002), p.5.
86 Ibid.
87 *SCMP*, (Hong Kong: March 6, 2002), p.17.
88 *SCMP*, (Hong Kong: March 10, 2002), p.5.
89 Ke Lin, op.cit., p.47.

90 *BR*, (Beijing: October 6–12, 1997), p.13.
91 *BR*, (Beijing: April 1–7, 1996), p.4.

Chapter Nine
China in the New Century

1 *BR*, (Beijing: November 28, 2002), p.25.
2 Lau, Lawrence J., "Gain without Pain: Why Economic Reform in the PRC Worked?", in Wang, Gungwu and Wong, John, *China's Political Economy,* op. cit., p.43.
3 *SCMP*, (Hong Kong: April 14, 1999), p.7.
4 *BR*, (Beijing: November 14–20, 1988), p.14.
5 *BR*, (Beijing: April 27, 1987), p.17.
6 Ibid.
7 Ibid.
8 Ibid.
9 *BR*, (Beijing: May 13–19, 1991), p.23.
10 Ibid.
11 Ibid.
12 *BR*, (Beijing: April 3–16, 1995), p.8.
13 *BR*, (Beijing: May 13–19, 1991), pp.22–3.
14 *BR*, (Beijing: November 14–20, 1988), p.14.
15 Ibid.
16 *Building Research & Information*, (London: Taylor and Francis Ltd, July–August 2001), p.294.
17 *Ibid.*
18 *BR*, (Beijing: March 20, 2000), p.19.
19 *BR*, (Beijing: November 14–20, 1988), p.14.
20 Ibid.
21 Ibid.
22 *BR*, (Beijing: May 13–19, 1991), p.23.
23 Ibid.
24 Ibid.
25 *BR*, (Beijing: May 13–9, 1991), p.23.
26 *BR*, (Beijing: April 3–16, 1995), p.9.
27 Ibid.
28 Ibid.
29 Ibid
30 Ibid.

31 *Building Research & Information,* (London: Taylor and Francis Ltd, July–August 2001), p.262; also refer to Hong, S.W., "Korea-China Cooperation in Housing Construction", (Beijing: International Engineering Contractor Symposium, 1998), pp.297–338.
32 *Asian Architect & Contractor*, (Hong Kong: January 2000), p.9.
33 Ibid.
34 *SCMP*, (Hong Kong: November 9, 2002), p.3.
35 Ibid.
36 Ibid.
37 *Business Week,* (New York: McGraw-Hill, December 2002); see also *HSBC Premier*, (Hong Kong: spring 2003), pp.9–10.
38 Ibid.
39 Ibid.
40 Ibid.
41 *BR*, (Beijing: January 17, 2000), p.38.
42 *SCMP*, (Hong Kong: May 20, 2006), p.A13.
43 *BR*, (Beijing: February 8–14, 1999), p.5.
44 *BR*, (Beijing: September 19, 2002), p.14.
45 HSBC Asset Management (HK) Ltd, (Hong Kong: Hong Kong and Shanghai Banking Corporation, November 2003), p.4.
46 *BR*, (Beijing: July 14, 2002), p.29.
47 *BR*, (Beijing: January 12–18, 1998), p.5.
48 *HSBC Premier*, op.cit.
49 Ibid.
50 *SCMP*, (Hong Kong: June 25, 2005), p.A8.
51 Ibid.
52 Vice Chairman Yang Changji, "China's Foreign Trade and Investment Policies", in *Pacific Rim Management*, (Hong Kong), p.21.
53 *BR*, (Beijing: March 29–April 4, 1999), p.20.
54 *SCMP*, (Hong Kong: June 21, 2003), p.E2.
55 *BR*, (Beijing: November 27–December 3, 1995), p.4.
56 Ibid.
57 *HSBC Premier*, op.cit.
58 Ibid.
59 *BR*, (Beijing: September 19, 2002), p.15.
60 Ibid.
61 Ibid.
62 Lee Kuan Yew, "The East Asian Challenge and Its Impact on Europe and North America", in *Speeches*, a Bimonthly Selection of Ministerial Speeches, (Singapore: Ministry of Information and the Arts, September–October 1994), p.33.
63 *Time* Magazine, (New York: December 23, 2002), p.34.
64 Ibid.

Bibliography

Chinese Sources

(a) Texts

Ban, Gu (班固) (of the Han dynasty), *The Han Book* (汉书), (Hong Kong: Chung Hua Press, 1970)

Deng, Xiaoping, *Deng Xiaoping Wenxuan, Vol. III*, (Beijing: People's Press, 1993)

___ *Deng Xiaoping Wenxuan 1975–1982*, (Hong Kong: Joint Publishers and People's Press, 1983)

Jiang, Zemin, *Jiang Zemin Wenxuan* (江泽民文选),three volumes, (Beijing: People's Press, 2006)

Li, Yinqiao (李银桥), *Beside Mao Zedong for 15 Years* (在毛泽东身边 15 年), (Hong Kong: Cosmos Books Ltd, 1992)

Li, Ying (李颖), and Cheng, Meidong (程美东), ed., *Experiencing History With Mao Zedong* (与毛泽东一起感受历史), two volumes, (Wuhan: Hupei People's Press, 2005)

Mao, *Mao Tse-tung Si Xiang Wan Su*i (Beijing: no publisher given, 1969)

___ *Mao Tse-tung's Works* (毛泽东集), The Research Section of Chinese Communism, ed., (Hong Kong: I Shan Press, 1976)

___ *Selected Works of Mao Tse-tung*, four volumes, (Beijing: People's Press, 1969); *Vol.V*, (Beijing: People's Press, 1977); *Vol.II*, (Beijing: People's Press, 1966)

___ *Poems of Chairman Mao* (毛主席诗词), (Beijing: People's Literature Press, 1967)

___ *Mao Zedong Wenji* (毛泽东文集), *Vols.6–8*, (Beijing: People's Press, 1999)

Zhou, Enlai, *Report on the Proposals for the Second Five Year Plan for Development of the National Economy*, (September 16, 1956, the 8th Party Congress).

Zhou, Enlai, *Selected Works of Zhou Enlai* (周恩来选集), (Beijing: Foreign Languages Press, 1989)

(b) General Reference

Chen, Jin (陈晋), ed., *Explaining Mao Tse-tung's Reading Notes* (毛泽东读书笔记解析), two volumes, (Shenzhen: Guangdong People's Press, 1996)

Chinese People's Liberation Army and the Liberation Areas During the Ant-Japanese Period, (Beijing: People's Press, 1954)

Li, Jui (李锐), *Comrade Mao Tse-tung's Early Revolutionary Activities*, (Beijing: The Chinese Youth Press, 1957); *see also* Sariti, A.W., tran., (New York: M.E. Sharpe, 1977)

(c) Periodicals and Newspapers

Chang, Kejia (臧克家), ed., *Poetry* (诗刊), (Beijing: People's Press, 1964)

Guangming Ribao (光明日报), (Beijing: January 1976, December 1978)

Hongqi Editorial, *Hongqi (Red Flag)*, (Beijing: February 1963, October 1978)

Kung Ming Jih Pao (昆明日□), (Kung Ming: May 1957)

People's Daily, (Beijing: February 1964, October 1955)

Poetry, Shi Kan Editiorial Committee, (Beijing: People's Press, 1959, 1976)

Ta Kung Pao (大公报), (Hong Kong: May 1957, December 1990)

Wen I Pao (文艺报), 24th edition, (Shanghai: 1952)

Wen Wei Po (文□报), (Hong Kong: May 19, 1991; February 16, 2002)

Yearbook of Chinese Communism Editorial Committee, *The Yearbook of Chinese Communism* (中共年报), (Taipei: Institute for the Study of Chinese Communist Problems, 1967, 1968)

Yenan Liberation Daily, (Yenan: 1941–45)

English Sources

(a) General Literature

Adie, W.A.C., "World Or Power? China As An Alternative Model of the International System", (Canberra: The Australian National University Seminar Paper, 1974)

Barnett, A. Doak, ed., *Chinese Communist Politics in Action*, (Seattle: University of Washington Press, 1969)

Baum, Richard, *Bury Mao: Chinese Politics in the Age of Deng Xiaoping*, (Princeton: Princeton University Press, 1994)

Bonavia, David, *Deng*, (Hong Kong: Longman, 1989)

Chao, Han, *On Rectification Campaigns of the CCP*, (Peking: Chinese Youth Press, 1957)

Chang, Kingyuh, ed., *Perspectives on Development in Mainland China*, (Boulder: Westview Press, 1985)

Cheng, Joseph Y.S., ed., *China: Modernization in the 1980s*, (Hong Kong: The Chinese University Press, 1989)

____*China in the Post-Deng Era*, (Hong Kong.: The Chinese University Press, 1998)

Chiou, C.L., *Maoism in Action*, (Brisbane: University of Queensland Press, 1974)

Conference on Problems and Prospects of the Asian Pacific Region, (Hong Kong: University of Hong Kong, August 1987)

Daubier, Jean, *A History of the Chinese Cultural Revolution*, tran. Seaver, R., (New York: Random House, 1974)

Deng, Xiaoping, *Selected Works of Deng Xiaoping*, 1982–92, (Beijing: Foreign Languages Press, 1994)

____*Selected Works of Deng Xiaoping* 1975–82, (Beijing: Foreign Languages Press, 1983)

____Report on the Rectification Campaigns delivered at the Third Plenum (Enlarged) of the 8th C.C. of the CCP, (Beijing: Foreign Languages Press, September 23, 1957)

Eckstein, Alexander, *China's Economic Development,* (Ann Arbor: The University of Michigan Press, 1975)

Eckstein, Alexander, Galenson, Walter, and Liu, Ta-Chung, *Economic Trends in Communist China,* (Edinburgh: Edinburgh University Press, 1985)

General Program of the New Party Constitution, (Appendix II, August, 24, 1973)

Goh, Chok Tong, "Positioning Singapore for the 21st Century", in *Speeches 95*, a bimonthly selection of ministerial speeches, (Singapore: Ministry of Information and the Arts, May–June 1995)

Goodman, David S.G., *Deng Xiaoping and the Chinese Revolution: A Political Biography,* (London: Routledge, 1994)

Gurley, John G., *China's Economy and the Maoist Strategy*, (New York: Monthly Review Press, 1976)

Han, Suyin, *China in the Year 2001*, (London: C.A. Watts, Ltd., 1967)

Harrison, James P., *Long March to Power*, (London: Macmillan Press, 1973)

Hinton, Harold C., ed., *The People's Republic of China*, (Boulder: Westview Press, 1979)

Hoffmann, Charles, *Work Incentive Practices and Policies in the People's Republic of China 1953–65*, (New York: State University of New York Press, 1968)

Hong Kong 1997, 2000 (Hong Kong: Information Services Department, Hong Kong SAR Government)

Hsu, C.Y. Immanuel, *Rise of the Chinese People's Republic*, 5th edition, (New York: Oxford University Press, 1995)

Huang, T.W., and Li, Z.Y., "The Changing Security Scene in East Asia – An Analysis of the US Perspective", in *ASEAN-China, Hong Kong Forum 1990*, (Hong Kong: Royal Park Hotel, August 7–9, 1990)

Huntington, Samuel P., *The Clash of Civilization and Remaking of World Order*, (New York: Simon & Schuster, 1996)

Il, Sakong, *Korea in the World Economy*, (Washington D.C.: Institute of International Economics, 1993)

Ikira, Iriye, *Across the Pacific: The Sino-American Crisis*, (Chicago: Imprint Publications Inc., 1992)

Kau, Michael Y-M and Marsh, Susan H., *China in the Era of Deng Xiaoping: A Decade of Reform*, (New York: M.E. Sharpe, Inc., 1993)

Khrushchev, Nikita, *Khrushchev Remembers: The Last Testament*, tran. and ed. by Strobe Talbott, (Boston: Little Brown & Co., 1974)
Khrushchev, Sergei Nikitich, *Nikita Khrushchev and the Creation of a Superpower*, tran., Benson, Shirley, (Pennsylvania: The Pennsylvania State University, 2000)
Kissinger, Henry, *Diplomacy*, (New York: Simon & Schuster, 1994)
____*White House Years*, (Boston: Little Brown, 1979)
Lam, Lai Sing, "A Short Note on ASEAN-Great Power Interaction", in *Contemporary Southeast Asia*, (Singapore: Institute of Southeast Asian Studies, March 1994)
____"From Mikhail Gorbachev's Policy to China's Regional Role", in *The Journal of East Asian Affairs*, (Seoul: The Research Institute of International Affairs, August 1993)
____*Mao Tse-tung's Purposive Contention with the Superpowers: The Theory of Ch'i*, (Lewiston: Edwin Mellen Press, 1995)
____*The Role of Ch'i in Mao Tse-tung's Leadership Style*, (San Francisco: Mellen University Press, 1993)
____*Mao Tse-tung's Ch'i and the Chinese Political Economy With Special Reference to the Post-Mao Modernization Revolution*, (Lewiston/Queenston/Lampeter, Edwin Mellen Press, 2000)
Lee, Kuan Yew, "Growth Opportunities in East Asia", in *Speeches 95*, (Singapore: Ministry of Information and the Arts, September–October 1995)
____"The East Asian Challenge and Its Impact on Europe and North America", in *Speeches 94, (op.cit.*, September–October 1994)
Lethbridge, Henry J., *The Peasant and the Communes*, (Hong Kong: Dragonfly Books, 1963)
Liu, Suinian and Wu, Qungan, ed., *China's Socialist Economy*, (Beijing: Beijing Review Press, 1986)
MacFarquhar, Roderick, *The Origins of the Cultural Revolution: Contradictions Among the People*, (London: Oxford University Press, 1974)
____*The Origins of the Cultural Revolution: The GLF 1958–60*, (Oxford: Oxford University Press, 1983)
____*The Origins of the Cultural Revolution: The Coming of Cataclysm 1961–66*, (Oxford: Oxford University Press, 1997)

Mao, *Fight For the Basic Improvement of the National Financial and Economic Situation*, (为争取国家财政经济状况的基本好转而斗争), (Beijing: People's Press, 1950)
____ *Mao Tse-tung Poems*, (Beijing: Foreign Languages Press, 1976)
____*Selected Works of Mao Tse-tung*:
Vol.I–IV, (Beijing: Foreign Lanugages Press, 1967)
Vol V, (Beijing: Foreign Lanugages Press, 1977)
Vol.III, (Beijing: Foreign Lanugages Press, 1954)
Vol.IV, (Beijing: Foreign Lanugages Press, 1960)
Maruya, Toyojiro, ed., *Guangdong "Open Door" Economic Development Strategy*, (Tokyo: Institute of Developing Economics, 1992)
____*A Decade of "Open Door" Economic Development 1979–89*, (Tokyo: Institute of Developing Economics, 1991)
Meisner, Maurice J., *Mao's China: A History of the People's Republic*, (New York: The Free Press, 1977)
Morley, James W., ed., *Driven by Growth: Political Change in the Asia-Pacific Region*, (New York: M.E. Sharpe Inc., 1993)
Nixon, Richard, *The Memoirs of Richard Nixon*, (New York: Grosset & Dunlop, 1978)
____*Public Papers of the Presidents of the United States: Richard Nixon,* 1969.
Oh, S.K., *Land Reform in Communist China and Postwar Japan*, (Philadelaphia: University of Pennsylvania, 1966)
Park, Woo-Hee, "The Role of Science and Technology in Korean Economic Development", in *Conference on Problems and Prospects of the Asian Pacific Region*, (Hong Kong: Centre of Asian Studies, University of Hong Kong, August 5–7, 1987)
People's Communes in China, (Peking: Foreign Languages Press, 1958)
Polomka, Peter, "Strategic Stability and the South China Sea: Beyond Geopolitics", in *The International Academic Conference on Territorial Claims in the South China Sea*, (Hong Kong: Centre of Asian Studies, University of Hong Kong, December 4–6, 1990)
Pradeep, Taneja, etc., *China Since 1978*, second edition, (Melbourne: Longman, 1998)
Richman, Barry, *Industrial Society in Communist China*, (New York: Random House, 1969)

Robinson, Joan, *The Cultural Revolution in China*, (United Kingdom: Pelican, 1970)
Ross, Robert S. & Jiang, Changbin, *Re-examining the Cold War: US–China Diplomacy, 1954-73*, [Cambridge, Mass. & London: Harvard University Press, 2001]
Salisbury, Harrison E., *The Coming War Between Russia and China*, (New York: W.W. Norton & Co. Inc., 1969)
____*The New Emperors, Mao & Deng: A Dual Biography*, (London: HarperCollins Publishers, 1992)
Schram, Stuart R., *The Political Thought of Mao Tse-tung*, (New York: Frederick A. Praeger, 1963)
Snow, Edgar, *Red Star Over China*, (New York: Random House, 1961; also Grove Press, 1973)
____*The Other Side of the River*, (London: Gollancz, 1966)
Teiwes, Frederick C., *Politics and Purges in China*, (New York: M.E. Sharpe, Inc., 1979)
____*Politics and Purges in China*, second edition, (New York: M.E. Sharpe, Inc., 1993)
Teng, Hsiao-ping (Deng, Xiaoping), *Report on the Rectification Campaigns*, (Peking: Foreign Languages Press, 1957)
The Party's Documents (的文献), (4th issue, 1959 and 5th issue, 1994)
Twitchett, Denis C., and Fairbank, John K., *The Cambridge History of China, Vol.14*, (Cambridge: Cambridge University Press, 1987)
Union Research Institute, ed., *CCP Documents of the GPCR*, 1966–67, (Hong Kong, Union Press, 1968)
US Consulate General, *Current Background*, (Hong Kong: 1950–55)
Van Ness, Peter, *Revolution and Chinese Foreign Policy: Peking Support for Wars of National Liberation*, (Berkeley: University of California Press, 1970)
Wang, Gungwu and Wong, John, *China's Political Economy*, (Singapore: Singapore University Press & World Scientific Press, 1998)
Welfield, John B., *Australia and Japan in the Sino-US Cold War, 1949–72, Some Notes and Observations*, (Canberra: Australian National University Seminar, April 1974)
Wong, John, *Land Reform in the PRC: Institutional Transformation in Agriculture*, (New York: Praeger, 1973)

(b) Periodicals

Asian Architect & Contractor, (Hong Kong: January 2000)
Asian Survey, vol.38, no.10, (Berkeley: University of California, 1988)
Asian Wall Street Journal, (Hong Kong: December 8, 1988)
*Beijing Review (Peking Review), (*Beijing, various issues)
Building Research & Information, (London: Taylor and Francis Ltd., July–August, 2001)
Business Week, (New York: McGraw-Hill, December 2002)
*China Daily, (*Beijing: February 1999)
China Perspective, (Hong Kong, various issues)
China Review 1997, 2000 (Hong Kong: The Chinese University of Hong Kong, 1998, 2000)
China Quarterly, no.36, (London: October–December 1968)
China Strategic Review, (Washington: The China Strategic Institute, September–October 1997)
China Today, (Beijing: China Welfare Institute)
Current Background, no.46, 1, (Hong Kong: US Consulate General)
Far Eastern Economic Review, (Hong Kong: February 7, 1975; March 1987)
Foreign Affairs, (New York: July 1996)
HK iMail, (Hong Kong: various issues of 2000)
Hong Kong Standard, (Hong Kong, July 2002)
Hongqi, (Beijing: 10th issue, 1958)
HSBC Asset Management Ltd, (Hong Kong: Hong Kong and Shanghai Banking Corporation, November 2003)
HSBC Premier, (Hong Kong: Hong Kong and Shanghai Banking Corporation, various issues)
Journal of Asian Studies, (Ann Arbor: November 1964, February 1965)
Macaubusiness, ed., Kareem Jalal, vol.1, no.12, (Macau: De Ficao–Projectors Multimedia, April 2005)
Modern China, An International Quarterly of History and Social Science, (Beverly Hills: January 1977)
NCNA, (Beijing: June, August, September, 1957, April 1996)
New York Times, (New York: August 5, 1953)

Newsweek Magazine, (New York: October 1, 1996)
Pacific Rim Management, (Hong Kong: 21)
Peking Review, (Beijing: 10th edition, March, 1975)
South China Morning Post, (Hong Kong: various issues)
Straits Times, (Singapore: July 24, 1993)
The China Journal, no.49, (Canberra: Australian National University, January 2003)
The Guardian, (London: December 1971)
The Journal of East Asian Affairs, vol.8, no.1, 1994; vol.6, no.2, (Seoul: 1992)
The Nation, (Sydney: December 1982)
The Star, (Singapore: July 24, 1992)
The Times, (London: various issues)
Time Magazine, (New York: December 2002)

Index